Praise for SERGEANT REX

"Briskly written . . . Dowling's account has many suspenseful moments as well as interesting facts about how dogs are selected, trained, paired with a human, and even ranked as service members."

—*The Washington Post*

"This is a truly heartwarming and moving story."

—*Hollywood Reporter*

"Punchy prose that takes readers into the heart of the action . . . a blend of harrowing action and a tender story about the close bond between a Marine and his dog."

—*Orange County Register*

"If you're in the mood for a brutal book with a heartwarming core, *Sergeant Rex* is the one to seek, seek, seek. Just keep it out of the bedroom, or you'll never be able to sleep."

—*Killeen Daily Herald*

"A touching memoir . . . Enhance[s] our understanding of the special bond between man and man's best friend."

—*Publishers Weekly*

"Dowling details [his and Rex's] training, their missions, and most important, their everlasting bond."

—*Library Journal*

"A straightforward telling of an unusual wartime narrative . . . A clear-headed view of the improvisational nature of combat in Iraq, and the brutal difficulties with which American military personnel contended . . . A unique testimonial from today's professional, highly specialized military, with a clear extra appeal to animal lovers."

—*Kirkus Reviews*

"Packed with colorful characters and dramatic incidents, *Sergeant Rex* is a moving story of true grit cast seamlessly amidst tough realism, rich insightful detail, and mutual respect."

—*Seattle Kennel Club*

"A story of a bomb-sniffing dog with a happy ending."

—*Smithsonian Air & Space*

"A first-rate buddy story from the front lines of the Iraq War."

—*Shelf Awareness*

SERGEANT REX

THE UNBREAKABLE BOND BETWEEN A MARINE AND HIS MILITARY WORKING DOG

MIKE DOWLING
with Damien Lewis

ATRIA PAPERBACK

New York   London   Toronto   Sydney   New Delhi

ATRIA PAPERBACK
A Division of Simon & Schuster, Inc.
1230 Avenue of the Americas
New York, NY 10020

First Atria paperback edition October 2012

ATRIA PAPERBACK and colophon are trademarks of Simon & Schuster, Inc.

For information about special discounts for bulk purchases, please
contact Simon & Schuster Special Sales at 1-866-506-1949 or
business@simonandschuster.com.

The Simon & Schuster Speakers Bureau can bring authors to
your live event. For more information or to book an event contact the
Simon & Schuster Speakers Bureau at 1-866-248-3049 or visit our
website at www.simonspeakers.com.

Designed by Rhea Braunstein

Manufactured in the United States of America

10   9   8

The Library of Congress has cataloged the hardcover edition as follows:
Dowling, Mike C.
    Sergeant Rex : the unbreakable bond between a Marine and his
military working dog / Mike Dowling.
    p. cm.
    1. Dowling, Mike C. 2. Iraq War, 2003—Campaigns—Iraq—Mahmudiyah.
3. Detector dogs—Anecdotes. 4. German shepherd dog—War use—Anecdotes.
5. Improvised explosive devices—Detection—Iraq. 6. United States. Marine
Corps. Marines, 2nd. Battalion, 2nd.—Biography. 7. Marines—United States—
Biography. 8. Dogs—War use—Iraq. 9. Iraq War, 2003—Personal narra-
tives, American. I. Title. II. Title: Unbreakable bond between a Marine and his
military working dog.
    DS79.764.M33D69 2011
    956.7044'345—dc23
    2011040947

ISBN 978-1-4516-3596-6
ISBN 978-1-4516-3597-3 (pbk)
ISBN 978-1-4516-3598-0 (ebook)

For Sergeant Adam Cann
and Joseph Patrick Dowling

Guardians of the Night

Trust in me my friend for I am your comrade.
I will protect you with my last breath
When all others have left you
And the loneliness of the night closes in,
I will be at your side.

Together we will conquer all obstacles,
And search out those who might wish harm to others.
All I ask of you is compassion,
The caring touch of your hands.
It is for you that I will selflessly give my life
And spend my nights unrested.

Although our days together
May be marked by the passing of the seasons,
Know that each day at your side is my reward.
My days are measured by
The coming and going of your footsteps.
I anticipate them at the opening of the door.

You are the voice of caring when I am ill.
The voice of authority over me when I've done wrong.
Do not chastise me unduly
For I am your right arm,
The sword at your side.

I attempt to do only what you bid of me.
I seek only to please you and remain in your favor.
Together you and I shall experience
A bond only others like you will understand.
When outsiders see us together
Their envy will be measured by their disdain.

I will quietly listen to you
And pass no judgment,
Nor will your spoken words be repeated.
I will remain ever silent,
Ever vigilant, ever loyal.
And when our time together is done
And you move on in the world,
Remember me with kind thoughts and tales.
For a time we were unbeatable,
Nothing passed among us undetected.
If we should ever meet again on another field
I will gladly take up your fight.
I am a military working dog and together
We are guardians of the night.

Anonymous

SERGEANT REX

Prologue

WE START THE WALK.

IED Alley stretches before us, a deserted length of rubble-strewn, sunbaked dirt. To the uninitiated, there's nothing obvious here that screams out violence and danger. To me, gazing down IED Alley is like peering into the very jaws of hell.

On either side of the route are the broken mounds of shattered earth and the craters where roadside bombs have blown themselves—and all too often their targets—to smithereens. But luckily, typically, Rex, my search dog, is out front alone and unperturbed, eager to sniff out the bombs.

I've felt fear every day that we've led these patrols. It's been my constant companion here in Iraq. But this morning, the terror had me gripped as never before.

It was Rex who gave me the strength to get up and to carry on. He sent me one look—*Come on, partner, we can do this; you got me by your side*—and I knew then that I had to raise my game to the level of my dog.

I look to my fellow marines as my own brothers, and Rex and I are tasked with keeping them safe from the insurgents' bombs out here. Having my courageous, crazy, stubborn, loyal, dedicated, devilishly handsome dog by my side helps me deal with the enormous stress of that responsibility.

I gaze down IED Alley and give Rex the command, the magic words: "Seek . . . Seek . . . Seek . . ." But right now they're rasping out from a throat that's dry and constricted with fear.

In response, Rex is off. His nose starts going like a suction pump: *slurp, slurp, slurp.* He's dropped his muzzle low to the ground, and he's vacuuming up the scent just inches off the dirt. His tail's horizontal behind him, the end flicked up just a fraction, as his head sweeps from side to side.

I'd know that posture anywhere: *Here I am on the search, and I'm loving it.* Rex always has loved sniffing out the bombs. It's like he was born to do this work. From the earliest days of training he was one of the few and the proud—an unbeatable Marine Corps arms- and explosives-detection dog.

I'm a couple of paces behind him, his lead looped around my left hand. My M16 assault rifle is slung over my back on its sling, and I'm gripping my Beretta M9 pistol in my right hand. My rifle's too long and unwieldy to use much when searching with my dog.

If Rex steps on an improvised explosive device, we're both as good as done for. But we've been ordered to clear IED Alley so our patrol can pass through it, and the two of us out front on foot is the only way to do it.

To Rex, clearing the route of death is all a fantastic game. I've shown him a flash of his rubber ball—his reward—and he knows if he finds the target scent he gets to play with it. It's only me who's racked with this visceral, heart-stopping fear, fear that the next step Rex's paws take may be his, and my, last.

Rex's whole focus is his sense of smell now, and that's how he's navigating. He's moving through a world defined by scent. He's tracking smells on the hot, dusty air, his footfalls dictated by the direction those odors are coming from. He lifts his head now and then to check on his location—that he's not about to walk into a wall or tumble into a ditch.

We're a third of the way down IED Alley. My pulse is thumping like a jackhammer. Every time Rex raises a paw and places it onto the baking-hot earth, I tense for the blast. But I force myself to keep moving forward with him, and the sweat's pouring off me in buckets.

It's shortly after first light, yet already the temperature out here must be pushing 100 degrees. If it's this hot for me, how must it be for Rex, all wrapped up in his thick, shaggy, charcoal-brown coat of fur? But nothing seems to faze my dog, not even the burning Iraqi sun that's beating down on his head and shoulders.

I see Rex approaching a small patch of dirt ahead of us that looks as if it might recently have been disturbed. The difference in this area is minimal, just a slightly different color from the earth all around it, as if it's been dug up and tamped down again.

An unusual area of terrain is one of the signs that an IED may be buried there. I'm hyperalert, and my threat radar is working overtime. I try to work out what might lie beneath that patch of dirt, because I can't let Rex go walking right over it. Not for the first time since we deployed to Iraq, I curse the fact that I don't have X-ray vision, that I can't see the bombs lying just below earth's surface.

Rex pauses just a few paces short of that patch of dirt. His nostrils flare, and suddenly he's sucking in great lungfuls of air. He turns his head this way and that, sampling the scent, until he's got his nose pressed up tight against the hot mud of the earth.

Rex snuffles hard a good few times, then glances back at me. His sparkling amber eyes are wide with the thrill of the search. There's an unspoken bond between us. I can read his every expression, and I figure I can pretty much read his mind.

This look means: *Hey, I really think I'm onto something here.*

"Easy, boy, careful," I whisper at him. "Easy does it, Rexy. What you think you got there, boy?"

He moves ahead a foot or so until he's level with the patch of dirt. His muzzle swings left and right, before he's staring right at it. He pokes his snout forward, until he's sniffing at the very surface of that disturbed area.

His entire body goes rigid. He gives me a quick, intense, piercing look: *Freakin' hell, get in here and check this out!*

I feel my blood run cold. Rex never false responds—signaling that he's found something when actually he hasn't. There's some kind of explosive device buried right in front of my dog's nose, of that I am 100 percent certain.

I don't know why I'm sure—it can only be in response to the unspoken message that's flashed between Rex and me—but I lunge forward, and with one hand I grab his collar and haul him backward.

In my mind's eye I can picture a gleeful Iraqi insurgent hunched over a detonator device, punching the firing pin, and hoping to blow the shaggy dog and his handler into shreds of flesh and gore.

With my free hand I reach for my radio so I can send out an alert to the rest of the patrol strung out behind us. I press the Send button and yell out a warning: "There's a—"

My words are lost in this deafening roar of an explosion. I hit the dirt and elbow myself forward and dive on top of Rex, to shield him from the blast. But an instant later I sense that it's not the bomb in front of us that's gone off. If it were, we'd both be dead by now.

Just to the east of us above the palm trees, a massive plume of smoke and debris is fisting into the sky. An IED has been triggered there, to one side of our road.

The harsh, juddering crackle of gunfire thunders out of the smoke and dust as the insurgents unleash a barrage of fire in a follow-up attack. I roll across Rex, getting my body between him and the pounding gunfire.

I'm wearing body armor; Rex isn't. I'm not about to let anyone shoot my best buddy. I wrap all six feet of me around him and pull his thick fur in tight against me.

As I hold him there, I whisper into his ear: "It's okay, boy, it's okay. It's all gonna be all right. . . ."

Chapter One

THE BILLOWING CLOUD OF DUST FROM THE DEPARTING CONVOY OF trucks drifts away, to be replaced by the blinding glare of the Iraqi sun beating down upon us. I'm surrounded by a pile of kit and dog food canisters, and Rex standing loyally at my side.

At first light this morning we'd hitched a lift on a Marine Corps convoy heading south from Baghdad. It's dropped us exactly where we've asked it to—in the Marine Corps base at Mahmoudiyah, the capital of the "Triangle of Death."

This is arguably the single most dangerous place in the most dangerous war in the world right now. And Rex and I have come here to do the most dangerous job in the world—tracking down the insurgents' caches of arms and explosives, plus their murderous improvised explosive devices.

Rex peers up at me, his head cocked to one side and his eyes burning with curiosity. I can read his every expression. This one means: *So what now, partner?* Rex isn't big for a German shepherd. He comes up to just above my knees when standing on all fours. But, boy, he is one good-looking animal.

I glance around and shrug: *How the hell do I know?* When dog and handler are as close as Rex and I are, emotions run down leash and up again. Man and dog can sense each other's every shift in mood. We're both of us unsettled now that we've finally reached Death Central.

We've volunteered to be here, and we know the vital, life-and-death importance of the task that lies before us. It's the spring of 2004 and IEDs—basically bombs hidden on the side of streets, in buildings, and in vehicles—have become the single biggest threat facing U.S. forces here. Rex and I have come here to outwit and defeat the bomb makers.

Rex and I are one of only a handful of military working dog (MWD)—or K9—teams deployed to the war in Iraq. We're among the first K9 units ever sent here. And with Rex's hyper-sensitive sense of smell, and my ability to read him, we hope to save countless lives—both Americans and Iraqis.

When it comes to tracking down explosives, nature has created in a dog's nose a device infinitely more precise than anything modern technology has to offer. No one knows for sure, but people say that a dog's nose is one thousand times more sensitive than a human's. Dogs have millions more scent receptors than humans, and the size of the part of their brain used for analyzing smells is 20–40 percent larger than ours. They can literally sniff out the bombs.

A handler trains his dog how best to use his incredible abilities, so the dog becomes a bomb-detection device with its own mind and driven by a brain. A good handler learns to trust his dog to lead the way, and to use his instinct and drive to track down the threat. A mechanical bomb-detection device—like a metal detector—goes only where the operator takes it. It offers a blunt, unintelligent form of search compared to a dog tracking a scent on the air.

Rex and I have every confidence in our abilities as an explosives-detection team, but we've proved ourselves only in training. We've had zero combat experience, and we've never been to war before. I just hope my dog and I will do well out here.

We've been dumped at the base of the Second Battalion, Second Marines—the 2/2, also known as "the Warlords." The 2/2 are a battle-hardened bunch of marines who fought in the 2003 invasion of Iraq. They are now on their second tour, and they've been given the responsibility to soldier in the Triangle of Death.

Rex and I have been allocated to the Warlords as their K9 team for the six months of our combat tour, and we don't know anyone here. All I know of the Warlords is that they're a tough combat battalion headquartered at Camp Lejeune, on the east coast of the United States. Rex and I are based out of Camp Pendleton, on the sunny California coast. We're from opposite ends of the country, and I've never even spoken to anyone from the 2/2.

But a part of me is hugely relieved finally to be here, and my worries are eased by my confidence in my dog. We've spent a week bouncing around Iraq hitchhiking lifts on convoys, and I'm keen to get Rex settled. Dogs appreciate routine, Rex more than most. He wants nothing more than to get his paws under the table and call somewhere home.

My dog is an extension of me. Wherever I go, he goes. As long as he's with me, he knows I'll take care of him. But as we wait for someone to come to meet and greet us, Rex gives me an odd, bemused look: *You know, it's hot as hell here, it stinks, and we don't know anyone. But hell, if you're here, that's good enough for me.*

Rex rarely sits at heel. He's always standing. He stands because he's curious and wants to have a good nose-around. I know he's getting assaulted by a whole cocktail of new scents. Even I can detect a few of them. This place smells like a rotting, festering sewer. God only knows what Rex's nose is making of it all.

There are eight hundred marines stationed at Mahmoudiyah. We feel distinctly of out of place, especially because I am a dog handler and not an infantry marine. The infantry are the backbone of the Marine Corps, and I'm aware that marines like me are known as Persons Other Than Grunts (POGs), which isn't particularly encouraging.

But the first thing that happens to us here is good. I tell myself it's an omen of things to come. A passing marine catches sight of Rex and me, and he stops dead in his tracks. He's got a buzz cut of bright red hair sticking up like his head's on fire, and sunburned, freckled skin.

He stares at Rex and lets out a great whoop of joy. "Holy shit, we got a dog!" He's got a thick Southern country-boy drawl. "Holy shit, it's great to have a dog here!"

He comes bounding over. He introduces himself as John Walls, but everyone knows him as Red. He's clearly a genuinely good guy, and his joy at seeing Rex does a lot to settle my nerves. I hope this is how the rest of the marines of 2/2 will react to having a dog team among them.

Red bends to pet Rex and I know what's coming. I'm a tall guy and Rex can look diminutive by my side. But despite his size, he's still the toughest, most prideful and stubborn dog you ever could come across. He has to get to know you real well before he'll let you pet him.

Rex stares the guy out and starts his low, throaty growl. Red realizes he's about to get chewed and backs off. I tell him if he hangs around Rex long enough, Rex'll get used to him and maybe let him pet him. Red grins and says that's good enough for him.

"Y'all look a little lost," he says. "Who you need to report to?"

I shrug. "I need to report into the two-two's headquarters, preferably the battalion commander, but I don't know anyone's name here."

Red tells me to wait here and he'll go fetch someone.

Rex and I wait. Rex knows we're here to meet a bunch of people for the first time. He's familiar with the Marines; he's stationed on one of the biggest bases in the United States. He knows the Marine Corps uniform well, but he also knows that there are no humans here—apart from me—whose smell he recognizes. He's standing here taking in his new surroundings, just as I am.

I often wonder whether Rex thinks he's a dog or a human. I reckon he knows he's a dog, but he figures that he's a very, very smart one—smarter, in fact, than a lot of humans. Or maybe there's part of him thinks he is human, but then he's got these doggy instincts he can't control, like when he was about to chew out Red.

Red returns with an officer in tow. He's a stocky major of medium build, and he's the Warlords' executive officer, or XO, the second in command of the battalion.

I put Rex at heel, come to attention, and give a salute. "Corporal Dowling and Military Working Dog Rex reporting for duty, sir."

The major returns the salute. "Corporal Dowling, you are most welcome here in Camp Mahmoudiyah. I'm excited to finally get a dog team allocated to my marines. We anticipate your being pretty damn busy around here—we got IEDs and bombs going off everywhere. We're eager to find out what you guys can do."

The major explains that Rex and I will be attached to the Headquarters and Service (H&S) Company, from which patrols and missions will be tasked to us. H&S should be able to get us out in the most timely manner possible and where we can best be used. I'm to report to the commander of H&S, a Captain Dahle (pronounced "Dawly").

The major jerks a thumb at a massive warehouse-like building behind him. "Meantime, best you go find yourself and your dog a billet in the chicken factory."

The Warlords are based in an abandoned poultry farm. That in part must account for the smell around here.

"Are there many marines billeted in there, sir?" I ask him.

"Absolutely. It's very tight around here. There are marines just about everywhere."

"My dog can be aggressive, sir. So if there's a way we could find just a little private space for us . . ."

The major laughs. "You find that space, you let me know; not even the battalion commander has privacy here. Take a look around you. We have tents full of marines and a chicken factory full of marines. Take your pick, Corporal."

"I'd still like to be able to let my dog off leash without worrying about him biting your marines, sir."

Among the pile of K9 gear dropped with Rex and me, the major spies our expeditionary kennel. It's a hulking piece of tan-yellow steel the size of a transit van, and the only way to move it is by forklift truck. This kit dates back to the Vietnam War era, the last time K9 units were deployed onto the front line of combat with the U.S. military.

Since Vietnam, the American K9 community has gotten out of practice conducting combat operations on the front line of war, and we have little of the right kit to do so. Myself and Rex—plus the handful of other K9 teams sent out with us— have been told that we are the guinea pigs. By trial and error we're to learn how to take K9 units into the heart of war once again.

I wasn't keen on bringing that expeditionary kennel to Iraq. It's got air-conditioning, but the aircon unit is outdated and un-reliable. If it malfunctions, that steel kennel will become like an oven in the burning sun, and Rex could overheat and die in a matter of minutes. But I was pretty much ordered to bring it by my kennel master. The argument was that we're the first K9 units deployed to the Iraq War, and no one knows what equip-ment might prove useful out here. So we take whatever we've got and see what works.

The major stabs a finger in the direction of the kennel. "That's some kind of kennel, right? Why can't you put your dog in there? He sleeps there, and you can rack out in the factory along with the other marines."

"With all due respect, sir, wherever my dog is sleeping, I'm sleeping. I need to be with him every minute of the day. I cannot be separated from my dog. Plus the aircon unit's real dodgy. If it fails, Rex would fry. I don't want to wake up to find him dead.

D'you mind if I take a quick look around the base for a suitable spot?"

I am being as tactful and respectful as I can be with the major. Even so, there's a long second where he gives me a probing look. It's not often that a corporal defies him this way. But he's in an odd situation here. I am in his command chain, but I'm not a part of his unit. As for Rex, a military working dog is answerable only to his handler. No one else can ever order my dog what to do—not that he'd listen to anyone else. The reasoning is simple: Only I know what's best for Rex.

The major gives a shrug. "Okay, be my guest. You find a spot, it's yours."

I need Rex in tip-top condition if we're to do our job, and that's to get out with the 2/2's infantry companies patrolling the city. They're the ones on the front lines getting blown up by IEDs and wounded and killed. I want us out there helping find those devices and saving lives. We've never done anything remotely like this before, but everyone has his baptism of fire.

Red offers to show us around the base. "Let's go see if we can find you guys a space."

As we walk, he explains that he's a country boy from North Carolina, but he's of Irish origin. There's immediately a bond forged between us, because my family also hails from the Emerald Isle. My dad comes from County Kildare, and his brothers still run the family farm there, which they call their "bog."

I spot this small hut in the corner of the base. "Who's in there?" I ask Red.

"That's the watchtower building."

A sandbagged platform on stilts is perched above the hut, one of the watchtowers to guard the base perimeter.

"Okay, but who's in the hut underneath it?"

"You know, I don't think anyone's in there. Let's go check it out."

It's immediately obvious why this is the one building on the entire base that's unoccupied. Squeezed beneath the watch-tower is a bare concrete cubicle. It has three tiny rooms, each of which has a door but no windows, no air-conditioning, no electricity.

To one side of the hut sits the hulking mass of the base's main generator, and to the other there's a rank of wheelie bins stuffed full of trash. A couple of feet behind the hut is the base perimeter, made up of concrete blast walls topped with razor wire. On the far side of that is the small brown ooze of a stream that doubles as a sewer. In short, the room is dark, baking hot, deafeningly noisy, and stinks to high heaven.

Red, Rex, and I take a few steps back to appraise it. The only way to keep the heat down will be to keep the door open, which will let the biting bugs and insects in. But if we ignore that, plus the generator, the trash, and the creek-cum-sewer, there's real privacy to the place. No marine in his right mind would want to hang out here, and the only through traffic's going to be marines going to and fro to relieve those on duty in the watchtower.

There are a couple of other upsides to the hut. One, the only tree of any significance on the entire base is right beside it. I guess it's got its roots in the creek-sewer. Whatever, it offers a rare piece of shade for my dog. Plus Rex can cock his leg against it when he needs to pee.

The other major advantage is that the door to the main hut opens onto the muster area, where the vehicles and men gather to go out on patrol. From there I'll be able to see exactly what's going on and whether there are missions preparing to head out that Rex and I should be a part of.

I tell Red that it's perfect and we'll take it. I'm being sarcastic, but in fact it is the best the base has to offer Rex and me. Red gives me a look, like I've got to be crazy if I want to spend the next seven months living in there. I shrug. I'd sleep on a bed of nails if I had to, as long as it gave me some private space with my dog.

We nickname the hut the Bunker. Red leaves us to sort out the Bunker as best we can, promising to see if he can get some aircon fitted for us. I tell him we'll need electricity piped in first, and he says he'll see what he can do.

I move in Rex's lightweight, plastic crate with wire mesh door and sides. It's got CAUTION—MILITAR WORKING OG stenciled across the top. Still, anyone reading that will get the message. In any case, it's one of the few bits of out gear that are actually proving useful. I can take it apart and reassemble it in a couple of minutes, which makes it good for overnight operations or for when we're on the move from one base to another.

I lug over Rex's plastic buckets of dog chow, plus my personal gear. I set up my cot on one side of the tiny hut and place Rex's travel kennel alongside it. That way I can reach out and touch him with my fingers through the bars, and he and I can have eye contact as we rest. I pile my seabags, rucksack, and CamelBak water container at one end of the cot, lean my M16 in the corner, and we're pretty much done.

It's midafternoon by the time I finally get a chance to have a breather and take stock. It's March 31, and we left our home base of Camp Pendleton on the 19th. We're approaching two weeks in and finally we're where we need to be. Camp Mahmoudiyah may be a dump at the end of the universe, but I wasn't expecting luxury. More important, I'm told there is as much action here as anywhere else in Iraq.

Camp Pendleton is the size of a small California city, both in terms of its population and expanse. It takes a good hour to drive from one side of the base to the other. Here you can walk from one end of the chicken factory compound to the other in fifteen minutes flat. But I don't for one moment regret having volunteered to come here. I'm 100 percent certain that this is where Rex and I will come of age as a K9 team, or die trying.

I make sure Rex is fed and watered, then give him a good ruffle on the back of his head just above his thick leather collar. As I scratch, his eyebrows move in time to the rubbing, and the end of his tail beats a rhythm on the hut's earthen floor. When I stop, his tail starts beating more wildly: *Come on, partner, what are you stopping for?*

I do my best to ignore the stench drifting in through the door of the Bunker and force a smile. "So what d'you reckon, Rex? Home sweet home. This is us for the next few months, eh?"

He does one of his doggy stretches, starting with his rear end up high and head on the ground, and swinging his body forward until his head's up high and his bottom's on the deck. He glances up at me: *See, there's room enough for a good stretch. And if I'm here with you, that's good enough for me.*

He cocks his head to one side and an inquiring look comes into his eyes: *I've had a good scratch and a good stretch, so what about it—any chance of a walk and an explore?*

I haven't seen anywhere remotely suitable for exercising Rex, so I grab his tug toy from my backpack and give him a good play with it. It's a tough red, sausage-shaped stuffed toy, and Rex has a big bite and a growl as he tries to wrestle it off me. Working dogs like Rex need to have their playtime. It's a vital part of building a close bond and a good relationship with your dog.

Having messed around with Rex for a while, we set out to find Captain Dahle, the H&S company commander. It's as good an excuse as any to take Rex on a walkabout. I'm stepping out of the Bunker and pulling my "cover"—my Marine Corps cap—onto my head, when I practically stumble into a three-star general.

I recognize him instantly. It's General James "Chaos" Mattis, the overall commander of the Marine Corps here in Iraq. It was on the general's convoy that Rex and I hitched our ride down to Mahmoudiyah. He's got most of the 2/2's top brass with him, including the major who told Rex and me to billet ourselves in the chicken factory.

I glance at Rex. "Rex: Heel! Sit! Stay!"

With my dog obediently perched on his haunches at my left side, I snap my heels together and render a salute. The general's got a huge grin spreading across his features.

"Well, if isn't a dog team!" he exclaims. "About time we got a dog team out here. You're the first Marine Corps K9 team I've seen in Iraq. I'm excited to have dog teams here in country."

"Oo-rah," I reply softly. That's Marine Corps speak for "yessir."

The general keeps walking toward us. He bends down and he's reaching out to pet Rex. "And boy, what a magnificent-looking animal you are."

I put my hand out, palm toward him in the universal gesture of *Stop right there*. The general pauses in midstretch.

"Sir, I'd love you to pet my dog," I tell him. "But with all due respect, he's a working dog, and I don't want to risk an accidental bite."

The general starts laughing. "Now, that's the attitude! That's good to go, Marine. Just make sure if he's gonna bite someone, it's some insurgent's ass!"

"Oo-rah."

"What's your dog's name?"

"Rex, sir."

"Fantastic. Rex. You know, there's no device on earth can measure up to a dog's nose when looking for explosives. You guys stay safe out there."

"Oo-rah."

"Carry on, Marine, and carry on, Rex!"

The general's XO hangs back to have a quiet word. He's a full bird colonel, and he asks me if I'm being taken care of out here. He knows I'm a lone marine who's been parachuted into the Warlords' base along with my dog. He wants to know if I've got my mailing address yet, so I can pass it to my family. I'm amazed and encouraged by how the highest ranks in the Corps are looking out for the lowest rankers and the newest arrivals— my dog and me.

I locate Captain Dahle in the H&S building, a low kind of prefab office block to one side of the chicken factory. At first he seems confused, like he's not expecting Rex and me. Then he makes some checks and tells me I'm to report to his deputy at H&S, Gunnery Sergeant Trotter.

Captain Dahle makes a call on the radio, and a couple of

minutes later Gunnery Sergeant Trotter appears with an expression like a charging rhino. He and Captain Dahle are like oil and water. The captain is a soft-spoken white guy, and I sense that he's smart and he's going to look out for Rex and me. Gunnery Sergeant Trotter is a squat black marine the size and shape of Mike Tyson. He'd been a drill instructor prior to joining 2/2, and he's genuine badass.

Captain Dahle tells him he's got two new marines to supervise—that's Rex and me. With that, the captain leaves us to it. The gunnery sergeant is the first guy we've met on the base who doesn't seem to dig my dog. He shows no interest or curiosity in Rex and doesn't even to want to pet him. He asks me where we've billeted ourselves.

I point out the Bunker. "That little hut over there."

He glares at it. "Who the fuck said you could billet there?"

I can tell what he's thinking: How can this corporal and his dog have their own room, when me, a gunnery sergeant, has to bunk with five other marines in one goddamn room?

"I told the XO I needed a place I could stay twenty-four-seven with my dog and not be disturbed. The XO said if I could find somewhere, it was mine. That's where we found."

"Good to go," snorts the gunnery sergeant, but I can tell that he's not happy.

He gives me a radio so we can communicate with each other across the base.

"Okay, so what are we doing with you?" he demands.

"I'm here at the battalion's disposal, so whatever they need me to do."

"Right. We'll have you doing gate duty and set up a rotation. I want you to change the hours you stand on gate every day, so if the insurgents are watching they won't know when to expect you. We'll let the infantry companies know you're here and if they need you we'll let you know. Every day you check in with me, two or three times a day. If you need anything, let me know."

"Roger that," I tell him. "Good to go, Gunney."

That evening I pen a letter home to my folks. Rex is snoring away beside me, and whimpering and snorting when he dreams one of his doggy dreams. He's probably off chasing a coyote somewhere on the hills around Camp Pendleton, which is one of our favorite places. I'm feeling pretty good in spite of the smell from the stream sewer and the buzz of insects all around us. They're drawn to my flashlight, but I can't close the door because of the heat.

"Everyone loves Rex and they're all excited that we're here," I write my parents. "They tried to separate us at first, but I found a funny kind of a room so that Rex and I can be together."

I tell them that I really hope Rex and I do a great job out here, because so many people are relying on us. I'm at a base where we're bang in the spotlight, and everyone's looking to my dog and me to track down the bombs. I'm nervous as hell, but at the same time I can't wait to get started. This is it. This is where Rex and I are going to get tested. This is where the rubber meets the road.

I've just finished writing when Red comes over to check on how we're doing. I ask him why this area is called the Triangle of Death. I've inquired of several people before, but no one seemed able to tell me.

"Easy," Red explains. "Look on any map and you'll see our area of ops forms a triangle shape. It's in there that you'll find the greatest concentration of firefights plus IEDs in all Iraq."

I ask him if Rex and I will get to see action. Red laughs, like it's a dumb thing to ask.

"Man, it's not a question of if you'll get to see combat. It's a question of whether you'll survive it."

Chapter Two

THAT FIRST NIGHT I WRAP MYSELF IN MY MOSQUITO NET, BUT COME morning I'm still bitten red raw by the insects. I glance across at Rex stretched out in his kennel. It looks as if he slept pretty much fine in there. I guess when there's a choice between the soft skin of a marine, or the tough, hairy flank of a dog, I'm the mosquito's first choice every time.

I'm relieved that Rex has slept well. We've got a big day ahead of us. First priority is to get Rex's nose in. I need to get him acclimated to searching in the heat, and I need to get his olfactory organs adjusted to the smells here. Rex is a dual-certified patrol and explosive-detection dog. That means he's trained to find weapons and to detect a range of explosive odors, as well as being able to secure bases and apprehend suspects.

It's the explosive-detection side of things that we're really needed for here in Iraq. Explosive-detection dogs need to maintain 95 percent accuracy when searching, to stay certified. They're required to have a certain number of "hits" on each explosive odor they're trained to detect. They need to be constantly training with those scents so they remain very recognizable to the dog.

Explosive scents tend to differ wherever you're searching, especially when you've got a nose as sensitive as Rex's. The scent of a bomb here in Mahmoudiyah is bound to differ from how it smells back in California. I need to train Rex with local arms and explosives—those that the insurgents are using here to build their bombs—to get his nose fully tuned in.

I go introduce Rex and myself to the Explosive Ordnance Disposal (EOD) team—the bomb disposal guys. By chance, their building is just along the perimeter wall from us, so they're our nearest neighbors. It's a stroke of good fortune. If there's one team Rex and I are bound to be working with closely, it's the EOD guys. Whenever we find something, they'll get called in to defuse it.

The guy in charge of the EOD team is Gunnery Sergeant Clyde Smith, a short, stocky white dude. As soon as I walk into their building, I hear this voice say, "All right! A dog team!"

I can tell immediately that Gunney Smith and his team really dig Rex. They're accustomed to working with K9 teams, and Gunney Smith's not the slightest bit surprised when I ask him if he's got any local explosives or IED-type devices I can use to do some training.

He takes me into a back room. They've got a wall racked out with wooden shelving, on which they've got all kinds of devices and explosives that their team has found around Mahmoudiyah. It's a treasure trove—every kind of training aid I could ever wish for in terms of the deadly kit that the local insurgents are using is here.

I ask Gunney Smith to show me the kind of devices they're

finding around Mahmoudiyah. He points me toward a typical cell-phone-initiated IED. There's something innately chilling about the look of the thing. It's a standard gray Nokia phone strapped to a small car battery with half a dozen loops of yellow electrical wire. The wire is attached to the phone's aerial, and I presume that the phone must send a signal to the battery in some way or another.

At the battery end, the yellow wire is soldered in to a number of electrical connectors, which in turn lead to the explosives. Gunney Smith explains to me that when the cell phone rings, it completes an electrical circuit that enables the car battery to punch in enough electrical current to set off the blasting cap or detonation cord, which in turn ignites the main body of the explosives.

This type of IED requires a watcher to initiate it, someone who's in visual range of the device. Here in the Triangle of Death the watcher waits for a U.S. military patrol to come along, and as it passes the IED he dials the cell phone—and *boom!* It's that simple. It's a horrendous killing machine, and a watcher can easily activate it when he spots a dog tracking an explosive scent to its source.

Planting IEDs is a cowardly, sneaky way to fight a war, as opposed to fronting up man-to-man to your enemy and saying *Bring it on*. The marines are getting hit by IEDs seemingly every time they get out around Mahmoudiyah. But it's a fact that 80 percent of those devices are killing innocent Iraqi civilians, mostly women and children. IEDs are banned under all the rules of warfare, because they're such indiscriminate maimers and killers.

What I'm most interested in getting my hands on is some

PE4. This is the Russian equivalent of our own C4 plastic explosive, and it has similar characteristics. It looks and feels like a lump of plasticine. It can be molded to fit into just about any nook or cranny, or any shape of IED-type device.

Gunney Smith confirms that PE4 is the main killer here in Iraq. They're finding more of it than any other type of explosive. The bomb makers are using detonation cord—"detcord"—to set off the PE4. When they can't get their hands on any PE4, they use TNT—dynamite—as a fallback option.

I get samples of PE4, detcord, and dynamite, and take them over to the supply room, a mini-warehouse inside the chicken factory. I figure it's the ideal place in which to set Rex some detection exercises. It's windless in there, so the scents won't get blown about, and there are acres of equipment within which to hide the various explosives. Plus there is no ordnance stored in the supply room, so there are no explosive odors to distract Rex from what I want him to find.

I've already met the supply room guy, Sergeant Bentley, and I figure he'll have no problem with Rex and me messing around in there. Sergeant Bentley's an Eminem look-alike who's big into rap music. He's actually a surfer dude at heart, although he doesn't look or act like one.

I ask Bentley if he minds Rex and me doing some search exercises in his domain. He tells me no problem. There are piles of kit everywhere, heaped on pallets and stuffed into crates and boxes. There's everything here that a Marine Corps battalion needs that's nonlethal and that isn't kept in the armory: Kevlar helmets, flak jackets, AC units, bunk beds, cots, flashlights, the works.

I hide the detcord under a pile of body armor, and I slip the

TNT into one of the helmets. It's the PE4 that's going to be the real tester for Rex. It's a new odor for him, because back in the United States we train using C4. Some explosives have powerful scents: for example, detcord smells pretty much exactly like a firework. But I've had a good sniff of the PE4, and the off-white puttylike substance has no odor, or at least not one that I can detect.

It contains RDX—an explosive chemical also found in C4—so I hope that Rex'll be able to pick up the odor of the RDX. I stuff the PE4 inside an AC unit, at the bottom of a stack of the things, and set Rex to work. I show him his rubber ball—a quick flash of it out of my trouser pocket where it lives at all times—and give him the command: "Seek, Seek, Seek." The actual command is "Seek"—singular—but Rex and I have gotten into the habit of doing the commands three times, real quick.

Rex lowers his head and goes to work, sifting the air expertly through his muzzle. This is a game to Rex, and one that he loves. His tail starts wagging, and he's smiling happily as he sets off on the search. Gradually, everything else around us seems to stop. One after another, Sergeant Bentley and his supply guys cease what they're doing. They are transfixed.

As Rex walks his search transects, I'm glued to his every move. I'm watching for him to show a change of behavior—the first signal that he's hit the "scent cone." At the outer limit of the scent cone the particles in the air are less concentrated, and that's what he'll pick up on first.

Every dog's change of behavior differs, and it's all part of the animal's unique character. With Rex I'm watching for an almost imperceptible pause, like he's double-checking that he's onto something. He'll "air up," which means his head will come up and his nose will be snorting away to check for the smell. Then his tail will flick straighter and his muzzle will point the way ahead, tracking the concentration of particles to the strongest point, the source.

The closer he gets to the explosive, the more frantic and fierce his snuffling will be. Finally, I'll be able to hear him sucking in the scent like a pig. He's reached the "saturation point"—the strongest concentration of the smell—and he'll get as close as he can without physically touching it. Then he'll sit before it. He'll stare at it for a second, then look back at me: *Come on, partner, it's right here!*

Rex does all of that with the detcord—the strongest explosive scent in the room—and I pluck it out from under the heap of body armor. I show Rex the find and throw him his ball, saying, "Oh, good boy! Good boy!" I'm speaking in my high-pitched "praise" voice, the one that Rex knows means what good a job he's done. Rex grabs the ball and runs off with it, doing a victory roll as he goes.

Behind me, Sergeant Bentley and his boys are laughing their heads off.

"Wow, man, that was awesome!" Bentley exclaims. "I never seen anything like it!"

I give a half smile. I'm used to people going ape over my dog. "He's not done yet."

I retrieve the ball and give Rex the Seek command again. He goes and finds the TNT. I reward him again, then tell him to seek once more. For a moment he gives me a look: *Hey, is there more here? I thought we were all done.* Rex never wants to stop searching, though, he enjoys it so much, and he's soon off again snuffling and sniffing about. It takes him a while, but eventually he plonks his butt down right in front of the stack of AC units.

He glances over his shoulder, his eyes twinkling joyfully: *New one on me, but whatever it is it smells a bit like C4, and it's in there.*

Rex hasn't missed it. His nose is working perfectly, and he's got a hit on the PE4, the main explosive that's being used here in Mahmoudiyah. Sergeant Bentley says that he has never in his life seen anything like Rex at work. It's totally riveting. He tells me that Rex and I are welcome to use his warehouse for training anytime.

"And whatever kit you or Rex needs from the storeroom, you just let me know," he adds, with a generous smile.

It's going to be a real help having made an ally of the storeroom guy. With Rex having got his nose well and truly in—getting hits on a fresh odor of the kind we're going to be searching for—we're pretty much ready to roll. Now all we need is a mission.

We return to the Bunker, and I give Rex a good groom. I start with his rake, a strong metal comb that I use to drag out the worst knots and tangles in his coat, plus any excess fur that he's ready to shed. After that I give him a good brushing down. When I'm done his coat feels smooth and looks glossy like dark silk.

As far as I'm concerned, how often you groom your dog is a crucial sign of a how good a handler you are. A bad handler doesn't put in the extra 5 percent that's required to forge man and dog into an unbreakable team, and grooming is a big part of that 5 percent.

If a dog like Rex isn't groomed regularly, his fur will get

matted, and he'll keep licking himself to try to clear and free it, which can give him hairballs. Plus the burs dogs pick up in the field can work their way into the skin and cause nasty infections. But most important, regular grooming is part of the physical closeness you need to bond with your dog, where you and he become as one. In my mind, grooming equates to a dog licking your face: It's one of the most powerful signs of affection a handler can share with his dog.

In a way, grooming my dog is comparable to the way a marine grunt cares for his rifle. A marine is taught to care for his weapon above all else, and to constantly clean it, check for damage, and remove any dirt or rust. Marines are taught "the rifleman's creed": "This is my rifle. There are many like it, but this one is mine. My rifle is my best friend. It is my life. I must master it, as I must master my life. . . ."

Likewise, a dog's weapons are his senses: teeth, eyes, ears, and nose. And grooming your dog is all part of keeping the animal at peak performance at all times. Grooming goes hand in hand with cleaning their teeth and ears, plus clipping their nails so they don't get caught in wire or on other obstructions and rip free. Every handler loves to do the fun stuff with his dog. Grooming is the more mundane side, but it keeps the animal in top form at all times.

It costs at least $50,000 to bring a dog like Rex to the stage he's at now, where he's the most highly trained animal on the planet. I'm 100 percent responsible for my dog here in Mahmoudiyah, for there's no kennel master to watch over us, and that's some degree of responsibility.

The twelve Marine Corps handlers who have been chosen to go to Iraq have the qualities to work and act independently, or so our kennel master told us. Good handlers have to be strong-minded and self-starters. They have to be happy alone with their dog, driving their own schedule day after day. They have to be able to show initiative and not to wait around to be told what to do. Handlers who haven't got those qualities probably won't have the commitment needed to build a strong relationship with their dog.

It's six o'clock by the time I'm done grooming Rex and the sun's setting bloodred. We walk the short way to the Internet room, which is set in the nearest corner of the chicken factory. I take Rex with me everywhere I go, to get him accustomed to his new home. We queue for a terminal and finally I get online. I e-mail my folks and tell them that the first priority in terms of care parcels for Rex and me has to be food.

En route to Mahmoudiyah we stopped off in Al Asad, Ramadi, and Fallujah, three massive U.S. military bases here in Iraq. Each has its own chow hall, with fresh meals cooked daily. Here at Mahmoudiyah I'm going to be eating MREs—Meals Ready to Eat, U.S. military ration packs—for the next five months. I ask my folks to mail me some real food: PowerBars, Gatorade powder, and beef jerky for me, plus some big juicy bones for Rex.

I've just hit the Send button when there's a massive explosion behind me. The detonation wave smacks through the open door, blasting sand and smoke into my face and half blinding me. All around me guys are grabbing their helmets and body armor. There's a rush for the door as everyone tries to evacuate all at once. I figure we're coming under heavy fire and Rex and I better go do the same.

I sprint across the vehicle staging area, which is where the smoke from the blast seems thickest. I figure they've dropped a mortar bang in between here and the Bunker, so pretty much on our doorstep. I slam through the Bunker's front door, and Rex is half freaking out. His eyes are rolling and showing their whites, and his head's flashing from the door to me and back again.

His jaws are shut tight, a sure sign that he's tense as hell. Normally, Rex is panting away, his mouth hanging open and his tongue lolling happily. I grab his collar and hug him, and talk him down from his fear. "Easy, Rex, easy."

I dig out his doggy flak vest, which is made of the same material as our own body armor. I Velcro it under his belly and around his neck so that he's strapped in real tight. It's the first time that he's had his flak on since we arrived here in Iraq, and I know how much he hates it. But if there's the slightest chance it might save him from death or injury, then Rex is wearing the thing.

That done, I grab my own Kevlar and flak—Marine Corps speak for helmet and body armor—and pull both of them on. I hear the thumping roar of a .50-caliber heavy machine gun starting up from the watchtower above us. Our guys are returning fire. I'm in no doubt how close that blast came to smashing us, and it's really hit home with me. Rex can sense it. It's the first time either of us has been under fire here in Mahmoudiyah, and we're both scared shitless.

The base is in a complete frenzy. Over in the staging area I can see marines in full battle rattle loading up Humvees. They're clearly heading out to take on whoever it is that's hit the base. I know Rex and I can't just shelter in the Bunker forever. Powerful diesel engines fire up, and as the front vehicle prepares to lead off, a marine leans out of the passenger window.

"Hey! Dog team!" he yells. "You and your dog wanna come? We're going out to get the bad guys! If we find where they launched it from, maybe you can track 'em from there, if you know what I mean."

I tell the marine to wait one, that I have to check with H&S whether we can go. Gunney Trotter has told me I have to clear it with him if Rex and I are heading out on missions. I try to raise him on my radio but he's not answering.

I wave my radio at the marine. "I can't get clearance! I can't go without clearing it up the chain—"

"No worries!" the guy yells back. The Humvee pulls away, the marine shouting a last few words. "But get your clearance procedures sorted, buddy, 'cause we're gonna need you out on missions."

I'm frustrated and angry that Rex and I can't just get out and do what we've come here to do. But I know Gunney Trotter isn't going to like me getting spontaneous on him. If I disobey orders, I'll get him on my ass. He'll start micromanaging Rex and me, which will make matters worse in the long run.

A couple of days pass, and I'm getting more and more frustrated and discouraged. Rex can feel it from me, and he's unsettled. He's such a happy dog whenever we're working—tongue lolling out luxuriously, tail wagging rhythmically, and all toothy smiles. But now he's stopped grinning, and his tail's rigid and upright. It's a sign he's feeling uptight, just like his handler. He'd like to be out there and getting used, just as I would.

We're spending our days standing duty at the gates, searching Iraqis and their vehicles on their way into and out of the base. Rex gets his front feet up on the sandbagged gatehouse, and he barks furiously at anything suspicious. The marines love it, and they love Rex—just as people do everywhere I've ever taken him. He's such a good-looking dog that the marines have nicknamed him "Sexy Rexy."

But we didn't need to come to Iraq to learn that Rex is a stunner, or to stand gate duty. We could be doing this back at Camp Pendleton. I can hear firefights sparking off all across the city, and the boom of exploding IEDs. I hear the radios nonstop, as those who've been hit call in their casualties.

Mahmoudiyah is certainly living up to the reputation of being Death Central. The 2/2 has lost two guys killed in action already and taken a good amount of wounded in the past week. I know Rex and I could be out there helping stop the carnage.

I keep hearing talk of patrols that have been hit in ambushes all across the city. One marine I come across has a hole through his camo pants, where a round went through but didn't hit him. We're getting mortared daily, and we're getting more and more injured marines through the gates.

I see the EOD guys leaving the base to defuse IEDs, but Rex and I are left on the sidelines, unrecognized and unused. Bombs are going off, and there's an explosives-detection dog team on base not being used. To make matters worse, marines keep coming up to me saying how they'd love to have us out on their patrols.

Every morning I report to Headquarters and Service seeking a mission, just like I was told to. "Corporal Dowling and Rex, checking in," I tell Gunney Trotter. Every morning I get the same response: Go stand gate duty. No one seems to understand what we're here for, or to realize what my dog and I can do. I'm boiling up with frustration.

Gunney Trotter is cool with me. He's not deliberately trying to bust my ass, he's just too busy to proactively sell what Rex and I can do to the infantry companies. Something's been lost in translation between him and the company commanders—that there's a K9 search team here and that we're dying to get out on patrol.

There's another reason why the stakes have just been upped big-time here in Mahmoudiyah. I've picked up on it via the news feeds over the Internet, and everyone's talking about it here on the base. A private military company called Blackwater has made headline news, and for the worst possible reasons.

Four Blackwater contractors—Scott Helvenston, Jerko Zovko, Wesley Batalona, and Michael Teague—were ambushed as their SUV passed through Fallujah city on a food delivery job. They were hit by machine-gun fire and grenades, and their burned bodies were dragged through the city streets before being hung from a bridge over the Euphrates River. It's pretty damn horrific.

I had no idea what Blackwater was, so I did some research on the Internet. It seems there are thousands of private military contractors working for Blackwater—and others—here in Iraq. They're getting paid a shitload of money pretty much to do the same job we're doing. I've seen these unshaven guys wandering about in combats and armed to the teeth, and I figure they must be some of those private operators.

The consensus among the marines of the 2/2 is that the Blackwater incident is not helpful to what we're doing here. Not helpful at all. We figure this incident will embolden the insurgency. Fallujah is like a tinderbox, and the U.S. military up there is looking to avenge those killings. If Fallujah blows, it's bound to make things a whole lot worse for us down here at Mahmoudiyah.

We're a week in, and I'm up on the roof of the EOD guys' building with Gunnery Sergeant Smith. It's late evening, and Gunney Smith's telling me about a mission they were on that day. They were called out to defuse an IED, but en route they got hit in an ambush. One of his EOD guys was shot in the arm by an enemy sniper. That's the end of his days defusing bombs in Iraq. He needs both his arms to be able to deal with defusing and dismantling IEDs. He's being medevaced back to the United States for urgent treatment.

Gunney Smith figures that the bad guys are deliberately targeting his EOD team. The insurgents know they can't beat us in open warfare, so their strategy is to smash us with IEDs, hit us with follow-up ambushes, and to kill the EOD guys who can defeat the bomb threat. It's pretty obvious that if Rex and I get out on patrol they're likely to start doing the same to us. But to me that doesn't matter. I have to start making a difference with my dog, or there's no point in us being here.

There's the distant crackle of gunfire over the darkened city, which sits about a mile to the south of us. I wonder which patrol is getting hit this time, and why Rex and I can't be out there sharing the load. I make a decision. Rex and I came here to find bombs and save lives. We can't do that unless we go outside the wire. I'm going to go see the infantry-company commanders myself, to offer our services direct.

It's midafternoon the following day when Rex and I finish standing yet another gate duty. There are three infantry companies in 2/2—Echo, Fox, and Golf. It's the marines in charge of those companies I need to go see. I head over to the first sergeant's office, because those are the guys who daily lead the fighting patrols out into the hell of Mahmoudiyah.

Military working dogs are given a rank one higher than that of their handler. (And if the handler is promoted, so is his dog!) Just as a soldier must treat a two-legged superior officer with respect, the same goes for his four-legged partner. I would never call my dog "Sergeant Rex" openly, but in my mind we've got every right to go make ourselves known to the first sergeants of the Warlords.

I stand by their open doorway and peer in. All three of the first sergeants are in there, and they're busy talking among themselves. I knock on the door to get their attention. They go quiet and glance up at Rex and me. They're staring. I can read the expressions on their faces: Who the hell is the dude with the dog?

I say, "Good afternoon, First Sergeants, my name's Corporal Dowling, and this is my military working dog, Rex. We've been attached to you guys for a week now, and we're here to help out—"

"Can that dog sniff out bombs?" one of the first sergeants cuts in.

"Yes, First Sergeant, that's what he's trained for."

"Great. I'm with Echo Company, and we're gonna use you tonight. Can you work tonight?"

I tell him we can.

"Great. We can sure use that dog. Damn, we didn't even know you guys were here. Meet in the briefing room at eighteen hundred."

"Good to go."

Next we head for H&S and root out Gunney Trotter. I tell him that I've got a mission scheduled for tonight. He gives me a look, like how the hell did you manage to get that? I explain that I went to see the first sergeants myself and got allocated the mission. Gunney Trotter shrugs. I guess he can't fault my initiative.

"Good to go, Dowling," he tells me, "and good luck. And, Dowling, report to me first thing in the morning and let me know how the mission went."

It's six o'clock and I'm in on the mission briefing. The commander of Echo Company outlines the plan to his first sergeant and one of his platoon commanders. Marines from Echo Company have been ambushed repeatedly in one area on the eastern side of Mahmoudiyah. They've received good intel as to who is responsible, and they've located the safe house where the bad guys are hiding out. The mission is to go in at dead of night and set up a Vehicle Checkpoint (VCP) and to raid that building.

One squad will dismount from Humvees at the rear and assault across the open bush. The other squad will hit the target from the front, in a pincer movement. Echo Company will be taking down a target in the midst of an area of intense IED activity, which is part of the reason they want me and Rex on tonight's mission.

Once the commander has finished outlining the mission, he turns to me. "Dog handler, we haven't worked with a dog team before, so how best can you be used?"

It's crucial I get my response just right here. I'm a corporal surrounded by staff NCOs and officers, and someone of my rank normally never gets access to such briefings. I'm here because I'm the only one who can advise on the use of Rex, and I want to say the right thing to give them confidence to use us again.

"My dog and I will man the VCP and search for arms and explosives," I tell him, trying to sound confident. "Soon as the target building has been cleared, we'll move up and search that and the surrounding area for arms and explosives."

"Good. Simple as that," the Echo Company commander confirms. "Is this your first time outside the wire?"

I nod an affirmative. "Yessir."

"In that case be sure you stay in the vehicle until the target building's been secured."

Echo Company will depart the base at two-thirty a.m. That leaves a little over seven hours to get Rex and myself ready. My first priority is to get my dog fed and rested, in preparation for the mission. As I fuss over him, I realize my mood has changed dramatically. I'm no longer itching to get used. Instead, I'm racked with nervous excitement. I'm a professional, as is Rex, and this is what we came here to do. I want to get out there and make my father proud of me. But at the same time I'm worried how Rex will react under combat conditions and facing fire.

As usual Rex wolfs down his chow, then cuddles up to me on my cot. It's so cramped he's half on top of me. Just as he's dozing off he jumps down and heads for his kennel. It's typical Rex: He's very particular about his sleeping arrangements. A couple of quick turnarounds and he flops down. Soon he's co-matose, making faint snoring noises and the odd grunt, twitch, and squeak as he dreams.

I leave the door of his travel kennel open, in case he decides he wants to come and cuddle up to me in the hours before the mission. It's rare that he doesn't come for a snuggle in the night. Maybe he's had a bad dream, or he's just in need of some com-pany. Either way, I'm here for Rex 24/7, just as he's always here for me.

In the year and a half that Rex and I have been together as

a team, we've done loads of detection work. We've been out training with the law enforcement agencies local to Camp Pendleton, because they have no bomb-detection dogs of their own, and we've been first on call to any potential bomb threat. We've responded to several, and Rex has always done well. Every time we went out he obeyed my commands, worked tirelessly, and always followed a good search pattern, so I knew he'd cleared whatever he was searching.

We patrolled the Camp Pendleton base for intruders—what we term "unauthorized personnel"—and worked around the area tracking down illegal immigrants, a lot of whom have crossed over the border from Mexico. And in the weeks prior to deploying to Iraq, I made a special effort to get Rex out on the ranges at Camp Pendleton, to try to get him used to gunfire and explosions.

But time and again, Rex would freak out at all the loud bangs and detonations. The nearer an explosion or gunshot was to him, the more it would spook him. I'm acutely aware that being on the ranges is a far cry from being in the midst of a fast-moving firefight, for which Rex and I have done no training whatsoever.

Normally, U.S. military units scheduled for deployment to the front line carry out intensive training and exercises—both shooting blanks and live firing—to simulate combat conditions. Troops in a unit bond "under fire," or as near as you can get to being under hostile fire without being at war. Plus those troops learn how to operate together as a team and how to respond to specific threats.

Rex and I—plus the other K9 handlers deployed to Iraq—have had none of that. There's been no time or opportunity or expertise on hand to provide such training. Our kennel master kept telling us that K9 units hadn't gone to the front line of war since the Vietnam era. As a result, we'd lost the know-how to do so, and there was no K9 training regime in place for deploying to war. It's our job to learn how to do it all again.

I start prepping my weapons—slamming rounds into the mags of my M16 and cleaning and oiling my pistol. I grab Rex's doggy flak jacket, plus his strap-over mesh muzzle in case we run into any strays. During the rides that we hitched down here, there were packs of mangy dogs everywhere, and Rex could smell and sense them. In spite of the years of training and his iron will, Rex is still a dog, and I need the muzzle to stop him barking at them.

I can't get the thought out of my head that here I am heading into action with a bunch of battle-hardened marines, and I'm a combat virgin with a dog that hates bombs going off and gunfire. I'm reminded of a saying of my father's: Beware of what you wish for—for you may end up getting it.

My kennel master had given me the option to avoid this deployment, because tragically, my father is dying from cancer. We're a small, tight-knit team at Camp Pendleton's K9 unit, and he is aware of how close I am to my dad.

"Corporal Dowling, I think you and Rex have been doing an excellent job," he told me when first he broached the subject of us deploying to Iraq. "I figure you have become one of our best dog teams, and I'm confident you guys will do a good job if I send you to Iraq. However, I'm aware of the situation with your dad. What's the prognosis right now?"

"Well, I'm told he probably won't live past the start of the summer," I replied.

"Okay, I'm giving you the option. I want you to go. You and Rex are my first choice to go on this deployment. But I'm giving you the option not to go so you can be here for your dad's funeral."

I'd anticipated this moment, and I'd thought of what I would say. "Staff Sergeant, I really appreciate you giving me the option to stay here, but I signed up for the Corps to do a job and my dad will want me to do it. Plus what good am I staying here waiting for him to die when I can be overseas saving lives? Why would I want to wait for the life I cherish most to pass away, when I can go and save life? And if I decide not to go and another team goes in my place and gets hurt or even killed, there is no way I will be able to live with myself after that."

My kennel master eyed me for a long second. "There's a good chance you won't be flown home for your dad's funeral."

"I think he'd find it okay, as long as he knew I was taking care of marines and saving lives out there."

"You're going, then?"

"Send me. I'm honored to go. And thank you."

I really respected and appreciated the care my kennel master had shown for me. He could have simply ordered me to go, regardless of how I felt or my circumstances back at home. Instead, he did his best to make sure I was mentally ready to deploy, and he'd shown real empathy with me over my father's illness.

Chapter Three

REX AND I EXIT THE DARKNESS OF THE BUNKER. THE SKY ABOVE US IS so star bright it dazzles. A bloodred moon hangs low on the horizon, and the constellations glitter close and crystal clear. It makes the California nights back home seem somehow muted and gray.

I take a second to catch my breath, admiring the beauty of the moment, and then I'm heading for the muster area, Rex trotting happily at my side. He glances up at me, giving me a look: *So, what adventures you taking me on tonight, partner?*

To tell the truth, I'm worried. It's our first combat mission and I've no idea what to expect. But I don't want Rex sensing that and picking up the bad vibes from me.

"It's Mission One, buddy," I tell him, reaching down to pat his powerful flank. "The Warlords are going looking for trouble. But you and I are ready for this. *We're ready.*"

We pitch up in the muster area. The Humvees have got their engines running and their headlights on. Beyond the base perimeter it's empty darkness, but here there's a halo of light, and I announce myself to the assembled marines.

"Hey, guys, this is my dog, Rex, and we're headed out with you on tonight's mission."

There's a chorus of enthusiastic responses.

"Fuck yeah!"

"We got a dog with us tonight to look after us!"

"So, he's gonna sniff out bombs and shit?"

"And how d'you get to be a K9 guy, anyway?"

They're real curious about Rex and me. I do my best to answer their questions. Most aren't even aware that the Marine Corps has K9 teams, let alone knowing what we're for. But when they ask me how I got into K9, all I tell them is that I "got lucky." If I told them the real story I doubt whether most of them would believe me. For now, at least, it's probably best left unsaid.

We're milling about as we wait to board the vehicles. The marines are going gaga over Rex. They can't help themselves, especially when they hear that this is our first time going outside the wire.

"Hey, it's Sexy Rexy!"

"Boy, you sure make me miss my Rusty back home!"

"You're one goddamn handsome dog!"

Rex is lapping it up, while at the same time trying to show that he's not up for a mass love-in. He's sniffing enthusiastically at the marines, but he's not letting them pet him. It's typical Rex. It's like he wants the marines to know he's one of the boys, while still keeping his cool.

Remember that kid at high school who was so damn good-looking and confident and funny that he didn't even have to try? Every school has one. Well, that's Rex. That's 100 percent Rex as we gather with the marines for this night mission.

There are two squads of marines, so about twenty-five guys in all. As I glance around them I realize that I am the only person here who was present at the mission briefing. The Echo Company first sergeant must have briefed his staff sergeant, who is the guy leading the raid on the ground tonight.

Come sunup, the marines tasked with this mission are going to be running security for the 2/2 battalion commander. So tonight, they want to get in and out as quickly as possible. They decide to dispense with the Vehicle Checkpoint and go straight to hit the target building.

We load up. There are four open-backed Humvees, six marines to each, plus Rex and me. Rex gets his front paws onto one of the bench seats so he can peer over the side. He turns his head toward me. I know the expression well: *Come on, let's get this show on the road!*

We head out of the base and into the night, Rex's nose in the speeding vehicle's slipstream. The streets are eerily quiet. At this hour everyone but us is tucked up in their beds, which is where any sane person should be. It's the perfect time to hit the target.

We head into downtown Mahmoudiyah. The tension in the vehicle crackles. The marines are dead silent, eyes forward, hands gripping their weapons as they psych themselves up for the mission. I glance at the faces in our vehicle. The guys seem ready but relaxed, and I guess for them it must be business as usual. I hope that my own fear doesn't show.

I ruffle Rex's ears and caress the soft fur beneath them. He flicks his long tongue out and gives my hand a few good licks. It's his way of telling me he's okay. Plus it's his way of reassuring me: *Hey, don't be so nervous, partner. I'm with you.*

It's the first time Rex and I have ventured into the city. The buildings are run-down gray hulks dotted between palm groves. There are piles of trash and debris everywhere, plus open sewers. The smell is ripe in our nostrils.

We hit an open, rural area on the far side of town. The blacktop gives way to dirt roads. The convoy of Humvees weaves its way between ranks of slender, arching palm trees. This place would be breathtaking in a sparse desert oasis kind of way if it weren't for the reason we're here.

We take a tiny track leading into the middle of nowhere, and the convoy starts to slow. We're almost at the target. I slip the mesh muzzle over Rex's snout. He barely reacts. He knows it's the real deal now. He can sense it.

The Humvees grind to a halt. In the stillness and silence that follows, the staff sergeant in charge gives a whispered order: "Okay, dismount!"

As the men pile off, Rex turns to me: *So are we going, or what?* He wants to be where the marines are. I shake my head at him, keeping a firm hold on his leash. Our orders are to stay with the vehicle until the target building is secured.

The staff sergeant glances over his shoulder. "Dog team, come with us."

I say, "The captain briefed us to stay with the vehicles."

"I don't give a fuck," he fires back. "Come with us."

I pile off, Rex one bound ahead of me and hyperalert. "Good to go," I confirm.

With a grunt of their big diesel engines, the Humvees pull away. In the few moments it takes the staff sergeant to orient himself, I realize I'm hugely vulnerable. The vehicles have gone, and we're on foot and unprotected in the heart of enemy territory. It suddenly hits me that Rex and I are in the middle of a hostile war zone, and in that instant my senses become hyperalert.

I glance around. There's a shallow culvert to one side of the track. I make a mental note of it. If the enemy hits us, it's there that Rex and I will go to ground. I'll shield him with my own bulk if I have to, encased as I am in my body armor. As long as I'm still breathing, no one's shooting my dog.

The staff sergeant signals for us to circle up. "There," he whispers, a finger jabbing the darkness, "the target house."

A couple hundred yards away is a squat building half obscured by palm trees.

"We got to get from here to there as fast as we can," he continues. "I want you guys over there in the blink of an eye. We got to double-time behind the rear of the house and get into position fast. You guys move fast and don't stop till you get there."

All I can think is that I have never trained for what we're about to do. I decide to shadow one of the marines and go wherever he goes. The marine on point cuts through some strands of barbed wire. We start running, a thin line of gray, moonlit figures flitting through the palm grove.

Rex knows this is it—a combat mission, red in tooth and claw—and as he runs he keeps swiping at the mesh muzzle with his paw. He wants it off badly. Like the rest of us, he wants his weapons ready. He can't fully protect us muzzled, but I don't want him barking and giving away our position.

As we run, my main problem is my M16. The other marines have their weapons held at the ready. Mine is slung across my front on a sling so I can keep a tight hold of Rex's leash. But it keeps slipping down and half tripping me and whacking Rex on the head. I sling it onto my back, and grab my Beretta 9mm pistol from my thigh holster. I grip that in my hand as we run.

Right away I know that for K9 teams to function properly in combat, we'll need shorter weapons. I guess that's what my kennel master meant by us being the "guinea pigs."

The other marines are all using night-vision kit, which enables them to see in the dark—but not me. I need to see things as Rex sees them. And there's no way I can strap a night-vision unit onto my dog.

Rex keeps glancing to the left. I look where he's looking. There's a thin line of weird double spots dancing like shining coals beneath the palm grove. It's the moonlight reflecting in the eyes of a pack of stray dogs.

To the marines this means nothing. Iraq is full of mangy mongrels. To me it means everything. The greatest threat to Rex right now is that dog pack, and he knows it.

There're a dozen-odd strays and they can sense and smell Rex. They know there's a strange dog in their territory and they hate it. Their hackles are up, the dog pack's aggression smoldering.

The strays have a shorter, wirier coat than Rex's thick, glossy fur. It's far more suited to the furnace heat of the Iraqi day. But now we're operating in the cool of the desert night, and Rex is at no disadvantage. He's more than a match for the average stray—but not a pack of twelve of them. I've got to do something.

I stoop as I'm running and grab a fist-sized rock. I'm about to lob it at the nearest strays when I stop myself. The marines are bound to hear it. They'll think we have hostiles on our left flank, which will blow the mission wide open.

The strays are closing in fast. Rex goes tense at my side. For him to be muzzled and facing a slathering dog pack is his worst possible nightmare.

He's going wild trying to paw off his muzzle. We can't keep running with him doing so. I reach down, flick it off, and finally his mouth is free. He shakes his head real quick, then turns to face the advancing dog pack, the most aggressive of which have started barking wildly.

It's now that every fiber of his canine instinct is fighting against the years of disciplined training. I know Rex is about to bark. He's hyperprotective of me and the other marines. But if he barks, the strays will read it as a challenge and pursue him ever more aggressively.

My sixth sense is screaming a warning at me that Rex is going to growl and bark. He is an extension of myself, and I know what he's going to do before he does it. I'm closer to my dog than I am to just about any human being. Without the need to speak, I can communicate with another species. It's incredible. Nothing comes close.

As we're running, I flick my boot up and rap Rex on the nose. A real quick tap. He glances up at me, and I make a move with my open hand, closing all four fingers and thumb into a tight fist. It's the signal for *Keep your mouth shut.*

At the same time I hiss a single word: "Quiet!"

As soon as I've said it, Rex turns back toward the target building, his jaws clamped firmly shut, and we're racing to outrun the killer dogs. We sprint for all we're worth, but the strays are closing fast—a snarling, slathering wolf pack.

Rex keeps glancing in their direction, back to the target building, and to the strays again. I know exactly what he's thinking: *Which are we gonna run into first?*

We reach the coiled razor wire perimeter of the target building just as the wolf pack is upon us. But the mass of marines gathered here and armed to the teeth halts the strays in their tracks. They can sense that Rex is one of us and that they're outgunned and outnumbered.

The strays stick to the shadows, pacing and snarling, fangs gleaming white in the moonlight. Up ahead, the target is like a fortress. I've got to get Rex's mind off the strays and onto the next challenge—the coils of deadly razor wire piled up to chest height before us. The marines start vaulting over, but I know Rex'll need a helping hand.

I grab the marine I'm shadowing. "I need help getting my dog over this!"

The marine shakes his head, confused. "Like how?"

"Jump over and I'll throw my rifle on top. I'll grab the barrel end, you grab the butt stock, and let's compress it as much as possible. Then I'll have him jump over."

The marine nods and vaults over the wire. Using all of our weight on the M16, we flatten the barrier as much as we're able. I unleash Rex and signal for him to prepare to jump. He doesn't need me telling him twice. He's already moving back the fifteen feet he needs to get his run up.

We practiced this a thousand times or more back at Camp Pendleton. The doggy obstacle course there includes a tunnel, a catwalk, hurdles, a window frame, and a six-foot wall. The wall is sheer on the one side, with a shelf halfway down the other for the dogs to land on. A slope runs off the shelf at forty-five degrees so the dogs can run to the ground.

The difference is that now Rex is facing a tangled mesh of wire coils, each sprouting mini–razor blades like talons. You

touch that razor wire stuff, it snares you. The more you struggle, the deeper the fanglike blades dig, snagging clothes and biting deep into soft body parts. It's lethal.

Rex isn't big for a German shepherd, and he never was able
to make the Camp Pendleton wall unsupported. Ignoring the
strays pacing in the shadows, he turns to face me. I go down
on one knee, crying gently: "Hup! Hup! Hup!" At the same
time I'm patting my thigh. It's the signal for him to use it as the
springboard from which to jump, just like we've done with the
wall a thousand times during training.

Rex runs forward, but I can tell that he's not going to make
it. I can read it in his eyes. He skids to a halt just short of the
wire. He's smart. He knows he doesn't have the momentum.

He sniffs the wire, then looks up at me, his trusting eyes full
of uncertainty, and a worry bordering on fear: *Are you kidding?
You want me to jump that?*

I bend down and whisper reassuringly in his ear: "You can
do this, boy. *You can do this.*"

From the opposite side of the wire I hear the staff sergeant
leading the mission urging us to get a move on. Rex turns and
prepares to make a second, longer run. But he knows what
that vicious wire can do to his soft underbelly, and it's un-
nerved him. He sprints toward me once more, falters for an
instant, then springs forward and touches off from my bended
knee.

Even before he's airborne I know he's going to straddle the
wire. I thrust both arms under his belly and heave him up and
forward and into the air.

Under Rex's weight, my arms crash down on the wire coils.
The blades rip through my combats like a thousand knives

through butter and tear into the soft skin of my forearms. I'm in agony, but I keep my teeth clamped tight shut.

The marine on the far side grabs Rex's collar and hauls him over the last. But as he does so I hear a pained, muted yelp from my dog. I vault across the wire and all my thoughts are for Rex. I stoop to check on him.

One of the strands of razor wire has slashed bloodred across the white velvety softness of Rex's belly. It's not life-threatening, but it sure is nasty, and I know it must hurt like hell. Yet my dog—God love him—has barely let out a whimper.

Rex knows this is different, that we're not on a training exercise anymore. He knows if he messes up it could spell death for either one or both of us. He has an incredible sixth sense for how I, his handler, am feeling. He knows I'm all keyed up, and he's raised his game and his attitude accordingly. What a dog.

We turn to follow the marine we're shadowing. But with my next step I stumble into an open drainage ditch that doubles as a sewer. Before I can stop myself, I've dragged poor Rex in with me. I'm up to my knees in stinking human shit and piss, but Rex has it up to his stomach or more.

He gives me a look: *Partner, you know what this smells like? No, I guess you don't—not with that nose.*

I think of all the stagnant water and dirt and shit that's seeping into Rex's open stomach wound. The thought, coupled with the smell of what we've blundered into, makes me gag. In the burning heat of Iraq, cuts can quickly turn septic. I'll have to clean, treat, and disinfect that injury just as soon as this is over.

Scrambling and slipping, I haul myself and Rex onto firmer ground. We're cut to shreds and covered in human feces, and the real fight hasn't even started yet. There's one upside: The pack of strays is on the far side of the wire and can't get to Rex anymore.

The marines on point are already at the rear of the target. Out front the Humvees are rolling to a halt, disgorging the other squad.

"Okay, move!" the staff sergeant signals. "Go! Go! Go!"

As the grunts hit the target building from two sides, the marine we're with signals for us to stay put. "We'll cover the rear," he mouths.

The crack of boots splintering wood cuts the night, followed by sharp screams and cries. Rex stiffens for an instant, then glances up at me. He gives me a half-worried gaze: *What the hell's that? And what do we do now?*

Rex is three years old, and during the last year and a half we've spent barely a day apart. He has become my life. He's at the peak of his fitness, and he'll never be sharper or quicker than he is now. I hope that as long as I stay calm and collected, my dog will too.

The noise is deafening as the first of the insurgents are bundled out the door, hands over their heads. I stroke Rex and talk to him, cooing and soothing him softly: "It's okay, boy, it's okay. . . ."

I spot a flash of movement out of the corner of my eye. A lone figure sprints from a side door to our left. I can't see a weapon, but I know that Rex has spotted him the same instant that I have.

As one, we turn our heads very sharply to the left. But it seems to take an age to do so. In the adrenaline rush of combat I'm hypersensitive to everything around me. Each second seems magnified one hundred–fold, each movement playing out in ultraslow motion.

I grab Rex's thick collar and mouth into his ear: "Watch him! Watch him! Watch him!"

Just as soon as he hears the command, it's like a light's been switched on. A low growl echoes in the depths of Rex's throat, and he's up on all fours, alert, tense, ears down, and ready to go. He's straining at the leash. As for me, my adrenaline's pumping bucketloads, for I'm about to release my dog.

The figure reaches the open street. I release both leash and collar: "Get him!"

Rex powers away like a bullet from a gun. His bunched muscles are firing him forward, his legs flashing through the thin grass, his leash trailing like a whip behind him.

Rex is closing on the target, sprinting through the bush to get to the open road. But as the figure passes under a flickering streetlamp, I see that it's a kid. No way can I live with myself if I set my dog on an innocent kid. I don't want that playing on my mind, and especially as this is the first time I've ever sent Rex after a live human being for real.

Above the deafening noise from the target building, I start screaming at the top of my lungs: "OUT! OUT! OUT!"

Rex slows, to show me he's heard me, but he keeps moving forward. He's been shown the target and he wants to do his stuff now. It's a battle of wills, and Rex is as stubborn as they come.

"REX—OUT!" I yell again. He turns to look at me, glances back at the running figure, then back to me again: *Oh, come on, let me get him.*

I respond by giving him the Sit command, and reluctantly he lowers his rump onto the dirt. I follow this with the Heel command, and slowly Rex returns to my side. He's got his head held low, eyes down. I grab Rex's collar and praise him for being such a good boy.

I see the kid running off down the street, and he seems oblivious of the fact that Rex was after him. If I'd used my rifle and taken the shot, the kid would now be dead. If you fire and realize it's the wrong target, it's too late. A dog is like a bullet you can call back again.

There's a huddle of captives out in front of the house, plus a growing pile of weaponry and ammo. The raid has gone in so swiftly and silently, not one of the insurgents has had the chance to open fire on us. It's a textbook snatch operation, and I'm starting to appreciate how good the 2/2 are at what they do.

The marines line up the captives and secure their wrists with plastic ties. As Rex and I move into the light, they are staring at us—or, more accurately, at Rex—like we've just beamed down from Planet Zog. They're wide-eyed with fear. They've clearly never seen a K9 team in action before, and they must be wondering what the hell we've brought the dog for.

I ask one of the marines if everyone's out of the house.

He shakes his head. "Dunno."

"Okay, we'll start searching for weapons and explosives outside. When everyone's out of the house, I'll take Rex in."

He nods. "Sounds good to me."

I pull Rex's ball out of my pocket. We handlers use a Kong, a solid rubber tennis-ball-sized sphere that's all but immune to a dog's chewing. The moment Rex sees the Kong, he lowers his rump and sits at my feet, gazing longingly at it. He knows we're moving into detection mode now. He knows if he doesn't find something he won't get to play with his beloved ball.

I give him the command: "Seek, seek, seek." I tuck the Kong

back into my pocket. Rex puts his nose to the ground. He's immediately trying to catch the scent of gunmetal or explosives. With a gentle tug on the leash I guide him where I want him to go.

Rex loves detection work. He's flicking his tail back and forth as he noses carefully through the bush. As for me, I am totally focused on my dog now. A dog reacts to detecting a target scent by a subtle change in the way he's searching. Each dog's reactions differ, so a handler must learn his dog's every mannerism and move.

In the dim light thrown off by the moon and the stars, Rex freezes momentarily: *Wait a second—I think I got something.* I pause with him. He sniffs the air, tasting the scent on his tongue: *Just a moment, let me work my nose.* His tail stops wagging, his nose is up, and he's ready: *Let's go for it!*

We move off together following the trail of the odor, tracking it to its source. And wherever Rex is leading me, I hope to God it's not going to kill us.

Chapter Four

REX'S NOSE IS FLARING, HIS LUNGS WORKING OVERTIME AS HE DRAGS in the scent of whatever it is that he's onto. His eyes have the look that I know—and out here, *fear*—so well. There's an intense, maniacal light burning in them as he tracks the killer scent to its source.

With every step his paws take, I'm poised to pull him back, to save him from stepping on a device that will blow us both to smithereens. But at the same time I know that if we don't push it to the max, it may be one of the marines who gets killed instead. Whatever he's onto here, we've got to find and clear it.

Rex slows to a crawl. It's a clear sign that he's right in the heart of the scent cone. My pulse is racing, heartbeat hammering like a machine gun as he inches forward, head swinging gently from side to side as he sifts the air. Suddenly I hear this voice yelling from behind me.

"LOAD UP! HEY, LOAD UP! DOG TEAM, WE'RE MOVIN' OUT!"

I turn to see the staff sergeant signaling me urgently from his Humvee. One of the Iraqi prisoners is crammed in there alongside half a dozen marines, plus there's a bundle of seized weaponry lying in the vehicle's footwell. I've been so focused on my dog that I haven't noticed the entire squad of marines loading up to leave.

I hesitate for an instant, so reluctant am I to call Rex off this far into the search. Then the staff sergeant starts screaming at me to shift my ass and to get the hell out of there. He's going ape about the amount of time we've spent on the ground in the heart of bandit country, and he wants us gone.

I turn with Rex and we sprint for the vehicle. A moment later we're in the back alongside the marines, and the staff sergeant gives the "Move out!" I settle onto the seats, Rex between my knees. I pet him and tell him he's done a real good job out there. He was onto something, of that I'm certain. It was just that time was against us.

My main concern now is for Rex's wounded stomach. As we ride through the silent, night-dark streets of Mahmoudiyah, I do my best to inspect it. I get my M9 pistol, flick on the flashlight attached to it, and take a quick look at his injury. The gash has bled out a little, but it doesn't appear to he bothering him too much. He lets me look it over without trying to nip at my hand. He's not yelping or licking the wound, and he's certainly not been limping.

As soon as we're back at the Bunker I grab some bottled water and soap and a sponge, and I clean where the razor wire gashed him. I wipe away all the grime and feces until the wound's good and clean. It's pretty much in the center of his belly, and I can tell that he doesn't like me messing with it much. But at the same time he understands and appreciates what I'm doing.

He knows I'm looking out for him, doing what I'm doing

with tenderness and love. I break out our medical kit and check and treat and disinfect the raw-red slash as best I can. There's no point bandaging it, because he'll only rip it off, so I leave it open to the air. I'll check in the morning that it's clean and that it doesn't look like it's getting infected.

When I'm done, we settle down to rest, both of us cradled together on my narrow bunk. Rex keeps trying to lick his wound, and there's no point trying to stop him. I think back over the mission. It's our first time in action, and we've yet to be in full-on combat, and already Rex is injured. As for me, I felt totally unprepared as the Echo Company Marines hit the target. I'm painfully aware of how Rex and I are yet to face a full-on firefight.

I console myself with the thought that so much could have gone so wrong for us out there. And by and large we did good. Rex faced a rabid dog pack, vaulted the razor wire, chased a suspect, and got called off, not to mention the search. We could hardly have asked for a tougher first mission. Rex has got his first war wound, he's got his feet dirty, and he's earned a scar to remember the mission by.

I'm immensely proud of Rex, and I figure he deserves a big treat. Most dogs would love a doggy snack or a biscuit at a time like this, but not Rex. For him it's a cow's bone or bust.

I've brought with me a stack of PETCO's vacuum-wrapped Mammoth Dog Bones. Wow! Rex really digs those bones. I find him one fit for a hero who's just survived his first combat mission. He'll be up half the night gnawing away on it and keeping me awake, but he's more than earned it.

When Rex and I first teamed up together, I had to learn what kind of treats he likes. But every kind of doggy snack I brought for him was rejected. He'd take the biscuit or treat in his mouth, give me a look, then drop it uneaten on the dirt. But when I got him his first big dog bone, he went to town on it.

It was big enough to stick out both sides of his mouth, and he carried it around with him everywhere like a trophy. In no time he'd gnawed it down to nothing. Everything else wasn't good enough, and Rex would settle only for the best. That's the stubborn side of my dog that I've come to know and love so well.

The morning after our first mission, it almost feels as if it never happened. Rex and I have slept late after the tension of that night-dark operation. I'm covered in bites from whatever critters have swarmed in during the hours of darkness, but I've slept remarkably soundly. Maybe it's the relief of finally getting used.

Rex also looks well rested—tongue hanging out and a big gummy smile as he grins at me from his bed. I get him out of his kennel and he gives me a look: *What kind of adventures can we get into today?*

First priority is to check his stomach wound. I clean it again, and it seems like it's healing well. I throw a scoop of Science Diet dog chow into his metal feed bowl. We're under strict instructions not to feed our dogs anything other than Science Diet, because changing a dog's feed can make him ill. Science Diet is precisely formulated to help keep dogs healthy, which is why the manufacturers of Science Diet are the military's chosen supplier.

Back at home I'd emptied out dozens of bags of the stuff into sealable plastic buckets. I've got five of those crammed full to the brim, which is about two months' worth of food for Rex.

Morning and night I feed him two big scoops of the crunchy dried food. I clean and sanitize his bowl after each meal, to stop him picking up infections. As a human I wouldn't want to eat off a dirty plate, and as handlers we're taught that a dog shouldn't have to either.

Every morning and evening Rex and I sit and eat together. It's a ritual, and Rex loves his routines. He also loves his chow. Normally, he consumes it so quickly that it's gone in a couple of mouthfuls. But ever since we touched down in Iraq he's been suffering from a light case of the runs. It's not serious, and I figure it's just the change of climate that's caused it. It often affects dogs that way.

But now that he's got that nasty gash to his stomach, I'm worried. I watch him like a hawk as I feed him his breakfast. If Rex was feeling real bad, then he'd be off his food. As he wolfs down the Science Diet, just like normal, I'm happy. There's nothing wrong with Rex. He's got his first war wound and it doesn't seem to be bothering him.

I rip the top off an MRE ration pack and settle down to my own meal. MREs aren't too bad—it's just that you have to eat them day after day and you get sick to death of them. The hot dog sealed in an airtight plastic bag is total garbage. But the spaghetti with chicken is pretty good, and I love the crackers and cheese. As for the little bottles of Tabasco sauce, those are to die for.

I've brought lots of beef jerky with me, because I had a premonition about living for months on end on MREs. The best you can get is Jack Link's Beef Jerky—Original, Peppered, Seasoned Hot, Sweet & Hot, and Organic varieties. My favorite is Peppered, because it reminds me of my mother's hot and spicy cooking back home. Being of Mexican Indian origin, my mom cooks the best tacos you've ever tasted.

I can't share the beef jerky with Rex, for fear that it'll screw with his digestion. It's bad enough with the diarrhea he's got. He needs to go more frequently, which isn't the easiest thing to deal with when living in the Bunker. Luckily, I've found a pile of sand around the back of the hut and that's become his break area.

Rex knows not to beg when I'm tucking into my beef jerky. He might glance my way, but he knows not to ask. I'll give him a bit of bread from the MREs, which I know won't upset his digestion. Anyway, Rex is too proud to beg, and he knows that's not that kind of relationship we have.

After breakfast, we head down to H&S. Captain Dahle is all smiles. "Good work, Corporal. I'm getting word they want you guys with them regular on patrols."

Even Gunney Trotter seems somewhat impressed. He asks us to stand a gate duty, but only while we're waiting to get allocated our next mission.

Everywhere on the base people seem to be warming to my dog. But there's no way I can seem to get the Iraqi interpreters to like him. Many Muslims consider dogs to be unclean. They would never have one living in the house as a pet, let alone dream of sleeping with one as I do. But I'm not used to people *not* loving Rex, especially the young, pretty woman with whom I'm sharing gate duty.

Suraya is in her midtwenties and she dresses in Western-style clothes, apart from her head covering. She's an English teacher by profession, but she can earn better money acting as an interpreter for us and she needs it for her family. At first she strikes me as being typically shy and reserved, but once she realizes that I'm genuinely interested in what she has to say, she switches right on.

Talking to her is the first time I feel like I'm actually connecting with a local. I've got loads of questions I want to ask, and most of them concern how the Iraqis see us. The trouble is Rex. He sees Suraya, he barks at her. In part he's doing it because she's not a marine. Anyone who isn't a marine is well outside of his dog pack. But in part he's doing it because he's jealous. He can sense that I like Suraya.

"Your dog is very rude," she remarks as Rex barks his head off at her.

I try a winning smile. "He's just very protective. Anyway, he's jealous of you."

That's my way of flirting with her. I'm not hitting on her as such, I'm just trying to make a connection. Anyway, it makes Suraya laugh, and I love making pretty girls laugh. None of the marines standing gate duty seems interested in engaging with her much, so I guess this makes me a bit of an oddity. Do I care? Not particularly.

Pretty quickly I figure out a way for Suraya and me to chat without Rex going crazy the whole time. I stand outside the gatehouse with Rex at my feet, and she stands inside. We can talk via the window, and Rex can't see whom I'm talking to, so he's got no excuse to start barking.

"You're the first person I've met who's a local," I tell her. I ask her if she minds me talking about some of the subjects that are foremost on my mind, like how the Iraqis see the American forces here. Suraya says she's happy to speak about such things.

"I'd like to know how you see things," I tell her, "and the

attitude generally to us being here, getting rid of Saddam, that kind of thing."

"We are excited that the United States got rid of Saddam," she tells me. "We wanted him gone for so long. Initially that is how we felt. But now we feel like there is so much fighting and we do not know if it is worth it anymore. So much violence, and we do not know how it will all end."

Suraya's one of twelve siblings, and she's a wholesome, family girl. She's university-educated and, surprisingly for an Iraqi woman of her age, she's not married. She's also big into Western culture. She loves American pop music and especially our movies. Her favorites are the timeless American thrillers and comedies. We reminisce over the classic eighties gangster movies, like *Scarface* with Al Pacino, and one of my all-time favorite films, *Top Gun*.

Suraya shares some of her flat unleavened bread with me. It's delicious, and it's real food as opposed to MREs. She offers to start bringing me some bread whenever she's working at the base. She tells me she wants to build bridges between the Americans and the Iraqis, and she feels it's her duty to help communicate to the people what our intentions are here. She also feels that because we are away from our families—especially our mothers and our wives—she has a duty to help take care of us.

The gate has a lot of traffic, locals demanding compensation for a cow that's been caught in the crossfire, that kind of thing. I watch Suraya translating their grievances, but at the same time she's also trying to help reach a settlement that's fair to all via her calm and straightforward interpreting. I guess I'm drawn to her by her worldliness and her Western-friendly ways, and she's drawn to me by my interest in her country, her people, and the impact of the war.

Suraya starts bringing me pirated DVDs. She can get her hands on all the current movie releases. They're terrible quality, but that doesn't matter when you're trapped in the backwater of Mahmoudiyah. She brings me local bread, and chicken kebabs wrapped in pita, which are delicious. We've been ordered not to eat the local food, but I can't resist.

I offer her MREs in return, and I can sense some kind of cross-cultural partnership flourishing here. Getting to know Suraya and her life fascinates me, and it feels important to me to understand what makes the locals tick. It's just Rex who still isn't pleased about our growing friendship. He keeps barking at Suraya, baring his fangs, and going *grrrr-grrrrr-grrrrr*. It's no way to behave with a lady.

I know what's going on here. Rex suspects that I'm flirting with Suraya, and in truth he's got a point. She is pretty, plus she's very, very friendly. When I talk to her she looks right into my eyes, as if she is really, really listening. And she's one of the only females on the entire base.

Suraya clearly loves our chats. The topics of conversation veer widely—but often it's about how we date so freely in America and do or don't end up getting married. Suraya tries to teach me Arabic words, and we end up laughing fit to burst, because it's so freakin' hard for me to pronounce them.

Rarely have I met a person who didn't love my dog, so having to get someone to *like* Rex is a whole new experience for me. I put the mesh muzzle on him whenever Suraya's around so she and I can talk more easily. But he keeps growling at her and trying to show his teeth, which is his jealousy shining through. I know how green-eyed and possessive Rex can be. I've seen him in action before.

Back in August 2003, we were tasked to help provide security for a presidential visit. The Secret Service had requested an extra explosive-detection dog team, and Rex and I were it. George Bush was holding a fund-raising dinner in Newport Beach, about an hour south of L.A. Rex and I had to check over the Four Seasons Hotel, clearing the room he was going to speak in plus the route he'd walk. That done, we had to check every car that arrived with the invitation-only guests, each of whom paid $5,000 to be there.

I was dressed in a dark suit with a special pin on my chest. Every Secret Service guy was wearing a pin, and they were color-coded to signify your level of security clearance. Rex and I were cleared pretty much up to all areas, which was a real buzz. The design of the pin was revealed only at the last moment so no one could copy it and bluff their way in.

Secret Service agents are notorious for wearing shades, like in *Men in Black*. I didn't have those, and neither did Rex. But otherwise, my dog and I looked exactly like we were members of their gang. The guys manning the Vehicle Checkpoint were ex-military, so they were big into Rex and me.

The guests were mostly very understanding that Rex and I had to give their top-of-the-range vehicles the once-over. I asked people to step out of their cars and to leave their doors and trunk open. I kept Rex on a very short leash so that I could yank him back and stop him from scratching their paintwork.

All was going well until a woman arrived in a brand-new luxury metallic silver Hummer H2. She was in her fifties and had a face plastered with makeup. She got out of the vehicle with obvious reluctance, and the first thing she said was, "That dog is not coming anywhere near my car!"

"Ma'am, every vehicle is subject to an inspection tonight," I told her.

"You can search it without the dog!" she snapped back at me.

The traffic had started to back up behind her. "Ma'am, you need to step to the side. The quicker you let us search, the quicker we get this done."

A voice cut in from behind me. "Lady, do as the dog handler says and move to the side. I need you to stand here with me, and I will need to see your driver's license and your ID."

It was one of the Secret Service guys. The lady stormed over and started haranguing him. The Secret Service guy was having none of it. He demanded to see her documents and warned her not to force him to "escalate the situation." She had her back to me and Rex, which was an opportunity not to be wasted.

I picked Rex up and threw him into the front of the Hummer. I said: "Hup! Hup! Hup!" He jumped all over the seat and the dash, sniffing everywhere, and then I got him to leap over the seats into the vehicle's rear, to do a repeat performance. The Secret Service guy could see what I was doing, and I could tell that he was loving it.

The backseats done, I got Rex into the trunk, so by now he'd been through the entire vehicle, leaving pawprints and dog hair. *That's my boy.* We searched around the outside and then we were done. The Secret Service guy released the woman, and she stormed back to her Hummer with an expression like thunder. She got in, fired up, and burned off. The Secret Service guy came over to me, and we cracked up laughing.

"Man, you should have had him take a shit on the front seat," he told me.

When we were done searching the vehicles, we moved inside. Rex and I had to stand duty outside the room where Bush was giving his dinner speech. A beautiful young woman approached. She was around five foot seven, with deep brown eyes and a cute face and an even cuter figure. She had great energy about her, and I could feel it bouncing back and forth between us.

She gazed at Rex. "Your dog is so beautiful. What a handsome dog."

I said, "Ma'am, meet Rex. He's my military working dog."

"You're in the military? What branch?"

I told her the Marine Corps.

"Ooooh, a marine."

"Yeah, a marine."

"Aren't you guys the toughest?" she asked.

"Pretty much, yeah."

"I love men in uniform. Marines in their uniform are so hot. What's your name?"

I told her I was Mike. She told me she was Annie and that she worked at the hotel. As we flirted, she kept glancing at Rex. He had his tongue hanging out and was looking all goofy and happy as usual.

"So, you like dogs?" I asked her.

"Oh, my God, I love dogs."

"I'm a marine and I love dogs, and you're a lady who loves dogs and marines. Looks like we're off to a good start already."

She smiled. "You're dog is *so* handsome. D'you mind if I pet him?"

"Actually, you can't pet him. I'd love for you to, but he

wouldn't 'cause he's a working dog. Plus I don't want to risk your getting bitten."

"Really? Are you sure I can't?" she asked. "He looks so cute, not that I'm saying he's a softie, but he doesn't look like he'd do that to me. . . ."

"Okay, if you really want to you can use one hand and stroke him on top of his head. But that's all, okay?"

Annie reached down and petted Rex as I'd instructed. Immediately, his tongue went in, his mouth closed, and he stopped smiling. He knew I was letting her do this, and he tolerated it for a short while. But he was looking at her hand and up at me, with an expression that said: *You know I don't do this kind of shit. Why d'you let her pet me?*

An instant later she'd thrust out her other hand and started rubbing both his ears. In a flash Rex freed himself, and *chomp*, he'd bitten down onto her hand. She let out a cry. She pulled back her arm and was holding the one hand with the other. She was gazing at it in horror to see if Rex has broken the skin. I could see the indents of his canines, but he hadn't drawn any blood.

"Urrgh, I can't believe he just bit me," she wailed.

"I told you not to do that," I replied.

She stared at me openmouthed, as if I was supposed to scold my dog. I had reprimanded Rex by saying, "No! Out!" But she obviously thought I was going to do more.

"I told you he's a working dog," I repeated, "and you weren't supposed to do what you just did."

She glared at me for a second, then turned and stormed off. I watched her go, then glanced down at Rex. He was looking up at me, a smug expression on his features.

"Way to go, buddy," I told him, shaking my head despairingly. "Way to go."

I loved the fact that Rex pulled in crowds, and particularly women. He was always getting compliments about how handsome he was. But then he'd get jealous of my getting any attention, and especially when it came from a pretty girl like Annie, and try to put a stop to any romance that might be in the offing.

I figure Rex is going to try something similar with Suraya, and that'll be the end of another beautiful friendship. But before he can try anything seriously devious and hostile with her, the insurgents have a good go at trying to kill both of us.

Rex and I are standing gate duty. Suraya's just finished her shift, and she's left to go home. I'm squatting on one of the concrete blast barriers, Rex sitting between my knees. From out of nowhere there's a massive explosion that feels like it's right on top of us. The insurgents have launched a rocket-propelled grenade (RPG) at the gatehouse, and it's exploded in airburst mode—in midair—halfway between us and the EOD building.

There's the deafening blast from above, and the exploding grenade showers the base with hot shards of jagged shrapnel. Luckily, there's a sandbagged roof over the gatehouse, so none of the shrapnel hits us. Rex is sticking very close to me and he's mimicking my every move. I've got an arm around him and I'm petting him and talking him down from his fear. I'm speaking real slow and calm, as it helps to quiet him.

"Easy boy, easy boy," I'm telling him. "Good boy, good boy." And with every soothing word I'm giving him a good, long stroke.

The marines on the gate ask me how Rex has handled the

blast. I tell them he's pretty cool with it. I'm sitting there thinking, Fuck, that was close, when there's an almighty great *BOOM* right in my ear. Something big and nasty has smacked into the opposite side of the barrier on which we're sitting.

This second RPG round blows me off my perch, and Rex with me, the massive blast wave punching us into the earth. I must've blacked out for a second, for I came to with Rex on his feet, eyes white with fear and searching wildly in the smoke and dust to find me. Then he's on top of me, madly licking my face. If Rex could talk, I know what he'd be yelling right now: *Wake up! Get up! Show me you're alive!*

We dive for cover as the mortars start slamming down all around our position. The barrage lasts for a good few minutes, but the marines in the watchtower can't return fire because the insurgents are way out of range. I can hear them on the radios calling the marines who are out on patrol so they can go check it out.

When the bombardment stops, I check over both of us. Miraculously, we're pretty much unscathed. Rex has some cuts and bruises and some scorched patches of fur, and I've taken the odd lump of blasted grit in my skin, but that's about all.

But I know how close we've both come to getting killed. A couple of feet higher, and the RPG round would have taken off my head, blowing Rex to shreds in the process.

Getting hit by that RPG makes me wonder whether the enemy has started to deliberately target me and my dog. We know they're aiming to kill the bomb-disposal teams. We've already lost an EOD guy to a sniper round. It would make sense for them to also target the K9 team.

But in a way it doesn't matter. All I know for sure is that

they've just come that close to killing me and my dog, and that means I've just come very close to breaking my promise to Rex. On deploying to Iraq, I made a solemn vow that I'd never let anything happen to my best buddy.

I won't be able to live with myself if I fail to keep that promise.

Chapter Five

THE FIRST TIME I LAID EYES ON REX WAS THROUGH THE SLATS OF HIS luggage crate, at San Diego International Airport, the nearest to Camp Pendleton. He'd been flown out from the Dog Training School (DTS) at Lackland Air Force Base, in Texas. Lackland's 341st Training Squadron oversees all U.S. Department of Defense K9 training, and it's the epicenter of the dog world for the American military.

I approached Rex thinking what a gorgeous-looking beast he was. He eyed me for a second, then let out his signature growl: *Stranger, stay away from the cage.* He wasn't big for a German shepherd, maybe seventy pounds or so, but boy, did he have attitude.

Rex had come to the United States as a puppy. He hailed from a top German shepherd breeder in Germany. A seasoned trainer from Lackland made regular journeys to Europe to purchase the most promising dogs. German shepherds, plus Dutch shepherds and Belgian Malinoise (what we handlers call "Mals"), are the only dogs the Marine Corps uses.

The German shepherd is the best known of the three breeds, but they all share similar qualities. They have everything you want in a working dog: stamina, loyalty, athleticism, intelligence, drive to learn and to work. Only the cleverest, smartest dogs make it through Lackland, so we start with the cream of the crop.

As a puppy, Rex had been fostered for a year with a local Lackland family. From there he'd gone on to DTS to learn the basics of being a patrol and search dog. The trainers at DTS are all seasoned handlers who return to Lackland to do nothing but train the new dogs. It usually takes about ninety days to get a dog through basic training as a dual patrol-detection dog.

They start by learning the very basic commands and the hand signal for sit, down, stay, and heel.

In patrol training, the dogs are taught to chase and bring down decoys—usually trainee handlers wearing a biteproof padded suit. And in detection work, they learn the basics of sniffing out various kinds of explosives hidden around the school. For detection work, Seek is the key command, plus you guide the dog using your palm to indicate where you want him to search.

Rex was shipped out to Camp Pendleton complete with his DTS handover file. I studied that closely, discovering that he'd distinguished himself even as a novice dog. "Rex is an independent dog who will search of his own accord if the handler allows it. He has excellent odor recognition and will track the odor until he pinpoints source. He will respond regardless of the handler's position, and has had significant drop-leash and off-leash work."

Drop-leash and off-leash work mean searching without the dog being on the lead, or the lead has been dropped to let the dog roam more freely. It's rare to get a dog fresh from training school who is that advanced. Many search dogs never get to the stage where they can do off-leash work. It's just too challenging for them.

When Rex arrived at Camp Pendleton, he was just one and a half years old, yet he was already trained to detect plastic explosives, water gel (an explosive slurry that's cheap to make and easy to store), sodium chlorate and potassium chlorate (chemical explosive compounds), detonation cord, smokeless powder, and TNT. His skills were highly developed, and I couldn't wait to start working with him.

I'd been through Lackland's military working dog handler course, doing my own basic training. Every new handler starts with a metal bucket that's a stand-in dog and practices how to enunciate commands properly. That's all you do in the first week. There's a six-foot fence to which you attach a leash so you can learn how to hold and handle it, then you get your ammo bucket filled with concrete, and you use that as your surrogate dog.

You learn to talk to the bucket with your "praise voice," your "correction voice," and your "command voice." In praise, you're high-pitched, which shows positive energy and excitement, because your dog just did something great. In command voice, you need your dog to do something, so you use an authoritative tone. And in correction mode, you adopt the deep-level threat voice of a pack leader, because your dog just did something wrong.

At first you feel pretty damn stupid talking to a cement-filled bucket and adopting all these different tones. But after a while you get into it, and it does help you train. It's as basic as it gets, but you have to start somewhere. After week one, you get assigned your dog. Most trainee handlers get an experienced dog to help them learn, but I lucked out. I got a "green" dog, which means he was there to train and get certified as a military working dog himself, just as I was there to get certified as a handler.

It's harder training with a green dog, because both of you are learning, but it's also more rewarding. You forge a real bond with your dog, and if you're lucky you graduate from the MWD handler course together. And if you're really lucky, you get to keep that dog when you move on to whichever K9 base you're assigned to.

My green dog was a Belgian Malinoise named Arco. Arco was young and fresh into the factory. There were twelve trainee handlers in my class, and our instructor spent loads more time with Arco and me, as he was training both of us. It was great—I received extra attention and I got to see how you trained a dog from scratch.

Arco taught me patience—that's the key lesson I learned from him. I loved that dog from the get-go, and it was such a great feeling when all of a sudden he'd get what I'd spent the past week trying to teach him. Pure magic. Arco would keep not getting a new command, and breaking position, and then suddenly, bam! He'd do it! We'd both realize at the same moment that he'd got it, and I'd praise him and he'd go wild with joy.

A good K9 handler needs bags of patience. Training and building a bond with your dog take a great deal of time. You have to work with your dog every day. You have to be constantly training with him; you can't expect the dog to become proficient on his own.

Arco was great: He was fresh and immature and a bundle of enthusiasm, and that meant that I could shape and mold him. All the other trainee handlers had old, experienced dogs, and there wasn't much of a bond they could forge with those guys. The older dogs were on autopilot and just going through the motions. I'd often catch the other trainees casting envious glances at Arco and me.

Lackland Dog Training School is an amazing facility. There are life-sized search terrains that look all too real. There are mock-up airports and warehouses and military barracks and vehicle parks. We learned to take the dogs through each of these, looking to sniff out one of the seven hidden explosives, those that Rex had been trained to find at DTS.

Detection work is a nightmare if you have a less than optimum dog. Some dogs get lazy, they won't keep their mind on the task at hand, they find the explosive but do not show any solid response. With a dog like that it can take forever to clear an area.

Rex's DTS report card showed he was the opposite of all that. From the beginning, he was a detection natural: He had a high drive to play with the ball, a highly sensitive nose, and a natural affinity for sniffing out bombs from day one. I couldn't wait to start searching with him.

The day after Rex's arrival at Camp Pendleton, I went into the kennel area. You have to build a rapport with your dog before you can start the special, intensive work to turn him into the most highly trained animal on the planet, which dual-trained patrol-detection dogs are. At the Camp Pendleton kennels, each dog has a large gated run with a sleeping area at the rear. I wanted to take Rex out so we could play, but he didn't know me yet and we hadn't started the bonding process.

In MWD school they tell you it's not a matter of if you'll get bitten by your dog, but when. I went into Rex's cage, talking softly to him the entire time. "Hi, Rex, how you doing, boy? I'm your new handler and we're gonna get to know each other real well . . ." Rex sat back in his run, coolly and silently watching the new arrival—me. The hair on the back of his neck was up, which is a sign of hostility. I slipped on his thick leather collar and attached his leash. I was just reaching for the choke chain when Rex attacked me.

In an instant he'd gone from cool and calm to a bundle of bunched muscle and snarling, flashing teeth, and he was doing his best to chew me out. I was alone in the kennels and there wasn't another handler around. Luckily, I'd seen Kollatschny, a fellow handler, deal with a dog attack just a few days earlier, so I had a pretty good idea what to do.

Kollatschny had been attacked by his new dog, Lobo. I realized what was happening and ran to fetch our kennel master, Staff Sergeant Greating. The staff sergeant was adamant: Kollatschny had to deal with it right then and there, and show Lobo who was boss. If he didn't, he'd never be able to handle the dog. Kollatschny managed to get Lobo out of his cage, and Greating taught him how to do an alpha roll on him.

As Rex went to attack me, I knew I needed to alpha-roll him. I managed to grab Rex's collar and wrestle him onto the ground. All the time he was going crazy trying to bite me. I got him onto his back with all my weight on top of him. With one hand on his throat forcing his head back, I took the lead and wrapped it around his muzzle several times, so his mouth was strapped shut. Then I grabbed his snout, got my face right up close to his, and stared into his eyes, to show him that I wasn't afraid.

I yelled in his face: "Out! Out! Out!"

This is the universal command meaning, Stop what you're doing right now. I had to do the alpha roll three times on Rex before finally he accepted that I was the boss.

The alpha roll uses the psychology of the dog pack to establish dominance. When puppies play, one's always trying to get on top of the others to wrestle them down and establish dominance. Rex now saw me as the pack leader. From being aggressive toward me, he'd now do everything in his power to protect me.

I guess because he saw his pack leader in the shape of a human, maybe he saw himself in that same image, pretty much as human too. Having done the dominance thing, I ran Rex around the obedience course a few times, just for fun and to take his mind off the alpha rolls that I'd just been doing on him. And so the bonding process began.

I started to feed Rex every day by hand, and spent hours talking to him and petting and grooming him. I knew already that Rex was different from the other dogs. As soon as a handler entered the kennel area, the other dogs would be going wild, barking and pawing at the wire walls. But Rex would be playing hard to get.

He would stand at his gate stock-still staring at me, his tongue lolling coolly. I'd give him the order "House!" He'd go into his kennel to give me the space to enter the run. Then with my arms held wide I'd yell, "Rexy!" in a high-pitched voice, and he'd come running to me. "How's it been, Rex?" I'd ask him as I got his collar and lead onto him, "How're you doing? You ready to go out and play?"

Finally he started to show how happy he was to see me. It was great having someone so pleased to have me around. Life had been pretty shitty over the last few years, and I needed Rex to make it sweet again. He was to be my salvation, and maybe I was Rex's too.

From the very start Rex loved detection work. He was a born natural, and all the other handlers could see that. He had a great nose. Seldom did he false-respond—pretending he'd found an odor just to get to play with the Kong. With me at his side, he didn't ever seem to tire of searching. I gave him his ball as a reward only when he took me to the very source of the scent. I kept it quiet from the other handlers, but I was determined to work my ass off with Rex so that we became one of the best K9 teams on the base.

When we did detection training, we couldn't always have a training aid in place—a hidden piece of explosives. More often when searching for real there is nothing to find, so your dog has to get used to searching and finding nothing. Often we did a forty-five-minute detection exercise, and Rex had a dozen training aids to find. But another time there might be only two, and sometimes I'd get him to clear a whole building and there was nothing at all.

Sometimes when working with Rex, I'd detect a change of behavior, but I'd pretend not to notice. I'd keep walking as if I hadn't seem him sit down at the source, and I'd give him a tug on the leash to make him follow. A less confident dog would at that stage give up and come to heel, but not Rex. He'd stand his ground and stubbornly refuse to budge, and when he did that I'd praise him to the roof and give him a good play with his ball. Over time it got to the stage where I'd tug on his leash with all my might, and there was no moving Rex. He was rock solid, a 100 percent detection dog.

It was November 2002 when I'd gotten Rex, so just over a year after 9/11. We'd had Operation Enduring Freedom in Afghanistan, the air war to drive out the Taliban and bin Laden, but the ground war hadn't yet started in either Afghanistan or Iraq. In the First Gulf War, dog teams had been sent to Iraq, but only to secure bases. So when we carried out our explosives search training, I was mostly imagining us searching places in the United States, or doing base security in some foreign conflict. I had no idea that a little over a year after getting Rex we'd deploy to the front line of war.

One thing was clear about Rex right off the bat: He loved playing the tough guy. Part of our K9 unit's duty was to patrol the Camp Pendleton perimeter for bomb threats or intruders. Rex and I were returning from one of our first patrols, and I pulled in to pick up a burger from a drive-thru McDonald's.

As we pulled into the McDonald's, Rex was in the rear of the jeep, in his travel cage. The girl in the drive-thru was a civvie, as most of the shop workers are on the base. She didn't notice Rex, and as she passed me the bag of food, he went wild: *AROOOOF! ROOF! ROOF! ROOF!* I knew what he was up to: He was protecting his pack leader. But the girl practically had a heart attack. She threw the food into the jeep and refused to take the money.

Right at that moment I was called to an incident on the base. I placed the food on the central console, and we set off. It was some domestic incident that turned out to be no big deal, and I left Rex in the jeep. When I got back I couldn't find the McDonald's anywhere. I searched high and low, before finally I spotted crumpled packaging scattered over the rear of Rex's cage.

I fixed him with a look: *Buddy, did you steal my chow?*

He had the guiltiest expression on his face that I'd ever seen. Somehow, he'd gotten his paw through the bars, reached out to full stretch, grabbed the McDonald's and hauled it back in, and eaten the lot. For a moment I tried to glare at him angrily, then I cracked up laughing.

By the summer of 2003, Rex and I had certified as a fully qualified patrol and explosive-detection dog team. By then, every handler in our K9 unit was well aware of the growing IED threat in Iraq. It was all over the news.

We were all thinking the same thing: If they deploy us with our dogs, we can search out the bombs before they can kill and maim. The rights or wrongs of the Iraq War weren't a consideration. This was a chance to go and save lives—both American and Iraqi.

Rumors started to fly that we might deploy to Iraq. For weeks our kennel master, Staff Sergeant Greg Massey, wouldn't confirm or deny those rumors. Massey was a good guy, but he was very much the boss. He was a tough-love kind of marine who didn't fraternize with the handlers. But I had great respect for Massey, and I knew we could count on him to back us up if we got sent to war.

It was November 2003 when Staff Sergeant Massey finally confirmed that Iraq was happening for us. Each Marine Corps K9 base had been asked to send a couple of teams for the March 2004 deployment. There were eight explosive-search teams in our unit, so Rex and I had a one-in-four chance of getting chosen to deploy. And boy, did I want to get sent to Iraq—just like every other handler in our unit!

My best buddies were handlers Adam Cann and Jason Cannon. Like me, they were both lance corporals, and we all had about the same time under our belts training and working with our dogs. Jason is a Tennessee lad, and he's a real country boy. Adam and I were forever teasing him: "If it walks like a hick and talks like a hick, it's gotta be a hick."

Jason took it all in stride and even played up to it. He tried getting me into country and western music, but it just wasn't happening. Adam, Jason, and I had become inseparable during our time at Camp Pendleton. We began to think of ourselves as the three dogs of war. In fact, Adam designed a tattoo that we were going to get done: It had the words DOGS OF WAR running around the imprint of a dog's paw. Adam and some other handlers got the tattoo, but I didn't—tattoos were never my style.

A lot of the handlers went and spoke to our kennel master and asked him to send them to Iraq. It didn't feel right to me to do so. A year earlier my father had been diagnosed with cancer of the lymph nodes, which had metastasized. He had a massive tumor in his throat that they could no longer operate on. They'd done all the surgery they could.

The doctors had told us we were in the endgame now. My father wasn't scheduled to last past the beginning of the summer, which would be four months into the Iraq deployment. If I asked Massey to send me to Iraq, I felt as if I would be tempting fate with my father. If he asked me to go, I'd go. But I wouldn't actively solicit it. And if I didn't get to go, at least I'd be here for my father's funeral.

When Massey told me that he'd chosen Rex and me to deploy, the first thing I did was go and see my dog. I sat cross-legged in Rex's kennel, with his head cradled in my lap. "Hey, buddy, we're about to go to war together," I told him as I gave him a good scratch behind the ears. I told him that I felt we were as ready as we'd ever be and that I couldn't have asked for a better dog to take to war in Iraq.

I like to think that Rex sensed something momentous was going down. I took him out on the hill behind the kennels. This was our favorite spot. It was where I used a tennis-ball thrower to hurl his ball this way and that, allowing him to run and to play. Rex and I did that for a while, just being a guy and his dog. I figured there wouldn't be a lot of time or space for this kind of thing in Iraq.

We came down from the hill and there were Adam and Jason, my fellow dogs of war. "You fucking bastard," they told me. "You and Rex got Iraq!"

But beneath those words they were smiling. They were happy for Rex and me. They had both been to Massey begging to get deployed, and now they'd heard that Rex and I had got it.

I'd been hoping one of them would be deploying with me, but instead I was going out with a guy called Charles Allen. Sergeant Allen is a black marine with a dog named Rocky. Rocky was a decent search dog, but it was no secret on the base that Rex was the best.

Chapter Six

THE FIRST CONCRETE SIGN OF OUR IMPENDING DEPLOYMENT WAS when a new kennel master turned up at Camp Pendleton. Staff Sergeant William Kartune was gathering all the K9 teams deploying to Iraq and running our deployment in the field. Kartune was short, muscular, and extremely fit, and it was clear from the get-go that he rated himself very highly.

That was not unusual in the K9 world, and not necessarily a bad thing either. We have a saying in K9: "If you put three dog handlers in a room, the only thing that two of them will agree on is that the third is wrong." In a way you needed your kennel master to have a big ego, especially when he was leading a group of you to war.

Kartune was around thirty years old, and he wasn't only a highly experienced K9 handler: He was also a Special Reaction Team (SRT) guy, the Marine Corps equivalent to the SWAT teams—those who carry out high-risk and highly specialized law enforcement operations.

Kartune knew his K9 stuff, he knew his elite combat skills from his SRT days, and he wasn't as stiff or by the book as Kennel Master Massey. He'd have a laugh with the handlers, and he was happy to go out and have a beer and shoot the shit. At Camp Pendleton he gathered together twelve K9 teams from Marine Corps bases all across the United States, to form the unit that would deploy to Iraq.

When we were assembled, Kartune gave it to us straight. "The last time K9 teams served on the front line was Vietnam. You're going into the unknown." Our mission was to discover the ground truth in Iraq, he explained, so the next wave of K9 guys could better prepare and deploy. And that's when Kartune said to us, "You guys, you're the guinea pigs."

I wouldn't say that I was thrilled at the idea of Rex and me being guinea pigs, but I liked being part of a historic "first in" deployment. That was some kind of a buzz.

All we heard on the news was that IEDs were killing and maiming soldiers and civilians in Iraq. In the year since the invasion, the nature of the war had changed beyond all recognition. No longer was it being fought between two armies wearing uniforms, in open battle. The rule book had been torn up. Instead, you had lawless militias and insurgents dressing like civilians and hiding among their number, and trying to lure American soldiers onto their IEDs. There was no need for sentry dogs in a war like that. It was a whole new kind of conflict, and K9 teams had one vital role to fulfill there: sniffing out the bombs.

In Vietnam, K9 teams had played a pivotal role. They cleared the tunnels that the Vietcong dug beneath the jungle, from which they'd emerge to fight and into which they'd melt away after the battle. They led patrols through the jungle, sensing by smell and by sound where the enemy was from hundreds of yards away. Specialist K9 combat tracker teams were tasked with tracking enemy units through the remotest hills and valleys so that nowhere offered them a safe refuge.

War dog teams were credited with saving ten thousand lives in Vietnam. But since then, the type of warfare K9 teams had pioneered in Vietnam had largely passed us by. High-tech warfare had come of age, and K9 teams were all about law enforcement and security, not front-line combat operations.

Kartune wanted us to get our dogs attuned to front-line battle conditions as much as possible, because that was where we would be operating, but there was precious little time or opportunity to do so. There are several different ranges at Camp Pendleton, and we did live-firing exercise on them all. But there were only four of us on the ranges at any one time, and the biggest weapon we got to fire was a shotgun.

More important, a one-way range is just that: Bullets don't fly in both directions. Only when you've got bullets and grenades zipping past your head do you really know what it's like to be under fire. We did what we could. We fired off our M16s, our Beretta M9 pistols, plus our M1014 Joint Service Combat Shotguns, but it still wasn't much like being in a real war.

From our sessions on the ranges, it was clear that Rex didn't like someone firing a weapon. I was able to do only one session with me firing my guns, and he absolutely hated it. He was barking wildly, which was his way of saying to me: *Partner, whatever you're up to here, I really, really don't like it.*

With our departure date fast approaching, I began to realize how ill prepared we were for front-line operations. We'd done no training for foot or vehicle patrols, for searching narrow alleyways, or for doing so under fire. We'd never been on any military exercises with tanks or helicopters or big weapons firing or bombs being dropped. In addition, we had no idea which units we'd be embedded with, or what kind of missions we'd be undertaking. We had no idea even where we were going in country. All we knew was Iraq.

I was spending my every waking hour with Rex. When we weren't training, we were up on the hill to the rear of the base. It was peaceful up there. I'd shoot a tennis ball this way and that, with Rex thundering after it, the grass and dirt flying from his speeding paws. I spent time hanging out, just letting him be a dog. We loved it up there.

When I saw Rex being so happy and so free, I wondered if I could live with myself if he got hurt in Iraq. And then he'd be there in my face trying to lick me. I'd grab his muzzle with the one hand and force his mouth closed. He'd pause for a second, then tear away, flicking out his tongue to sneak in a slurp. I'd start twisting my head from side to side to avoid his tongue. Then he'd get his front paw up on my face in an effort to hold me still while he got a good few licks in.

Before deploying to Iraq, I had to say farewell to my father. Dad was in and out of the hospital, but I got to spend a good few days with him.

"I got called to deploy," I told him, "and I feel like Rex and I can do real good out there."

He asked if I felt ready. I told him that I did. He was happy with that. He was absolutely supportive of my going to Iraq, because it was what I wanted to do. "God bless" were his last words to me.

Mom threw a barbecue and most of my family and friends were there. My hometown is in the San Francisco Bay Area, a very, very liberal part of the country. There had been huge protests locally against the war. I'd grown up in that liberal environment, but I'm my own political party. I don't classify myself as on one side of the fence or the other. Some of my old school friends were there, and they told me that they didn't support the war. They asked me if I really believed in what I was fighting for.

"The way I see it, I'm not thinking about the rights and wrongs of this conflict," I told them. "I consider my fellow marines like my family, like brothers in arms, and what would you do if you had family in harm's way, and you had a critical skill set to help bring them back home to their families? Wouldn't you want to go out there and save lives?"

People got that. Whatever their political views, it made sense to them.

Before we said our final good-byes, my father gave me his rosary beads to keep me safe in Iraq. They were from Ireland, and my father hailed from a long line of Irish Catholics. He wasn't a military man. In fact, he'd trained and served as a Catholic priest before deciding that he wanted to have a family.

My father had met my mom at a Catholic church in Los Angeles, then they'd moved to the Bay Area to raise a family. He'd never expressed an opinion on the Iraq War. I presumed he thought that war was not the answer, but no matter what, he would always be supportive of me. My father was my rock, and that was one thing I had always been able to rely upon.

Before I returned to Camp Pendleton, my mother gave me a turquoise-and-black carved stone bear, which was small enough to fit into the palm of my hand. She is of Mexican-Indian descent, and in her tradition each animal signifies something special—the bear being protection and safety. She kept a whole bunch of different animals at home, and each year she'd go to Apache powwows and return with a few more.

Both my parents were big animal lovers, and they had bequeathed that to their kids. My father had grown up as one of sixteen children living on a farm in Ireland. They'd had cows, sheep, ducks, chickens, and lots of dogs on the farm, and my mother had always been a dog lover. I knew she didn't want me to go to war, but she knew that wasn't what I needed to hear. That barbecue send-off was her way of showing her support and her love.

Before I left home, there was one thing I wanted to grab from my room. In 2001, Captain William Putney had published a book called *Always Faithful*. It's the story of the Marine Corps K9 teams of World War II and I'd read it several times. Putney was a captain and veterinarian who trained and commanded seventy-plus dog teams in the Pacific theater. Putney's book is full of incredible stories of the heroics of the handlers and their dogs, and how they saved so many lives.

Back at Camp Pendleton, I stuffed *Always Faithful* in my kit bag, along with my father's rosary beads and my mother's stone bear. They were going with me to Iraq. Putney's war dog platoon had fought in a much more honest, straightforward kind of war, one where both sides wore uniforms and typically adhered to some basic rules of war. We were getting sent into a much harsher, murkier kind of conflict. But I hoped I could draw on some of those stories to stiffen my resolve when I reached Iraq.

On March 19, 2004, we headed for March Air Reserve Base, in Southern California. We loaded our kit onto a giant Boeing C-17 Globemaster III transport aircraft—twelve cages, twelve dogs, lined up together in the center of the aircraft. We handlers sat along the side, where we could keep a close eye on our dogs.

Rex's crate was right in front of me. He could see me and I could see him. He was lying down, resting but alert. He knew something serious was happening. Rex trusted me 100 percent, in that unique bond between man and dog. Yet he had no choice in my taking us to war, and he had no idea of the dangers we were flying into.

As the engines powered up on the giant aircraft, another worry took over completely. There were twenty-six hours of flying ahead of us, and my biggest fear was whether I would last the flight without flipping out. I have a total phobia of flying, something that dates back to my childhood when an aircraft I was traveling in almost fell out of the sky in a bad storm.

In that C-17 jetting off toward Iraq, I felt as if I were strapped into a giant metal coffin with no windows. I was blasting music on my CD player to cover up the fact that I was freaking out. I was playing Dave Matthews and the Red Hot Chili Peppers at top volume to drown out the screaming in my head.

It reached the stage where I unbuckled myself from my seat and lay on the floor of the aircraft next to Rex's cage. My father had always told me that dogs were the greatest stress relievers, and it did seem to help being close to Rex. Eventually I drifted off into an uneasy slumber.

The C-17 flew via a stopover in the United States onward to Germany, and from there into Iraq. At each stop we got our dogs out and gave them a break from the kennel crates. But as soon as we entered Iraqi airspace, the plane's main lights went out, to be replaced by dim red bulbs, the signal that we'd arrived in enemy territory. We were ordered to put on our flak and Kevlar.

Finally, the plane began its combat descent into Al Asad air base, in northern Iraq, corkscrewing out of the heavens in an effort to avoid enemy ground fire, doing a heart-stopping nose-dive. I looked around, and the other handlers were all in their own little world. I was sure that no one was in the same place as I was—on the verge of vomiting my guts up and freaking out.

We touched down in the dead of night, and I managed to just about hold myself together for the landing. We were shown to tented quarters to get some shut-eye.

We were back at the airstrip the following morning to collect our gear. We'd just started loading up the trucks with our K9 kit when there was a faint boom, followed by the whistle of something falling and the sharp crack of an explosion.

We peered around the crates of gear and saw a plume of smoke a ways down the runway. No one knew quite what to say. A few seconds later there was the howl of something else incoming toward us.

"Holy smoke," remarked one of my fellow K9 guys, "are we under fire?"

The marines doing the air base security started yelling for us to take cover. Take cover where? We're in the midst of the god-damn runway! Twenty minutes later the all clear was given, and we crawled out from in between the packing cases.

I was laughing nervously with one of the handlers, and we started cracking some bad jokes: We've been here less than twenty-four hours, and already someone's trying to kill us! That's how much they don't want us here. Welcome to Iraq. But at least we'd got the most important thing unpacked from the crates—our Science Diet dog food, which meant we could feed our dogs.

We were warned to be ready to deploy farther into Iraq, but days passed, and I got the distinct impression that no one had a clue what to do with us. Our kennel master started to do some SRT-style combat training with us, in part to kill the time. Kartune taught us how to transit from using our M16 assault rifle to our pistol, all in one fluid move. He showed us how to repeat the drill time after time, until it became part of our muscle memory, and we could do it without thinking.

He taught us hand-to-hand combat and how to take down an enemy by either hitting his joints or using a knife. Most useful of all, he showed us how to move "tactically"—safely transiting from one hostile area to another on foot. Basically, if one guy and his dog moved forward, the guy to the rear would cover him, and then reverse the procedure.

After a week at Al Asad, we finally got our marching orders. Staff Sergeant Kartune and his second in command, Sergeant Nester Antoine, would be heading south to the Marine Corps headquarters at Camp Fallujah. We all knew that Fallujah was insurgent central, where the U.S. military had fought some of its fiercest battles in Iraq. Their plan was to set up a headquarters there and coordinate all twelve K9 teams serving across Iraq.

Sergeant Allen was left in charge of the remaining handlers in Al Asad. Two teams would head north to the Syrian border, two would go to Ramadi in central Iraq, two would head east and west, and three would stay in Al Asad. Rex and I, plus two other K9 teams, were getting Al Asad. I'd pretty much figured that apart from the odd mortar, Al Asad was an easygoing kind of posting. It wasn't quite what Rex and I had come here for.

I went to have a word with Sergeant Allen. I asked him if he really thought that Al Asad was the best place to utilize a dog of Rex's abilities. There was little or no action here, so was this really the best place to use him?

"Yeah, I guess you're right," he told me, once he'd heard me out. "Maybe we do need to get Rex into an area where he'll be more productive."

There was a handler named Goers within earshot, a guy who was scheduled to go south to Ramadi or Fallujah.

"Goers, how d'you feel about staying in Al Asad instead of going south?" Sergeant Allen asked him.

Goers shrugged. "I don't give a fuck where you put me."

"Okay, Dowling, you're swapping with Goers," Sergeant Allen declared. "He's staying here, and you and Rex are coming with us to Fallujah."

Of the twelve handlers deployed to Iraq, Goers was the one I'd got to know least well. He came across as a real country-boy type who didn't socialize much with the other handlers. He kept to himself and his dog, and he didn't seem to care about much else. We were all strong dog teams; some of the best had been sent to Iraq. And we were all unusual characters, as dog handlers often are. I guess people saw me as the laid-back California beach dude who went with the flow, but what they made of Goers I've no idea.

When all was said and done, he worked well with his dog, which made them a good K9 team. In any case, Goers seemed happy to stay here in Al Asad, and Rex and I were heading south. That was where the shit went down big time. Everyone knew that. So maybe it was a case of beware of what you wish for all over again.

A Marine Corps convoy was forming up to head south, and they offered us a lift as far as Ramadi. We loaded up with our dogs. There was Sergeant Allen with his dog, Rocky; handler Darin Cleveringa with his dog, Rek; handler Donald Paldino with Santo, plus a couple of other handler-and-dog teams, and me with my buddy, Rex.

The ride south was hours of hell in the closed canvas of a truck back, the air billowing thick with dust from the desert roads. We were coughing our lungs up and the dogs were burning up. More worrying, we were traveling blind in the rear of the trucks, so if the insurgents hit us we were pretty much defenseless in there. Sure enough, there was an IED scare en route, our first concrete sign of the threat that we'd come here to counteract.

We had to overnight at the marine base in Ramadi, which was situated in what had once been a vacation resort for Saddam Hussein and his sons. There was an ornate, imposing palace set on the riverside. It had been smashed by a missile that one of our jets had slammed through its roof, but it was still half standing, and it served as the headquarters for the marines based here.

We six handlers were called into the palace for a briefing. We presumed it was going to be run-of-the-mill kind of stuff, until "Attention on deck" was called by a marine standing duty, and Colonel Joseph Dunford walked in. Colonel Dunford's reputation preceded him. He's nicknamed "Fighting Joe," and he commanded the Fifth Marine Regiment, which had spearheaded the invasion of Iraq.

The colonel has an enormous presence. With the silver eagles of rank on his collars he had the bearing of Jack Nicholson in

A Few Good Men. It was rare for a full bird colonel to brief a tiny unit of marines of our rank. Normally, he'd be speaking to entire regiments or battalions, and I had no idea what was coming.

"Marines, you're most welcome 'cause we know what you guys can do out here," the colonel told us. "It's extremely dangerous right now, with marines getting hurt and killed, and one of the most common ways that is happening is IEDs. We're confident that K9 teams are the way forward. Dogs have proved themselves in the past, and we believe you guys will prove yourselves again here in Iraq."

Dunford paused and eyed each of us. "Marines, you should know that K9 teams have been talked about at the highest level of U.S. military command. We see you as the key to combating the IED threat here in Iraq, and we see you as vital to limiting casualties among both the marines and the Iraqi civilian population. I want you to know how excited everyone is to finally have you here."

The marine on duty called "Attention on deck" again. We all snapped to. "Good luck out there, Marines," Colonel Dunford told us. "Semper fi." *Always faithful.*

The colonel had talked to us for a good thirty minutes. It was an awesome experience. Having arrived in Iraq feeling as if no one realized we were here or what to do with us, now we knew differently. Fighting Joe was exactly what I'd imagined a front-line commander would be like. He was the kind of man I'd happily have followed to the ends of the earth.

The palace was a place of real historical significance. The room we'd had the briefing in was where Saddam Hussein used to meet with his tribal sheikhs. I'd always thought I was part of something special being in K9. But to hear it from a man of the stature of Fighting Joe Dunford—well, what could ever top that?

After the colonel's talk we got a briefing from one of his aides, a major. He described Colonel Dunford as a "legitimate badass" and I couldn't have agreed more. The major welcomed us into the territory of the First Marine Division, "one of the most respected fighting forces in the world." He explained the rules of engagement: Don't fire unless fired upon; positively identify an enemy with a weapon; minimize collateral damage and threat to civilians. It all seemed like common sense to me.

Having finished briefing us, the major told us that a convoy was heading south to Fallujah, and it was happy to offer us a lift.

It was a huge relief finally to make it to Camp Fallujah, the sprawling base on the outskirts of that battle-torn city. This was where our kennel master has set up his HQ, and it was here that Rex and I were going to be operating for the remainder of our tour. Or at least so I thought. But it didn't work out that way. Kartune was there to meet us off the convoy, and he had some unexpected news for Rex and me.

"Dowling, don't bother unpacking too much," he told me. "You and Rex are going thirty minutes southeast, to a place called Mahmoudiyah. It's a small base half an hour from here, and you'll be attached to an infantry battalion, the two-two Marines. Here's my e-mail address. If you can get online, check in with me when something significant happens. You and Rex are a great team, and that's why we're sending you to Mahmoudiyah. I believe you'll be fine down there."

I told him Rex and I were good to go. If the e-mail didn't

work we had no way to communicate with our kennel master. I didn't have a radio, a satphone, or even a cell phone. I'd asked to not get an easy posting but to go somewhere where Rex and I might be most effective—where marines were seeing action and taking casualties, and where Rex and I might be able to save lives. In Mahmoudiyah, I figured I'd got what I'd asked for.

I was shooting the shit with a couple of the marines in Fallujah, and I asked if anyone knew much about this place I was going to—Mahmoudiyah. No one seemed to know a damn thing. All anyone could tell me was its nickname: "the Triangle of Death."

"The Triangle of *what*?" I asked.

The marine who'd told me shrugged. "The hell do I know. Go figure. I guess it's Death Central."

It was via the third lift that we'd hitchhiked on a convoy that Rex and I finally made it to our posting. I felt like some drifter cadging rides with my dog. We might as well have been standing by the roadside, me with my thumb out and Rex with his paw. We had no transport of our own, we didn't know a soul here at Mahmoudiyah, and we had no way of communicating with our kennel master or headquarters.

We were on our own, a couple of K9 vagabonds in the heart of bandit country.

Chapter Seven

WE'RE TWO WEEKS INTO OUR TIME IN MAHMOUDIYAH. WE'VE GOT THE mission to raid the insurgent safe house—where Rex injured his stomach—behind us. And we're feeling less like the greenhorn newbies we were when we first arrived. We're keen to get out on more patrols and get used.

Our next tasking is to go to the aid of a resupply convoy that's got into trouble in downtown Mahmoudiyah. A truck's overturned, throwing equipment all across the highway. A bunch of marines from 2/2 are heading out to throw a security cordon around the stranded convoy while the spilled cargo gets cleaned up and reloaded. Rex and I are scheduled to join them. It sounds like an easy enough task, but you never know when you're heading out onto the streets of Mahmoudiyah.

Rex and I ready ourselves, then head for the muster point. The first thing I notice strikes me as bizarre: There's what looks like one of our Iraqi interpreters perched in the turret of a Humvee, behind the big .50-cal machine gun. I do a double take. The guy's got a thick Saddam-style mustache and classic Arab features. Then I notice that he's dressed in Marine Corps uniform.

Rex and I approach him. I'm curious to find out more about the coming patrol, and it's as good an excuse as any to start a conversation with the Saddam look-alike. He's staring off into the middle distance, and he pays not the slightest attention to Rex, which strikes me as odd. Marines *always* react to my dog. Even Gunney Trotter reacted in a way that told me he didn't much dig Rex. This guy doesn't even seem to *see* him.

"Say, buddy, you know where we're headed today?" I ask.

He punches out an answer, making no eye contact at all. "Nope."

"You know any details about the mission?"

"Nope."

I try a few more questions, but to each I get "nope" or "dunno."

I end the conversation thus: "Thanks for all the help, buddy."

The guy shrugs. He's making it quite clear that he doesn't give a damn. All marines wear name tags, but I can't get a glance at this guy's because it's covered by his flak. He's been morose and sullen to the point of being rude, and I'm curious who he is. I go find a marine I can get some response out of. I ask him about the Arab-looking guy perched in the Humvee's turret.

The marine laughs. "Him? That's Corporal Wassef Ali Hassoun, or some such. Chatty guy, ain't he?"

Corporal Wassef Ali Hassoun is going to become the most famous marine on our tour, and for all the wrong reasons. But I don't know that yet.

The patrol's going out in the burning heat of the afternoon. I'm worried about Rex overheating, and I'm aware that we're not even into the Iraqi summer yet. Five of the six vehicles are open-backed, while the sixth is up-armored (the rear is enclosed in a metal shell). It has the advantage of having aircon, but the disadvantage is that it's the lead vehicle of the convoy.

Rarely do vehicles leave the base and not get targeted by IEDs. The Humvee on point is the most likely to get hit—always. Still, I ask the staff sergeant in command of the convoy if we can travel with him up front so Rex can take advantage of the air-conditioning. I'd rather be blown up than have my dog fried to death in the sun.

Rex seems totally unfazed by the heat and the crush. He hops into the rear of the metal coffin and turns to me: *Come on, partner, let's get going.* We take up our positions. Up front there's the staff sergeant with his radio, plus the driver. Behind the driver is the gunner on the .50-cal heavy machine gun, his head and shoulders out the turret. I take the place next to the gunner, and Rex is right beside me.

Or at least that's where he's positioned as the patrol pulls out of the base and onto the main highway. But just as soon as we're under way he sneaks between the front seats and gets his head nudging the windshield. His tongue's lolling out and he's staring out the glass. Rex's thick, powerful tail is slamming into me and the gunner's legs as he beats it back and forth happily.

I try to pull him back into line, but he throws a glare over his shoulder: *Hey, I'm enjoyin' the ride.* The staff sergeant sitting in the front passenger seat grins. The driver starts laughing. They love having Rex there sandwiched between them. It's destressing the team.

But the trouble with Rex is he's like a devil in disguise. He looks so happy and so goofy that the staff sergeant can't resist getting an arm around him to pet him. He nips at the staff sergeant's arm. And when the guy goes to grab his radio, which is hanging from the roof above Rex, my dog takes a playful chew on the guy's hand.

The staff sergeant can't help laughing. "Hey, dawg, you look like a great big teddy bear, but you're the tough guy, eh?"

He turns to me. "So, like I hear your dog can sniff out IEDs and bombs?"

I tell him that he can.

"Great. We'd like you out front checking a route for us."

The vehicles roll to a halt. Up ahead there's a narrow dirt track threading around a couple of low, shedlike buildings. Our convoys have been hit repeatedly here by IEDs, the staff sergeant explains. This is where he wants us to search. We're to clear the road.

This is what we came here for—to save lives. At the same time I know Rex could die out there. I know that if we mess up it could cost the lives of my fellow marines. And I know that I could die here too.

I stand in the beating sun surveying the route. Rex is at my feet, to my left as always. I pull out the Kong, and instantly Rex knows that we're here to search. But he can sense my indecision, and it's unnerving him.

I have no clear idea how we're going to go about doing this. I've gone over scenarios like this time and again in my head, but this is our first live search on the front line of war. We've never trained for this, and there's no standard operating procedure as far as I'm aware.

All I do know is that when we start the search I will be totally focused on my dog. I cannot look left or right; I need to keep my eyes on Rex. But how will I be able to concentrate on him when I'm worried about us getting shot or blown to pieces?

And for sure, I'm worried. My stomach's knotted tight as a fist and my legs feel like jelly. The seconds tick by and the marines are bunching up behind Rex and me. I've got to do something.

I have a flash of inspiration. I explain to the staff sergeant what I'm thinking. I need two marines, one to either side of the track, say, fifteen paces behind us, providing security for me and my dog. All my senses will be centered on Rex. That's what I'm here for. If Rex or I trigger a device, we'll take the blast. The marines should be far enough away to survive.

The staff sergeant asks for volunteers. A couple of marines step forward.

"Guys, I can't look to left or right," I tell them. "I got to be focused on my dog, or we'll walk right into an IED. I need you to be my eyes, scanning for the bad guys."

They nod. *Good to go.* They've got it.

I place the Kong back in my pocket and turn to the dirt track. I take the first step, Rex stepping out beside me. We start the loneliest walk.

Over the last few days, Gunney Smith has told me more about the types of IEDs they're finding here. The most common is the cell-phone-triggered IED, like the one he showed me back in his storeroom.

Cell-phone-triggered IEDs are usually hidden at the roadside, often under a mound of rubble or trash. When the bomb maker sees a patrol passing, he dials the phone. His call sends the circuit live, which detonates the bomb. If it's a vehicle convoy moving at speed, it's hard to time it right. Much easier with a patrol on foot moving slowly down a road, led by one man and his dog.

Rex and I are out front on our own. I've got my eyes glued to my dog. He's a couple of paces in front of me; the leash is six feet long, and I've left it loose so he's free to follow his nose. He starts snuffling through piles of garbage and rubble on both sides of the road, any one of which could conceal an IED.

We inch forward. I'm sweating buckets. My combats are soaked and plastered to my skin. A crowd of onlookers gathers in the bush, staring. I pause for a second and speak to one of the marines on my shoulder.

"Guys, you see anyone get a cell phone out, you better aim in on them and tell them to get the hell off the phone."

They eye the crowd more closely now, their weapons in the shoulder.

I'm hyperalert to Rex's slightest change in behavior: a pause and his tail going rigid for an instant. Every second out here seems to last a lifetime. I'm moving through a slo-mo tunnel vision of pure fear. I've never experienced anything like it before. It's like rolling the dice. It's evil, and it's only my link to my dog that's keeping me together. If Rex can do this, so can I.

I'm so concentrated on the search that I almost forget that Rex is an animal, a dog, and not a mechanical bomb-sniffing machine. We're twenty minutes into the task when Rex starts to show all the signs of heat exhaustion.

It's the furnace of midafternoon, and the Iraqi sun is beating down on his thick fur. He's suffering terribly, but I've missed all the vital warning signs. It's his tongue that finally alerts me. It's swollen to almost twice its normal size. Plus he's panting heavily and gasping for air.

I steer him into the shade of the bush at the roadside. I tell the guys we've got to take a break. I've got to help my dog. A dog can sweat from only the pads of its feet or its tongue—hence Rex's tongue swelling like it has. But before the tongue could expand enough to choke it, a dog would simply collapse from heat exhaustion.

I pull out a doggy ice pack, a kind of tray-sized freezer sack that I packed full of ice. It's supposed to be a cushion for your dog to lie on, as an emergency cooling aid. But as with most of our K9 kit, it turns out to be utterly useless. The ice has melted into a lukewarm slush.

I grab a bottle of water from my pack. I've got six liters in there, and it's all for Rex as far as I'm concerned. I pour the water into his mouth and I rub it into his fur to cool him, paying special attention to the pads of his feet. He's slumped in the shade and he's rolling his eyes at me in pleasured relief. It's like he's saying: *Okay, so I'm whacked. Just give me a couple of minutes, okay?*

I squat in the shade and stroke him, telling him to take as long as he needs. Rex is such a great dog he hasn't once complained or faltered in his task. He'd let me work him to death if I were dumb enough to. I'm consumed by guilt at his suffering.

Once he's recovered enough, we finish the walk. By the time we reach the end of the road, Rex has shown not the slightest sign of finding anything. Rex is superfast at detection work and he's superthorough, and I'm 100 percent certain that the route is clear. The job is done, at least until the insurgents plant their next crop of deadly IEDs here.

I can tell that Rex is disappointed. He was dying to pick up a scent so he could play with the Kong. He more than deserves a reward. As we wait for the marines to join us, I pull out the Kong. I show it to Rex, then toss it on the ground. It's closer to me than to him, and he knows exactly what's coming.

"Get your ball!" I tell him. "Get your ball!"

I dive for it at the same instant that Rex does. Dog and handler collide as I snatch the Kong and stuff it beneath me. Rex starts digging furiously as he tries to unearth it from under my body. I'm laughing fit to burst, and it's fantastic just to rid myself of the gut-wrenching tension of doing the walk. Finally, Rex gets the Kong gripped in his teeth, and he strides around like a champ, tail thrashing from side to side.

It's then that I notice we've got a crowd of Iraqis on hand. The kids are closest. It's always the kids who come first. They've seen Rex and me playing and can't resist a look. I get Rex to do a couple of obedience moves: Sit down; Stay; Heel. He kind of likes playing to the audience, and the kids are pointing and laughing and charging about excitedly.

They're yelling stuff at their buddies at the tops of their voices. I can't understand the Arabic, but I can guess what they're saying: Come look! It's so cool! There's this American soldier can talk to his dog, and his dog can understand him! That's the great thing about Rex: With the kids, he's perfect for winning hearts and minds.

We're in a rural area on the city limits, so the kids crowd in from the surrounding farmland. They're completely captivated by what I can do with my dog. They remind me of myself when I was a boy. From my earliest years dogs had won my own heart and mind.

I move on to showing them the hand signals: I move my arm one way and Rex goes down on his belly; I make a move with my hand and he's instantly at my heel; I make a gesture with my palm and he's sitting obediently at my side. As Rex responds to each silent gesture, the kids go wild and cheer. They're acting like the Rex and Dowling show is the coolest thing they've ever seen.

But all too soon it's time to move out. I tell the kids that Rex and I have to go. All of them back off, except one Iraqi boy. He looks about six or seven years old, he's missing one of his front teeth, and he's got wild, dusty hair. He's dressed in an ankle-length robe called a *thobe*. He stands there with a happy smile on his face, pointing at Rex and begging me to do one more thing with my dog.

I've got a pad in my pocket, which I use to note down any useful information to help us refine how we search. I take it out and scribble on it: "U.S. Marine Corps, Military Working Dog Rex, Number E168." Last, I sign my name. I rip out the page and hand it to the boy. I pass him my notebook, and mime him to write something for me. He scribbles some words in Arabic and hands it back.

I turn to our interpreter, who's stood nearby. I ask what the kid has written.

"It says Ali Hamid Khidur," the interpreter tells me. "The boy's name. And the date. That kid really loves your dog."

Like children everywhere, these Iraqi kids adore Rex. The intense dislike many Iraqis show for dogs seems to gets inculcated only at a later age. I guess it's all down to dogs being "unclean"—*haram*—in Islam, and it being wrong to have any close contact with them. It's a pity to think that Ali will end up thinking that way.

These kids loved my dog, and they loved the thrill of being

so scared of him when he showed off the snow-whites of his ca-nines. At his age, little Ali is completely mesmerized by Rex. He keeps mimicking my hand signals, and he's dying to get some response from my dog. Rex sees Ali doing the hand gestures and notes it with disdain: *Yeah, and who are you kidding?*

I point at Rex and say, "Rex." I repeat it until Ali is say-ing "Rex" pretty much as well as you could ever expect from a seven-year-old Iraqi boy. And then it really is time for us to mount up the Humvees and be on our way.

I wave good-bye to Ali and the other kids. I've got the scrap of paper with his name and other details stuffed deep in my combat trousers. I'm going to keep it safe. It's like a talisman for me. Proof that not everyone here hates us, and that with Rex on hand maybe we really can win some hearts and minds.

We complete the mission to secure the convoy that's thrown its load, and we return to base. I discover that there's been a mail delivery. There's an envelope addressed in the unmistak-able hand of Rosie Trujillo, my grandma on my mom's side. I rip it open to find a birthday card enclosed. I glance at my watch. It's April 18. I'd forgotten. It's my birthday.

The card has a kind of a poem with it: "One little smile can sometimes make a special difference in a person's days. . . . By the power of this little smile I hope you'll see many sunny mo-ments brightening up your corner of the world today." Well, I guess I just had that happen to me: Winning Ali's heart and mind was today's sunny moment here in Mahmoudiyah.

Grandma's sent a letter with the card. There's no specific news on Dad's health, which has to mean he hadn't taken a turn for the worst. It's a massive relief, because every day I'm dread-ing hearing bad news. Grandma's letter ends: "Easter Sunday I reminded everyone to write to you. I hope they do. I said 'the more mail, the better.' That's all the news for now. Take extra care of yourself and Rex. Love, Grandma."

Rex was born in April too, but I don't know which day. So we made a pact that he and I will celebrate on the same day. That evening I give Rex a mammoth-sized bone from PETCO as his birthday present. I treat myself to one of my favorite MREs—spaghetti with meat sauce. I put the card from Grandma on top of Rex's kennel, and that's it—birthday celebrated.

I'm twenty-five years old today, which means Rex is three years old. Three years of a dog's life is essentially twenty-five years for a human. We've just turned the same age, my dog and I.

Getting Grandma's letter gives me the urge to phone home. I've got no means of doing so, but I know the EOD guys have. I go see Gunney Smith, and he lets me use their satphone. The first call I make is to my unit back at Camp Pendleton.

I've promised to report in all that I learn as we K9 teams deploy to war, and I figure I've got a few tips I should share with the guys. If I can tell them one thing that'll help my buddies Jason and Adam better prepare for their own Iraq deployment, it'll make what we're doing out here all the more worthwhile.

A gruff voice answers the call: "Staff Sergeant Massey here."

"Hey, Staff Sergeant, it's Dowling."

"Hey, Marine, you ready to come home yet? You not dead yet?"

I laugh. My kennel master asks how we're doing and how Rex is faring, and if there's anything he can send out for us.

I say, "We've been going on raids and doing checkpoints, and the weather's hot as fuck. But when you send more handlers, do not let them come with their M16s, 'cause they're too long and they get in the way of the dogs. Send them out with M4s."

"Good to go," he confirms.

"We've been exposed to lots of loud fire—mortars and rockets. It would be great if the next batch of handlers can get down on the ranges with the mortar teams and infantry guys and get loads of exposure to live fire—a lot more than we had, anyway, 'cause—"

BOOM! My last words are drowned out by an explosion that rocks the base. We've been getting hit by rockets, mortars, and small arms daily, and I'm kind of used to it by now. But this one's loud enough for my kennel master back in Camp Pendleton to hear it over the echoing satphone connection.

"Holy shit, Dowling, what was that?"

"Oh, that's a mortar that landed on the base."

"Holy shit! You need to take cover or something?"

"No. It sounds like it was just the one."

At that moment several more mortars slam into the base. I can hear Massey going ape over the phone line, every blast punctuated by one of his expletives.

BOOM! "Holy shit!"

BOOM! "Holy shit!"

BOOM! "Holy fuck, Dowling!"

I say, "Give me just a minute."

There are half-concrete pipelike shelters scattered around the place. I run over and dive under the nearest one. I wait out the mortar attack sheltered under there. When it ceases, I talk some more to Massey. He seems kind of shocked that we're under such heavy and persistent fire.

"But that just goes to prove what I was saying," I tell him.

"You got to train the guys and their dogs for being under fire every day."

My kennel master asks me how my dad is doing. I tell him that he's hanging on, which is as good as can be expected. He puts Jason and Adam on the line. Adam keeps telling me how he can't wait to get out to Iraq and start working with his dog.

"You'll be out here soon enough, buddy," I tell him. "Your time will come. All right, brother, take care, I got to go."

I ask Gunney Smith if I can make one more call, this time to my folks. I speak to Mom and tell her that Rex and I are doing fine out here. She gives me an update on my favorite local baseball team, the Oakland A's. Then I ask her the question that's foremost on my mind: How is Dad?

"He's doing pretty much the same," she tells me, "and, you know, we're lucky to keep having him around still." She puts him on the line to say hi to me. He's real sluggish at talking now. I can sense that his voice has slowed further over the month that I've been away. But it's great just to hear him.

He says a few words and finishes with a heartfelt "God bless," just like he always does with me.

Chapter Eight

I'M THE FOURTH OF SIX KIDS AND WE GREW UP AROUND ANIMALS. Home was as near to being a farm as you could ever imagine with only a small suburban backyard. The yard ran away from the house into a rough area of small bushes and dirt and grass. We had dogs down there and guinea pigs, turtles, hamsters, and rabbits, plus cats in and out of the house, and parrots, tropical fish, and a snake.

The dogs were my pride and joy, but that snake—a Brazilian rainbow boa constrictor—sure was a new challenge to take care of. Sadly, it didn't get to grow so big. I loaned it to a friend for a few weeks, and the guy let it die. He loved animals as much as I did, and we had no idea why it perished. I wasn't overly heart-broken; my greatest affinity always was with our dogs.

We had Murphy the Irish setter and Brandy the cocker span-iel. They were puppies when I was an infant, and they were an absolute constant in my young life. Home was in Richmond, California, a city just north of Berkeley. San Francisco lay across the bay, and you could see the Golden Gate Bridge from our liv-ing room window.

Just down the road from us was Point Isabel, a beautiful stretch of hilly parkland rolling down to the sea. It's also the largest off-leash dog park in the nation. Point Isabel is split almost by an inlet, and people let their dogs frolic in the sea. I spent my weekends there with my father, brothers, and sisters, playing with Brandy and Murphy. All that ever took us home was the need to eat and to sleep.

It sounds like an idyllic California childhood, and in a way it was. But Richmond is actually a violent place. It isn't all bad, but one area in the city center has one of the highest murder rates in America. It's called the Iron Triangle, so named because of the railroad tracks that meet there to form a triangle. The Iron Triangle was a few minutes' drive from where we lived and it was known as a war zone.

I hung out with kids from the Iron Triangle, but I was never really a part of the place. I played basketball with these seriously dangerous guys and often was the only white kid on the court. We went to different schools and had different aspirations, and we knew each other only because of the sport.

I wasn't a hard case as a kid. My mom said I was the easiest kid to raise. I was easygoing and laid-back and did my own thing. I was the fourth of six children, so I learned from my older siblings what I could get away with and what I couldn't.

My mom and dad were strongly Catholic. We went to a Catholic church and a Catholic school, and we had nuns as some of our teachers. We all were baptized and confirmed, and all the boys did their stint as altar boys. But my absolute passion was sports. I played constantly, basketball and baseball my early favorites. But once I discovered football, I knew that was the game for me.

By the time I was in high school, there was only one thing I wanted to do with my life; to be an American pro football player. Unfortunately, I tore the cartilage in both knees the first season I played. I'd shot up real fast between the ages of twelve and thirteen, and the doc said that my physical abilities just couldn't keep pace with how fast my body was growing.

At junior high I got interested in Guide Dogs for the Blind. My older sister volunteered there and I tagged along. They had a center twenty minutes' drive away, and we fostered one of their puppies, a tiny Labrador named August. Working with August helped get my mind off my football injuries.

I started going once a week to the Guide Dogs for the Blind center, to train with August. I loved watching him and all the other puppies running around playing and tumbling—just being dogs. I was amazed at how clever August was. It was cool when he learned to respond to my verbal commands. It was like I could talk to him.

I didn't want to give him up, but I knew that at the end of the year August would have to go to work as a guide dog. The people at Guide Dogs for the Blind promised us we could adopt him when his working life was over, so that kind of consoled me.

At the end of the year, August graduated as a full-fledged guide dog, and our entire family went to the ceremony. August met the blind person for whom he would become a guide. I was happy that August went to a lovely lady who really needed his help, and they seemed somehow made for each other.

I had a buddy in high school named Daniel, and all he ever wanted to do was join the Marine Corps. He kept talking about how the marines were the toughest of the brave and the few, and about how joining up was the only way to truly test yourself. He was going to enlist as soon as he finished high school. For some reason, Daniel's words really hit home with me.

The Marine Corps had tried to recruit my older brothers when they graduated from high school, but they hadn't gone for it. But I was sorely tempted to follow Daniel's lead. I was pretty certain by now that a sporting career was a nonstarter. I figured in the Corps I'd still be able to push and challenge myself physically, which was what I craved.

My high school grades were good enough to get me accepted to college, and I figured I'd pay a visit before making my decision. I drove over to the University of California at Santa Barbara together with my best buddy at the time, Pooya. Pooya is an Iranian American and we'd known each other since we were small. We'd been to high school together and played on the same school sports teams.

The university is perched right on the ocean, a gorgeous campus crammed full of young, bright, beautiful people. We couldn't help noticing all the pretty young girls hanging out, and it didn't take us long to decide that this was the life for us.

Holy smoke, I thought, forget the Marines! I'm coming here.

Yet in less than two years my life would fall apart. I'd flunk out of college, and in an effort to find my way again I'd sign up for the Marine Corps. I'd lost myself completely at college, the first time in my life that I'd ever been separated from animals, especially dogs. In joining the Marines I was on my way to discovering a special closeness with dogs—in particular, Rex.

The night after Rex and I cleared the road and did our show-and-tell for the Iraqi kids, we're hit by another random mortar strike. We're learning that these attacks can come at any time of day or night. The first few times, there was the scream of an incoming round, and Rex went rigid with fear. But day by day he's learning to live with the bombs.

Getting mortared is part of everyday life in the Triangle. The indiscriminate violence comes with the territory. The irony doesn't escape me that I grew up living next to the Iron Triangle, and now Rex and I are serving in the Triangle of Death. And it sure as hell is living up to its name and reputation.

Rex and I go out on patrols daily now, and daily we're getting targeted by IEDs. Luckily, we've been traveling fast in convoy and they've yet to nail a vehicle. Rex does his best to take those IED blasts in his stride. There's a worried glance in my direction, but he sees me trying to act calm and it's from me that he takes his lead. I just pray we don't take a direct hit, proving Rex's faith in me horribly unjustified.

The road leading out of our base is code-named Route Jackson. Where it hits the main highway interchange it's the Mixing Bowl. Route Jackson forms one side of the Triangle of Death, running north to Baghdad. Route Michigan runs west out of Baghdad, and the third side is the Euphrates River. Take Route Tampa east from the Mixing Bowl and you hit IED Alley—the main road into Mahmoudiyah. It's here that the enemy is hitting us real bad.

Running IED Alley is like playing Russian roulette. Every time. Just off IED Alley is an area of hilly scrubland fringed by a couple of blocks of run-down low-rise housing. The area's a hotbed of insurgent activity, and we figure that's where they've got the bomb factories for building their IEDs. The trouble is, we can't seem to track down the explosives or the bomb makers.

Time and time again we return to that same patch of territory. The marines do cordon-and-search operations of all the buildings, and Rex and I go in on detection sweeps. We've found stacks of assault rifles and ammo but nothing remotely suitable for manufacturing IEDs, the devices of ultimate indiscriminate murder here.

The Iraqis hate Rex and me sniffing out all their weaponry. They keep screaming at us and pelting our vehicles with stones as we're driving away. But with Rex on hand, the heaviest situations can switch to hilarity in an instant.

We're in a building when Rex shows a massive change of behavior. I feel the hair on the back of my neck go up and my pulse start pumping.

Rex is rooting under a bed, and I'm convinced he's found the bomb-making kit we're after. There're a couple of marines with me and all eyes are glued to my dog. Then his head pops out with something gripped tightly in his jaws. He turns proudly toward us. It's a soccer ball! Rex grips the ball with this goofy grin and immediately it punctures in a *whooof* of expelling air. The marines dissolve into laughter.

We complete search after search and turn up nothing more than a few small arms and ammunition. Wherever their bomb-making kit is, they've got it exceedingly well hidden. We know the clock is ticking. As we refine our tactics to search for and combat the IED threat, so the bomb makers evolve their tactics to better hit us. It's a vicious—and deadly—circle.

We know the enemy is targeting our bomb-disposal guys. They've already put one in Gunney Smith's team out of action. It stands to reason that the more often they see Rex and me at work, the more they'll realize what K9 teams can do out here, and the more likely they are to start trying to hit us directly.

Here I am holding my nephew, flanked by my parents and two sisters, at boot camp graduation, Marine Corps Recruit Depot, San Diego, November 9, 2001.

Me with military working dog Joris (pronounced Yori), a brindle-colored Dutch shepherd. Our old kennel office Building 1712 is behind us, and in the parking lot is my 2000 Ford Mustang—the one that my brother totaled while I was on deployment in Iraq!

Rex hanging out in the hills of Camp Pendleton with the K9 kennels in the distance behind him. We spent the majority of our time in these hills exercising, training, and bonding. Taken February 23, 2003, about one year before our deployment.

Camp Pendleton K9 unit, winter 2002 (*from left*): Private First Class Matt Luyando; Sergeant Lester Huckey (chief trainer); Staff Sergeant Greg Massey (kennel master); Sergeant Vincent Amato with MWD Masto; Lance Corporal Mike Dowling with MWD Rex; Lance Corporal Sean Demoe with MWD Rita; Lance Corporal Jason Cannon with MWD Robby; Sergeant Charles Allen with MWD Penny; Lance Corporal Mario Cardenas with MWD Rokka; and Lance Corporal Adam Cann with MWD Bruno.

My kennel master Greg Massey and me at the Marine Corps Ball, November 2004. Because my father was dying of cancer, Staff Sergeant Massey gave me the choice of deploying to Iraq or staying behind. I told him to send me so that Rex and I could save lives out there. I knew it was what my father would want.

Staff Sergeant Chris Greating with "Winchester," our K9 unit mascot at Camp Pendleton, summer 2002. Staff Sergeant Greating was my kennel master at Camp Pendleton prior to Staff Sergeant Massey. I learned a tremendous amount from him that I applied when training Rex.

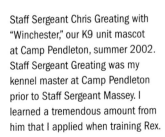

The dogs in their kennel crates, which are strapped down onto the floor of the US Air Force C17 transport aircraft. This is how Rex and the other military working dogs were transported from the USA to Iraq so we could start searching for the bombs.

Ramadi, Iraq (*from left*): Me with handlers Corporal Donald Paldino and Corporal Darin Cleveringa. Our dogs are loaded in their crates behind us for the move south to Camp Fallujah.

Here I am doing some training with Rex, using Sergeant Brian Stokes as the decoy—a volunteer "suspect" who wears a bite-proof sleeve so Rex can grab and detain him. The "bunker" we lived in while at Mahmoudiyah is directly behind us. There is a watchtower above it and the base generator is at right. Peaceful it was not, but at least it gave us some privacy where I could care for and bond with my dog.

Me, Rex, and Sergeant Brian Stokes of CAAT (Combined Anti-Armor Team) White, the Warlord's heavy weapons company. We patrolled in Sergeant Stokes's Humvee more than any other while with 2/2, and Rex and I built up a real bond of trust with those guys.

Sergeant Brian Stokes pretends to bite off a chunk of C4 plastic explosive that he picked up from the EOD (bomb disposal) truck. The C4 was used to blow up caches of enemy weapons and bomb-making kits that we found.

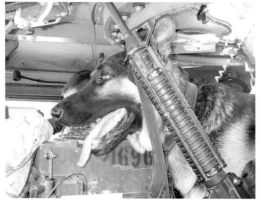

Rex in his favorite position, gazing through the windshield of the Humvee. Sergeant Stokes is behind him, the radio is in the middle and the handset is hanging from the roof—perfectly placed for Rex to bite whenever Stokes tried to make a radio call. Stokes and Rex were forever messing with each other, and it broke up the tension of the patrols.

Rex standing with his head stuck out the turret of a Humvee while I show him his Kong—the chew-proof ball I used as his reward whenever he found arms, explosives, or IEDs. Rex loved his Kong, and it was the promise of a play session that kept him so focused on his task of finding the deadly devices before they could maim and kill.

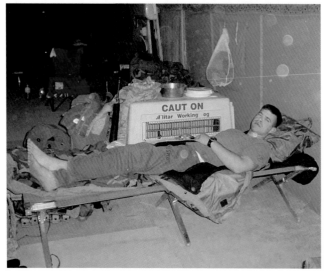

Spending the night under canvas in Ramadi before we headed to Camp Fallujah and eventually to Mahmoudiyah—the so-called Triangle of Death. Rex is in his crate beside my cot, where I can keep a good eye on him, and he on me.

The military working dog we dressed up at Camp Fallujah for our Iraq kennel master, Gunnery Sergeant Kartune. He would use the image in a PowerPoint presentation to the Marine Corps high command to bring attention to the dog teams and get them used more. Rex and I never had that problem down in the Triangle of Death, where we were always getting outside the wire.

Rex and I take a break after a morning-long search of a suspected insurgent area near Fallujah. Note the captured weaponry piled against the fence behind us. This is one of those days when we'd pull in a great haul of arms and explosives, and the combat engineers would blow it up with C4 so as to deny it to the enemy.

Holding a brand-new-looking rocket-propelled-grenade (RPG) round, one of several that Rex found buried on the outskirts of Fallujah. Rex's happy gaze is fixed on those rounds, as if he's saying: *See, I found them! I found them!* What a dog.

My favorite of all my deployment photos. Camp Fallujah, June 2004 (*top row, from left*): Sergeant Nester Antoine with MWD Boda; Air Force handler Daniel Adolf with MWD Jimmy: Lance Corporal Mike Dowling with MWD Rex; Air Force handler Stephen Hudson with MWD Tina; (*bottom row, from left*): Corporal José Chavez with MWD Luki; Air Force handler Breon Shird with his MWD; Air Force handler Cleophus Gallon with MWD Alan.

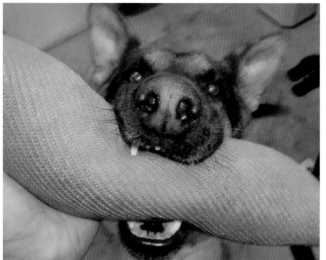

Playing tug-of-war with Rex inside the bunker at FOB Mahmoudiyah, Iraq. Rex is biting on his much-loved chew toy. It's important to keep playing with, grooming, and petting your military working dog to maintain and grow that unbreakable bond between dog and handler—that's what enables man and dog to keep going into harm's way and searching out the deadly IEDs.

Lance Corporal Bob Tincher of CAAT White, handing out coloring books and toys to children in Mahmoudiyah during a patrol. The kids loved watching Rex obey my commands, and interacting with them was one of the more fun parts of being in Iraq.

A couple of days after Rex ate the soccer ball, we return to the same area. This time I decide to head up into the scrubby hills overlooking the ragged blocks of housing. We're searching under the scorching midday sun, and Rex is suffering. He's loving the work, but he's showing signs of heat exhaustion. My backpack is stuffed full of bottles of water, and I keep hosing him down. As it evaporates from his thick coat, it helps to cool him.

The marines adore Rex. If one patrol sees that another has got him, they're immediately jealous: How come you guys got Sexy Rexy today? In part it's their innate love of animals, but it's also that they can see how hard he works to protect them and to try to defeat the bomb makers. They keep asking me why I don't shave off his fur, to make him cooler. The answer's simple: He'd get terrible sunburn, and that would be the end of Iraq for Rex.

We're searching for hours up and over the dry scrub. We're far from the vehicles and I've run out of water. I've brought twelve one-liter bottles, but Rex hasn't drunk much of it. Mostly, I've used it to splash his underside, to cool him. It's pushing 130 degrees, the only shade is the distant vehicles, and I'm out of water.

I'm seriously considering canning it when Rex shows just a faint change in behavior. There's the pause; the tail flicks straighter; his muzzle probes the way ahead. I let Rex lead me. Slowly, back and forth across the parched landscape, he tracks the scent. Rex figures he may be onto something, but I can tell that the scent is faint and intermittent and that he is far from certain.

It reaches the point where Rex is dying for a drink. One of the two security marines with us—our eyes and ears out here—pulls a CamelBak water carrier out of his backpack. He cuts the top off a plastic MRE container, empties out the contents, and crafts Rex a makeshift bowl. We slop the water in, and the marine holds the bowl for Rex as he laps thirstily.

Rex appears refreshed, and he perks up mightily. He's back on the search, and a few minutes later he comes to a halt. He glances at the ground at his feet, then up at me. I've seen this expression on his face a hundred times before, during training: *Partner, I think there's something right here, but, you know, I just can't be certain. . . .*

As carefully as I can, I part the grass and bush. There's nothing. I poke around in the dirt, still no sign of anything. Maybe it's a false respond. Maybe Rex is so pooped he's pretending he's found something so we can all go home.

But that's so unlike Rex. He's got more pride in his profession, and more faith in me, ever to try to do that. I try to lead Rex away, but he's refusing to move. I call up the combat engineers. There's a short delay before they arrive, complete with their EBEX 410 metal detectors. They check the area beneath where Rex is standing, passing their machines back and forth across the sunbaked dirt. Sure enough, just in front of Rex's paws one of the things starts bleeping.

Carefully, one of the EOD guy starts digging. Three feet down he hits a stash of detonation cord. Over the next hour we unearth scores of buried sandbags stuffed full of rocket-propelled grenades, mortar shells, and parcel after parcel of explosives. It's a bonanza of IED-making materials. No doubt about it, we've found the IED Alley bomb makers' secret stash of explosives. The bomb makers had to dig real deep in an effort to defeat Rex's sense of smell, but still Rex's nose has outfoxed them.

The marines love what we're doing—sniffing out all of this deadly material. The insurgents hate it. We're getting IED strikes and ambushes every day now. Marines from 2/2 are getting wounded and killed, and I know Rex and I have got to up our game.

With the help of the EOD guys, we try to refine and improve the way we do things. Gunney Smith makes Rex a set of carefully crafted training aids. They're empty chewing tobacco tins, with holes pricked in the lids, each of which is stuffed with the type of explosive the insurgents are using to build their bombs. I hide them around the base and set Rex to find them.

These training aids live in a special box in the EOD office. I can't keep them with us in the Bunker, or Rex would keep smelling the explosives and trying to dig them out. He can't stop himself from being a search dog. He loves what he does, and he does it so well.

With practice we're getting better and better at how we search, and we're getting more and more visible around the base, and that in turn boosts Rex's popularity. The marines love watching Rex at work, and they're full of curiosity and questions. As Rex bonds with the marines, so he starts to allow them to play with him too.

Play for Rex is roughhousing: It's like a play fight in which if you didn't know better, you'd think Rex was trying to kill you. There are all the snarls of a dogfight, but he's never actually biting. Marines have to watch me roughhouse with Rex, and come out unharmed, before they'll try it themselves. Rex earns himself another nickname now, from the marines in the roughhouse gang: "T-Rex."

We're six weeks into our deployment, and Rex and I are on

an incredibly steep learning curve. At times it feels near vertical. I'm feeding all that I'm learning to my kennel master back at Camp Pendleton. But the simplest lesson is also the most challenging: We are in desperate need of more K9 teams out here in Mahmoudiyah.

Rex and I are doing patrols every day. We're daily making the walk. Sometimes we're out on both a day and a night mission. The constant fear and the tension are getting to us. It's exhausting. Psychologically, the fear of blundering into an IED is almost as bad as the reality of being hit by one.

Rex and I are in danger of burnout, and we need backup. Hell, the Warlords could easily use a dozen K9 teams out here. We've been promised that a second wave will deploy, but they won't be ready for at least a month or more. In the meantime, Rex and I will have to hang on.

Just as it seems the pace of operations can't get any more frenzied, the Warlords are tasked to relocate the entire battalion. They are to move up to Camp Fallujah. The Marine Corps is poised to spearhead the taking down of Fallujah city, the single biggest Al Qaeda and insurgent stronghold in Iraq. The 2/2 is going to be an integral part of that operation, and a regular army unit will take over at Mahmoudiyah.

Rex and I are ordered to move to Fallujah along with the 2/2. We've been blown up by rockets, mortared, and targeted by IEDs, but we've yet to be in a major firefight. With the Warlords heading into the cauldron that is Fallujah, I'm certain that it's soon coming. I wonder if I'm up for it, if I'm ready. But it's Rex, the dog I love, that I'm worried sick for.

It's the end of April when we form up in a massive convoy to make the trip north. We move out at last light, the entire battalion pulling away from Mahmoudiyah in a riot of grunting engines and dust. Rex and I have been in Iraq less than two months, and we're on the road again. The difference is we're not like hobos this time: We don't have to hitch a ride up to Fallujah. We've got reservations on the Warlords' convoy.

We've had to pack up everything and ship it out so the army lot can move into the Mahmoudiyah base. It's been a real pain in the ass. And another thing is bothering me: In the rush to move, I haven't had a chance to say a good-bye to Suraya.

But on one level I'm happy to be heading to Camp Fallujah. I'm keen to see my fellow handlers again, especially my kennel master, Kartune. I've been able to send him the odd e-mail update, but there's been no communication otherwise. I wonder how the other handlers are faring in their various postings, plus I'm looking forward to a little luxury for me and my dog.

Camp Fallujah has a massive chow hall: real, fresh-cooked meals three times a day. In spite of Suraya's food parcels, the weight has been dropping off me, and I've had to tighten up a couple of inches on my belt. The K9 billet in Camp Fallujah has permanent aircon, so that'll be some relief for me and my dog. Plus I'm keen to do some refresher training with Rex. Kartune is a very experienced dog handler, and I want to get his advice on how Rex and I have been going about doing our search patrols.

By the time our convoy reaches Camp Fallujah, we're well into the hours of darkness. I'm eager to find the K9 quarters, but the XO doesn't want me to. We get into an argument. He wants me there with his marines 24/7. But the marines are pitching canvas, and there's nowhere private for me and my dog. The XO tells me to use the expeditionary kennel. He is adamant: My dog and I have to stay with the Warlords. We're not going anywhere.

That night I sleep out under the stars, bedding down on the rocks in my sleeping bag with my best friend by my side. The next morning the XO repeats what he's told me: He wants Rex and me there with 2/2. I go see Gunney Trotter. I tell him I need to run over to the K9 billet to fetch some supplies that I urgently need for my dog.

It's a couple of minutes' drive to where the rest of the handlers are based. I see immediately the luxury they're living in. Kartune shows me around. The whole place is fortified with sandbags and HESCO, behind which each handler has his own room complete with 24/7 aircon, plus a bathroom.

One of the things I've most been nagging my folks to send me in their care parcels is wet wipes. At our Mahmoudiyah base there were a handful of showers for eight hundred marines. On the rare occasion you did manage to get in one, you were rationed to two minutes of water. Most days, the nearest my body has got to a wash is a wipe-down with a baby wipe.

Now that I'm here in the luxury of the Fallujah K9 quarters, I'm dying to get into one of those rooms and dive under the shower and scrub off all the accumulated dirt and grime.

I explain to Kartune there's no way Rex can live at Camp Fallujah in a Vietnam-era expeditionary kennel, with an aircon unit that's on the blink. If Rex and I can billet with the rest of the K9 guys, we can get in some great training and brush up on tactics. We can check in with the 2/2 every hour of the day to see if we're needed.

I tell Kartune that I can't win the argument with the XO, because he's a major and I'm a corporal. I ask him to come and argue the case on our behalf. Kartune does just that, outlining all the benefits of our staying with our fellow K9 teams. The

XO hears him out and agrees to let us go. The one condition is that we check in first thing in the morning and all through the day with the 2/2. He gives me a voice-comms radio so I can get through to the Warlords at any hour of the day or night.

Rex and I move into the "Fallujah Hilton," as I've nicknamed the K9 quarters. It feels great to be there. Rex has an extra-special reason to be happy: One of the working dogs, Boda, is a female.

Rex reacts to Boda in the way I've come to expect. At first he's all cool and doing his best to make an impression: standing tall, mouth firmly closed, tail erect and still, then swishing gently to and fro after a few seconds. But as soon as they start sniffing each other's undersides, Rex loses it.

He's got a big loopy smile on his face like he's all embarrassed—the typical awkward gentleman. The bitch doesn't have any such qualms: She's hitting on him outrageously. Rex gives me a look: *So what do I do now?* I think back to Suraya, and how Rex always seems to scupper my romantic liaisons.

But after the stress and danger of the last two months I reckon he's earned a little playtime.

Chapter Nine

ALTHOUGH MOST MILITARY WORKING DOGS ARE MALE, THERE ARE some females. All the females are neutered, but the males are not. So we allow our dogs to have a little innocent flirtation, but no intimate fraternization. Rex and Boda seem to know they can take their relationship only so far.

We're two days into enjoying life at the Fallujah Hilton when I check in with the 2/2 and we get our first mission. It's two o'clock in the afternoon, and Gunney Trotter tells me we're heading out in three hours. Most of the 2/2 is moving to Karma, a suburb of Fallujah to the north of the city. Rex and I are going with them.

No one's told me what the mission is. I've just got to ready myself and my dog for the move, which could last a couple of days to a couple of weeks. We head out at last light. After a twenty-minute drive, we pull up at a deserted low-rise school building, which is where we're going to base ourselves. Rex and I search and clear the entire place, just in case it's been booby-trapped with an IED.

The only bit of the schoolhouse that is remotely suited to

my dog and my setting up home in is a tiny storeroom. Every wall has shelves that must have at one time contained school supplies. There's barely room to swing a cat in there. I can just about squeeze my sleeping bag in.

After a cramped night, Rex and I are up at the crack of dawn for the first mission. We've been allocated to Fox Company, Second Platoon. We're to drive west to the far side of Karma and to clear back through the area on foot until we reach the Combat Operations Center (COC), as our school base has now been designated.

Our orders are to clear the streets back to the base, block by block, until we're done. We hit the first run-down apartment complex and pound up the stairs to the top floor. The guys begin the search, but there's broken glass and debris everywhere underfoot. I've no idea where it's come from, and it's no big deal to the marines. But it could cut the pads of Rex's feet to shreds.

I have protective dog booties to save Rex's pads from getting injured. They're like wet-suit boots or reef shoes, with a ribbed rubber sole and Velcro strips that fasten around the ankles. We crouch down on the concrete floor, and Rex lifts each paw so I can slip them on.

He looks a lot happier now. He can charge about without being worried about getting injured. Rex is no sissy, but the last thing he wants is to damage a pad, because that would spell the end of this patrol for him, and he'd need several days in recovery.

There's one problem with the booties. A dog releases heat by sweating via the pads of its feet. In hot weather, a dog will lie belly down on a cool surface, with arms and legs splayed out, to cool itself. The booties lessen Rex's ability to sweat via his feet, and so the heat will prove even more debilitating. It's approaching high summer now, and it's 130 degrees or more at midday.

The marines are knocking on doors, and if they're not opened promptly they're booted in. It's brutal and relentless. Rex sniffs out an ammo crate hidden in some guy's home. It's stuffed full of rounds and explosives, prime bomb-making material. Finding it makes us search that house even more thoroughly, and we uncover a hidden stack of AK-47s wrapped in old blankets.

The more weapons and explosives we find, the bigger the crowd of Iraqis that's following us. At every juncture there's a huddle of sullen Iraqi men watching Rex and me work, plus gangs of kids charging about excitedly.

I remove Rex's booties whenever we're in a patch of terrain clear of glass, just to give his feet a moment to breathe. But by midday the sun is beating down from a cloudless sky with a blazing, furnacelike heat. I have to check the sidewalk with the palm of my hand before I can remove Rex's booties. More often than not it's burning hot, and Rex can't proceed with the search barefoot. The booties have to stay on.

By midafternoon we're a couple of blocks away from the Combat Operations Center, and Rex and I are out front clearing a road, with two security marines to either side of us. Way back are the Humvees, crawling along in our wake. Rex is close to exhaustion. We've been searching for seven hours under a blistering sun, with few breaks.

I can't believe that Rex is still tirelessly doing the search. Each of the homes we've had to clear seems to have an old broken-down fridge in it. Phew! The stench in those places has to be smelled to be believed. And I know the whiff is one thousand times stronger for Rex.

Rex's nostrils are being assaulted by powerful odors on all sides. Of course, a stench that I find revolting may not bother Rex. What smells good or bad to humans might smell the other way around to him. Most important for Rex and me, whatever he smells gives him vital information about what's in the vicinity, including the arms and explosives for which we're searching.

We turn into a street lined with a scatter of ramshackle buildings on one side and some scrubby bush on the other. It's eerily quiet. Creepy. I have a horrible feeling that the enemy is watching and waiting, and choosing a time to strike.

As we start the walk, all I can think about is getting Rex back to base so we can take a break. I'm pooped and so is Rex, and I tell myself that once we've cleared this road we're more or less done. But it's when you least expect something bad to happen that it so often hits you.

We press ahead, me forcing myself to concentrate and to watch for a change in Rex's behavior. Halfway down the street this sudden high-pitched snarl cuts the air as a bullet rips past just inches from my head. I know instantly that it's a sniper, even before I've heard the follow-up bark of the weapon firing.

Because the bullet travels faster than the speed of sound, when the round is that close to your head you hear and feel its passing before the crack of the weapon firing reaches your ears. It would be freakin' terrifying if the adrenaline hadn't kicked in, instantly transforming my exhaustion into a hyped-up, pumped-up frenzy.

"SNIPER!" the marine on my right shoulder yells. "SNIPER!"

He starts screaming at Rex and me to take cover. But take cover where? I've had all my senses focused on my dog, and I haven't the slightest idea where the round came from. More than likely the gunman is using a Soviet-era Dragunov sniper rifle, which fires a ten-round magazine. There're plenty more bullets where that came from.

Another round tears into the dirt, this one at Rex's feet. I feel a red mist of rage sweep over me. *They're trying to kill my dog.* The shots are coming from the built-up side of the road, and I want nothing more than to sprint in that direction, find the gunman, and shoot him in the head. But I've got to think of Rex's safety first.

I tug on his leash and we make a mad dash for the bush on the opposite side of the street, bullets kicking at our heels and snarling after us. We dive into the cover of a mud hut, the security marines on our shoulder piling in directly after us.

One of them fixes me with a look. "Dude, that fucker was trying to shoot you *and* your dog!"

"No shit."

"Yeah. I saw where the rounds hit and the direction they were firing from. You and your dog were the targets."

I force a smile. "Then it's good they can't shoot for shit."

A squad of marines charges into the building from where the gunman was shooting at us. It all goes quiet, and for a moment I reflect upon how Rex and I have just used up another of our nine lives. Having unleashed those high-velocity rounds at us, the enemy sniper must have rapidly made himself scarce, for the marines fail to find him.

The guy in charge of the patrol decides we should jog the remainder of the way home. It's a good call. It would be insane to put Rex and me out there again to finish the search, knowing that a sniper is trying to put a bullet into us. We'll come back and clear the last part of the route another day.

But right now we have to get back out there on the streets. As we inch our way onto the exposed emptiness of that bullet-pocked road, I feel horribly vulnerable and exposed. I try to hide my gut-wrenching fear from Rex: I don't want my terror running down leash to my dog.

"Come on, boy," I tell him as we regain the hardtop. "Only one more block and we're home."

Rex and I push ahead at a fast trot. I'm bracing myself for more shots. Finally, we round a bend and we're in sight of the COC. We reach the gates and thunder through into comparative safety.

Rex and I have done a whole day patrolling on foot with Fox Company. We've lasted the course and we've survived being shot at by an enemy sniper. I realize how much I feel like a real infantry marine now, and I realize how not getting killed out there is a massive buzz.

One thing is crystal clear. K9 handlers and their dogs are at the top of the insurgents' hit list, along with the EOD guys. We always presumed it would be the enemy's priority to kill Rex and me, because we're always at the front of patrols sniffing out the bombs. The more effective we get at finding their arms and explosives, the more they'll want to hit us.

After that daytime patrol, the Fox Company commander asks if Rex and I are willing to go out again, this time under cover of darkness. Third Platoon is mounting a night patrol, and it's heading out in a couple of hours. Rex is exhausted, and we've both just survived getting sniped at. But I want the guys to see how keen we are to search and to go out with them where the risk is greatest.

I tell the commander that we're up for it. It's a night op, so the heat will be less. If Rex gets overly exhausted, I can sit him in a Humvee. It's also a chance to test Rex and see how long he can keep going. Plus it's that riding-the-bike thing: I've got to get right back on the search again after those sniper rounds all but smashed us.

Rex and I eat and rest, and then we're heading out on night patrol. It's a repeat of the day mission but without the sniper attack. It's a short, intense foot patrol, and we're back around midnight. We crash out exhausted in the storeroom. I'm so tired I'm falling asleep in just my underwear. I've got Rex's leash knotted around my wrist, and he's snuggled up half on top of me.

Today has been a day of days, a big bonding moment for Rex and me. We've worked all day and half the night, and mostly on foot. We've been shot at and survived, and felt the buzz of cheating death out there on the brutal streets of Iraq. I feel closer to my dog than ever before, and more exhausted than I've felt in months. But there's little time to savor the moment, for Rex and I are instantly comatose.

I wake with my sixth sense screaming at me that something is wrong. There's a figure in the open doorway staring at us. Head fogged by sleep, I'm only aware of the stars gleaming on the marine's shoulders. Shoot. This is some kind of general, and there are only a couple of them in the whole of Iraq.

I jump up, Rex springing to his feet beside me. I try to come to attention, half forgetting that I'm in my underwear. I wonder if I should salute or try and get decent first.

It's Lieutenant General James T. Conway, one of the top Marine Corps commanders here in Iraq. He's a three-star general in charge of the First Marine Expeditionary Force. Here he is confronted by a marine in his boxer shorts, and a sergeant who happens to be a dog.

"Corporal Dowling and MWD Rex, sir," I announce. "We've been out on operations all day and all night. . . ."

We exchange glances for a moment, and then the general starts laughing good-naturedly.

"Good to go, Corporal," he tells me, returning the salute. "Keep up the good work—you and your dog."

I'm relieved that I woke when I did. If the general had taken just a step into our room, and Rex had spotted him first, my dog would more than likely have had a good chew on his uniform. As far as Rex is concerned, I'm the pack leader, and he's my second in command. I'm the equivalent of his commander in chief, so I guess it's hardly surprising he doesn't give a damn about anyone else's authority.

As Rex and I settle down to sleep again, my mind drifts back to a similar incident, one where Rex tried to chew out a similarly high-powered individual.

It was May 2003 and President Bush had flown down to Coronado Naval Base in San Diego. The carrier USS *Abraham Lincoln* was moored off the coast, and the president was scheduled to land at the naval base and transit by helicopter onto the carrier.

Secret Service had requested an extra bomb-detection dog, and my kennel master had sent Rex and me. We were tasked to secure a sector of the air base. As *Air Force One* landed, Rex and I joined the line of officers waiting to receive the president.

I'd never shaken a U.S. president's hand before, and I figured Rex and I had as good a right as anyone to be there. After we'd got eye-to-eye with the president, one of the pilots of *Air Force One* came wandering over to us.

"That is such a beautiful dog," he remarked.

He explained that he was one of the Presidential Aircrew, from the Presidential Logistics Squadron, part of the Air Mobility Command's Eighty-ninth Airlift Wing, based out of Andrews AFB, Maryland. I explained that Rex and I were part of a Marine Corps K9 unit based at Camp Pendleton.

I asked if we could get a look inside *Air Force One*. He apologized, saying that only the Secret Service guys were allowed on board. The presidential helicopters are known as *Marine One*, and by now there were rotors turning and chomping into the sky as Bush was airlifted off toward the carrier.

Unbeknownst to me, the pilot returned to *Air Force One* to fetch us a souvenir pack. He jogged up behind Rex and me with the package. He tapped me on the shoulder, and at that moment Rex presumed the pilot was attacking me. I had him on a six-foot leash, one end held in my right hand and the other looped over my left. As Rex lunged for the pilot, I just managed to rein him in.

"Whoa!" the guy exclaimed, dropping the souvenir pack in alarm.

He knew how close he'd come to getting chewed. Carefully, he stooped and retrieved the package.

"Erm, this is for you guys," he told me shakily. "Say, that sure is one hell of a badass dog."

He apologized for coming up behind us like that; he knew

he was at fault and said he appreciated how protective Rex was of his handler.

I looked through the souvenir pack. There was a fact sheet on *Air Force One*, telling me it was a modified Boeing 747-200B, containing an executive suite for the president, complete with dressing room, lavatory, and shower, plus a presidential office. There was also a copy of the *Presidential Entertainment Library* for March 2003, with a picture of Halle Berry looking vulnerable but real cute on the front of it.

Bush went on to make his now infamous "Mission Accomplished" speech from the deck of the carrier, in which he basically told the world that major combat operations in Iraq were over. It was a little premature, to put it mildly, but no one knew that yet. I saw it that evening on TV, and I thought to myself: That's it, it's all over, and we're never going to get out there.

Which only goes to show how wrong you can be.

After Lieutenant General Conway has left our schoolhouse base, Rex and I visit the room where all the confiscated weapons and explosives are stored. It's crammed full of AK-47s, RPKs, mortar tubes, makeshift rocket launchers, and explosives. Seeing this big pile of weaponry makes me feel like Rex and I have done good out there, that maybe we've saved a good number of lives here in Karma.

With our mission done, it's time to head back to Camp Fallujah. Rex and I arrive at our K9 unit to find something of a circus unfolding. Kartune, our kennel master, is concerned that the Marine Corps high command doesn't fully realize that dog teams are here or what we can be used for. He's asked the handlers to help him prepare a PowerPoint presentation about K9, which he will make to the Marine Corps top commanders.

He wants to open with an amusing image, so he's asked one of the handlers to dress his dog up like a marine grunt so that the first photo in the presentation will really grab attention and raise a laugh. He asks a handler fresh into theater, Jessie McClurr, to dress up his German shepherd, Rebel.

It's a bit of light relief and so we all pitch in. We get a pair of khaki boxer shorts on Rebel's rear end, a Marine Corps T-shirt on his body, plus a floppy jungle hat perched on his head. It's topped off by a pair of sunglasses propped on Rebel's nose. Rebel stands for the photo with a big toothy grin, and one leg thrust slightly forward in a catwalklike pose. He's clearly loving it, and we've had fun dressing up McClurr's dog.

I appreciate the struggle that Kartune's having getting his K9 teams used. It was tough for Rex and me to get noticed by the Warlords, even in a tiny little base like Mahmoudiyah. Camp Fallujah is more like an Iraqi version of Camp Pendleton. Trying to get out on missions here must be one hell of a challenge. In fact, the K9 teams stationed here seem to be standing gate duty only, as opposed to getting outside the wire to track down the bombs.

Kartune asks me all about the kind of patrols that Rex and I have been out on with the Warlords. It's vital intel for him, because it's the kind of work he wants his PowerPoint presentation to secure for his K9 teams. I ask him if there are ways that Rex and I can refine how we patrol and search, to reduce the threat to man and dog. Kartune figures there may be.

He gets us out doing long-leash training. He shows us how we can have the dog on the end of the 360-foot leash and allow him to search at a distance from the handler. The technique is similar to the way we normally search, just that the human is removed a fair way from his dog. The thinking is simple: If the dog triggers an IED, the handler's going to be far enough back to likely survive the blast.

"If you think you're gonna get blown up, use the 360," Kartune advises us. "That way, you limit injury to the dog team."

I coil the 360-foot leash and stash it in my backpack. I've already decided I'll use it only if I absolutely have to. I've got several reservations. First, it's fine doing this in Camp Fallujah, where the buildings are identical rows of clear, clean concrete structures. It's a very different proposition trying to do so out on the streets of an Iraqi city, which are invariably full of rubble and garbage and thronged with people and animals.

A 360 leash is going to keep getting tangled and snagged. It can easily catch on barbed wire or razor wire. And while Rex is a superintelligent dog, that's not going to stop him getting tangled in a leash that long and that cumbersome. When he's searching, he's 101 percent focused on the scents he's drawing into his nose. He doesn't need to be worrying about getting his feet all snarled in a 360.

I also figure it's better to be close to your dog so you can spot the all-important change of behavior. If it's a big respond—like sitting down at source—you'll see it anyway, even from 360 feet away. But not if it's a marginal response, like the one Rex had when we were searching the waste ground above IED Alley and he detected the buried bomb-making materials.

Plus if you're not up close with your dog, you may fail to spot something that the dog's about to stumble into. There can be danger up ahead of the type that only a handler can spot. I've no doubt in my mind that if I use Rex on a long leash, I'll increase the threat to him. I may be safer, but he won't be. And that's not something that I'm willing to countenance with Rex.

There's no alternative but to keep searching as I've always done—up close and personal with my dog.

Chapter Ten

WE'RE A WEEK INTO FALLUJAH AND I'M HAVING AN EARLY BREAKFAST in the chow hall. It's paradise in there. I've got scrambled eggs, sausage, and bacon heaped high on my plate, and I'm hoping to pile on some of the weight that I've lost. I'm halfway through the mountain of food when a marine from 2/2 pauses by my table.

"Hey, Dowling, you heard the news?" he announces. "We're leaving Camp Fallujah and getting into Fallujah proper tomorrow."

"Who, your platoon?" I ask through a mouthful.

He shakes his head. "Nope. The entire battalion."

It's the first I've heard about it, but it looks as if the Warlords are on the move again. I finish my chow, then head over to see Gunney Trotter. He pretty much confirms what the marine has told me.

"Better grab your shit, Dowling. Meet us here tomorrow morning at oh-eight-hundred sharp. The CO of the two-two has decided we're gonna head into Fallujah."

"How long for?" I ask.

He shrugs. "No one knows. Maybe as much as a month. We're moving in."

The CO of the Warlords, Lieutenant Colonel Keyser, has decided to relocate to the outskirts of the city so we can be poised for the coming assault into Fallujah itself. Lieutenant Colonel Keyser has the reputation of being a real cowboy. He's not the kind of commander ever to back down from a fight, which tends to make the marines in his battalion feel and act the same way.

In April, the U.S. military had launched Operation Vigilant Resolve, the trigger for which was the killing of the four private military contractors from Blackwater in central Fallujah. The U.S. high command reacted to that incident by ordering Fallujah city to be taken down and "pacified." It hadn't quite worked out the way they'd planned. Instead, forces from the First Marine Expeditionary Force had fought street by street in a series of bloody battles, leaving scores injured and twenty-seven American combatants dead.

The civilian casualties were far higher, and at the end of the fighting less than half the city lay in American hands. When a cease-fire was finally declared, the mission was judged more to be a victory for the insurgents than for us; they had retained control of the city, while the U.S. military had opted to withdraw.

That conflict has become known as the First Battle of Fallujah. No one has said as much officially, but the marines of 2/2 figure we've come here to launch the Second Battle of Fallujah and to take down the city once and for all. Lieutenant Colonel Keyser's decision to move our entire battalion into the outskirts of the city tends to confirm that view.

That night I make sure I call my folks. I have no idea how

long we'll be out on the coming mission, or how full-on murderous it's going to be. But if we're going into anything like the First Battle of Fallujah, it's sure to be heavy in there. I line up for the bank of booths, punch in my calling-card ID, then dial the number for home. My mom answers. It's great to hear her voice.

There's an extra-special excitement back home right now. My older brother Kevin works as a PR guy in the wine industry, and his wife, Maria, is pregnant. She's due to give birth any day now. My mom tells me that Maria's doing fine with the pregnancy, and she's looking real healthy. I'm happy to be able to speak to my father. He tells me how excited he is about the impending birth, which will be his second grandchild.

I don't tell either my mom or my dad that we're going into Fallujah. Even though the United States is so many thousands of miles away from Iraq, that city has achieved a darkly mythical status back at home. It's become known as the heartland of the insurgency and the stronghold of the forces that are battling America's finest—the Marine Corps.

There are some twenty hard-core insurgent groups operating in Fallujah—from the Madhi Army to Al Qaeda. Everyone knows how violent it is there. I don't want my folks worrying any more than they are already, and especially not my father, which is why I keep this coming mission all to myself.

It's one o'clock the following day by the time the massive convoy of seven-ton trucks and Humvees has formed up for the run into Fallujah. I speak to the convoy commander and offer Rex and me to walk the route ahead of us, to clear it of IEDs. He tells me it'll be too slow, and it'll make us too much of an easy target. Instead, they'll have a trigger vehicle pushing out front of the convoy—an up-armored Humvee that aims to set off any IEDs.

I throw a couple of canisters of Rex's chow into the rear of the lead Humvee at the head of the sixty-vehicle convoy. There's not enough room for Rex and his kennel plus me, so I'm forced to put him in a cargo vehicle some six behind. I hate being separated from my dog. It's the first time that he and I have been parted since we arrived in Iraq. But I figure it shouldn't prove a major drama. I've been told it's only a ten-minute drive, and we won't be going into Fallujah proper, so the chances of any fighting are minimal.

We have snipers, a mortar team, and a squadron of massive Abrams main battle tanks positioned at our new Combat Operations Center. They've gone ahead to secure it, and ours should be a simple drive down there. I explain to Rex what's happening, then place him in his travel kennel and load it onto the rear of the cargo vehicle.

"It's just a short ride to our new home, buddy," I tell him. "We'll be there in no time, and we'll be reunited. Okay?"

I wriggle my fingers through the bars, and Rex has a nervous lick at them. I can tell by his expression that he's not happy. Once he's in the Humvee he knows he's going somewhere, so why isn't he traveling in the company of his pack leader—me?

I try telling him that's it's only for a few minutes and a very short ride. We'll be there real soon. I hear engines revving at the front of the convoy and know we're about to move out. I give him one last reassuring look, then I race down the length of the convoy and load up in the lead Humvee.

The trigger vehicle moves off, zigzagging ahead of us. I'm in the one immediately behind it, with Rex coming after us.

We're several minutes into the drive and we're almost at the COC when there's a sharp crack of gunfire up ahead. The trigger vehicle disappears in a hail of bullets, which go sparking and ricocheting off the Humvee's armored sides.

Moments later, rounds start thumping into our own vehicle. From the inside, it sounds like a thousand metal spears are being slammed against the Humvee's metal flanks. Up ahead there's a wall of lead pounding into the Combat Operations Center, so we're being smashed on all fronts.

It's immediately clear that this is no shoot-and-scatter attack. It's a massive, concerted ambush, and it sounds like the entire city of Fallujah has opened up on us. Our vehicle is rocking with bullet impacts, and it's clear that we're dead if we stay here much longer.

We bail out and dive for the cover of a berm, a ridge of sand running along one side of the road. I stick my head up over the berm, and it's like I'm in the heart of a movie. There's a mad, chaotic scene all around us, with marines opening fire with their M16s and unleashing Javelin rockets at the enemy.

Gunney Trotter is screaming orders to marines all around us and sorting out our defenses. He's hard as nails, and he's come into his own now that the shit's going down. I may have had my differences with him, but right here and right now I can see what a great asset he is for a Marine Corps unit. Nothing beats seeing a professional do his job, and Gunney Trotter embodies true professionalism.

A series of massive booms sound off, drowning out even Gunney Trotter's screamed instructions. The Abrams battle tanks at the COC have started pounding the enemy positions with their massive 120mm guns. The M1A1 Abrams boasts steel-encased depleted uranium armor, and it weighs in at over sixty tons. It also carries a .50-cal heavy machine gun and two 7.62mm M240 machine guns.

The tanks are pretty much immune to anything the insurgents can throw at them. But that doesn't seem to deter the enemy fire. Rounds start smashing into the dirt right next to me, kicking up hot spurts of sand. I risk a look back up the line of our convoy toward Rex's vehicle. It's slightly less exposed to the firefight, but still it's getting hammered.

I see the fiery spark of rounds ricocheting off the open rear of the Humvee, just a few inches above Rex's cage. I can't keep my head up for long, for danger of getting it blown off. All I can think is, Shit, Rex has gotta be going crazy back there. I've got to get to my dog before an Iraqi bullet gets him.

Part of me wants to grab my M16 and return fire. The marine in me wants to fight. But the K9 handler side of me is stronger, as is the bond with my dog. I have an enormous responsibility for Rex, one enshrined in all the promises that I've made to him.

I'm also acutely aware that if "their" dog team gets shot up, that's the end of the Warlords' ability to sniff out the IEDs and the bombs here in Iraq. I turn to the marine beside me. I have to scream to make myself heard above the smack and thump of battle.

"Hey! I got to go check on my dog!"

For a moment he gives me a look: *Has he gone freakin' crazy?* But everyone in 2/2 knows what their K9 team is like by now and to expect the unexpected from me and my dog.

"What the hell, go check on Rex!" he yells back at me. "But, Dowling, be damn sure you make it back alive with Rexy, okay?"

For a moment I'm frozen with fear. Then I think of Rex alone in that bullet-hammered vehicle, and I'm on my feet sprinting for the cover of the nearest Humvee. I use it as a shield, moving along the length of it, then dash to the next. I move down the column sprinting from one vehicle to the next, bullets tearing into the hardtop at my feet wherever I'm exposed to enemy fire.

Each mad dash takes me a step closer to Rex. Six vehicles down I reach his. I peer over the open side. Through the mesh in his crate I see him seeing me. He fixes me with a lonely, frightened gaze, like he's convinced he's been abandoned: *Where were you? What the hell kept you? And what the hell's going on out there?*

It's fair enough, really. Here we are in the midst of a massive firefight, with hot lead ripping all around us, and I was nowhere around when Rex needed me most. But the most amazing thing is that Rex isn't totally freaking out. He's not clawing and biting at his cage to get free, or barking and howling his head off. It's like he knew in his heart that I'd never abandon him, that I was coming to rescue him all along.

I crawl into the rear of the Humvee, keeping my head and back below the level of the fire that's rippling across us. I flip open his cage. I let him flick his tongue around my hand for an instant so he can get a reassuring taste of me. Then he jumps out beside me and I've got the leash on him. We're lying in the rear of the Humvee as it rocks with the impact of enemy fire, and I'm hugging my dog.

"You're okay, boy, you're okay," I keep telling him. "I'm here for you now."

I peek out the rear of the Humvee. The berm's right beside us; it runs all the way up the road. Rex and I make a run for it, bullets hammering after us. An instant later we've dived into some good cover. I check him and pet him, and then I let him have a much-needed piss in the cover of the sun-blasted sand.

We move up the convoy at a low crouch, sticking to the cover of the berm. Rounds slam into the sandbank beside us and kick up off the hardtop, throwing pressure waves up from the road. Every few seconds there's a deafening roar as one of the tanks opens fire. It vibrates the very ground we're walking on.

Each time Rex hears the roar of the guns, he stops dead. He stares at me, wide-eyed and fearful: *What in God's name was that?* I force myself to keep calm and to keep moving ahead. And Rex, God love him, follows my lead. I realize that even in the midst of a crazed firefight like this, Rex will follow me. If I move calmly and without showing fear, he'll trust me completely. It's just like our instructors used to teach us back in K9 school: Trust in your dog.

We rejoin the marines at the front of the convoy. By now the gunner's up in the Humvee's armored turret, and he's pounding the enemy positions with the .50-caliber heavy machine gun. The *thud-thud-thud* of the big gun firing right next to us rips the air apart. I grab Rex and ruffle him around the ears, whispering into them to keep him calm: *It's all gonna be okay.*

His mouth is closed, his eyes are wide, wide open, and his ears are pricked forward toward the roar of the battle. He's glancing all around at the marines as they fight fire with fire, and he's hyperaware. But he's not barking, he's not panicking, and he's not out of control. On the ranges he used to slather and snarl and go crazy at the sound of gunfire, and compared to this that was just a quiet dress rehearsal. This is the full-on real deal, and I'm amazed at the attitude of my dog.

I glance over the berm, and every window in the city is alive with the flash of a muzzle firing. The marines push forward a few feet, Rex and I shadowing them. The Abrams tanks keep pounding the enemy positions, but it isn't enough to silence their guns. Every time a shell slams into a window that's spitting fire at us, the smoke clears and the target has been obliterated. But there are only two tanks, and there are so many insurgents in so many houses it's impossible for the tanks to nail them all.

There must be thousands of enemy fighters out there in Fallujah, and it feels like every one of them is trying to smash us right now. We reach a point where we're pinned down by murderous fire. An enemy gunner's got a bead on our position, and he's hammering us with what sounds like an RPK.

The RPK's a light machine gun with a muzzle-mounted tripod. It's pouring bullets out of its seventy-five-round drum, and the fire's murderously accurate and sustained. We can't move.

One direct hit from the RPK and that's the end of my dog. I've got body armor on, but Rex hasn't. I get my torso between Rex and the enemy gunner, using my bulk to shield him from the bullets. I'm hunkered down below the berm, pressing myself into the dirt, and I curl myself around my dog.

I know this is desperate, but somehow Rex seems to be cool and collected now that he's here with me at his side. I've always worried how Rex would react to being in a full-on firefight, and now I know. Instead of him freaking out, I find myself drawing strength from my dog.

Finally, there's the scream of jet engines high above us, and a flight of F-18s comes tearing through the skies. They dive onto the enemy positions all around us, unleashing five hundred-pound bombs. Each impacts with a massive thumping detonation, throwing a plume of shattered masonry high into the air. The powerful blast waves roar over us, and after several attack runs the battlefield falls silent.

The firefight has lasted for two and a half long hours. Rex and I raise our heads from the dirt. We join the marines as we advance on foot into the COC. We drop our gear in a building along with the rest, and we assess our casualties. We've got some guys lightly injured, but incredibly, not a marine among us has lost his life in that fearsome firefight.

I marvel at just how professional the 2/2 are. Every marine has remained calm and cool during the battle, doing exactly what was needed. Marines have been giving orders, and responses have been immediate and effective. Rex and I are honored to be serving here with the Warlords.

I take Rex out for a familiarization walk around our new position. I have a supreme feeling of confidence in myself and my dog now. We've just experienced what we were least prepared for and what I was dreading most—full-on combat. We've got through it and survived. We've done it. We've arrived.

My worries about Rex flipping out or not obeying my commands when we were under intense fire have all gone out the window. It's almost as if I didn't have to give him any orders. He knew instinctively what I wanted and needed him to do, as if he were reading my mind. If he'd hesitated or frozen for a moment when we needed to move, Rex could have endangered our lives. Instead, he's just had his baptism of fire and he's passed with flying colors.

It's Headquarters and Service's role to provide security for the Combat Operations Center 24/7. Rex and I have to stand our share of guard duty just like anyone else. I'm appointed corporal of the guard (COG) for our first night in our new position. As COG I have to make sure everyone remains in position and alert during my four hours of night duty.

The easiest way is to radio-check everyone, but I prefer doing walkabouts. My COG duty begins at four-thirty in the morning. It's pitch black outside, with only the barest sliver of a moon. As I walk the compound, I can hear gunfire, mortar rounds, and bomb blasts echoing across the city. Some of it sounds pretty close to us.

There's a big old house set in one side of the compound, and I take Rex for a nose inside. As we walk through the darkened corridors, I pass one room where a light's still burning. I glance in, and there's the CO of 2/2, Lieutenant Colonel Keyser, deep in conversation with the battalion sergeant major. Sergeant Major Swann is hard-core, and I'd seen him chew a lot of ass while down at Mahmoudiyah.

I keep walking, but a voice calls me back: "Hey, Marine, how's Rex doing?"

It's Lieutenant Colonel Keyser. I pause. "He's doing great, sir."

"How did he handle that fight today?"

"He's just like all the other two-two marines, sir. He's excited to get some."

The lieutenant colonel gives a tired smile. "Good to go. We love having him here."

"Oo-rah, sir."

The sergeant major comes out of the room. He follows me to have a private word. "How you doing, Dowling?"

"I'm good to go, Sergeant Major, and so is Rex."

He nods, satisfied. "Good, good. Carry on what you're doing, Marine."

This is my first interaction with the CO of 2/2 and his sergeant major. It's great to see the guys at the very top of the battalion caring for the lower-ranking marines. Again, it makes me feel like 2/2 is a fantastic home for Rex and me, the very best.

I walk from guard post to guard post, checking that the marines are all present and alert. After our separation earlier in the day, I want Rex with me at all times. It's a large compound, and in the still darkness of the walk from post to post I feel like we're alone in the universe, just me and my dog. It's a weird, isolated feeling, and I'm doubly glad that I've got Rex by my side.

All of a sudden there's a *whoosh-roar* from out of the darkness, and a massive flaming arrow comes screaming through the air right above our heads. It feels like the back blast from the rocket's motor has seared a scorch mark across my hairline. The rocket slams into the branches of a tree a few dozen yards beyond us and directly above where a bunch of marines are laid out sleeping.

It detonates in a ball of flame, hot shrapnel pounding down. Rex and I race over, expecting to find a scene of bloody carnage. Unbelievably, not one of the marines has taken a serious injury. There are cuts and lacerations, but other than that they're all unharmed. Luckily, the RPG round hit high in the tree, and the branches took the brunt of the blast. Had it detonated on the ground, we could have lost a lot of marines here.

Rex and I return to where we're billeted, and I put him into his travel kennel to sleep. I'm dog tired myself, but I take a few moments to reflect. My dog and I were that close to a rocket blowing our heads off. It's a repeat of the rocket that smashed into the H-barrier at the Mahmoudiyah gatehouse. It's just one more crazy brush with death that we've had here in Iraq.

Absentmindedly, I reach into the front pocket of my Kevlar to finger the rosary beads given me by my father. I can't immediately find them, and as I dig deeper I can feel the beads lying loose at the bottom. Sometime during today's battle I must have dived onto my front and shattered the rosary.

I glance at the handful of broken beads in the dim light of my flashlight. I can't help letting out an awkward laugh. They kept Rex and me safe down at Mahmoudiyah and for today's battle, but now what? I feel around for my mother's bear statue. It's made of marble, so surely it must be pretty much indestructible.

I pull it out and it's intact. I remember my mother's words as she gave it to me, the day I left Richmond to return to Camp Pendleton: The bear is for protection and safety. Keep it by your side. It strikes me as only right that Rex and I still have the bear unharmed to protect us.

I never had been able to deal with a life separated from animals.

Chapter Eleven

IN MY FINAL YEAR AT HIGH SCHOOL I INJURED MY SHOULDER PRETTY badly playing football. I had been hoping to play professionally, but by the time I went to Santa Barbara I wasn't able to make even the college teams. I missed sports, plus I found myself missing all the animals at home, especially my dogs.

I fell into a dark mind-set. I surrounded myself with negative people, and I started to smoke and drink too much. I was at a beautiful college surrounded by these beautiful young people, but I felt the lowest I'd ever been. No matter where I was in the world, inside my head I was not in a good place. I still felt like shit. I was down, and it was hard to get out of the dark place that I'd fallen into.

The one person who remained a steadying influence throughout this period was my father. He made it clear that he wanted me to stick it out at college, but he understood that I wasn't having a good time. He told me that together we would get through this and that whatever I chose to do he and my mom were there for me.

One day I headed home for term break. I took August—

who'd finished his work as a guide dog for the blind and come back to live with our family—for an evening walk on the beautiful beach near our house. It was April and my birthday was approaching; I was just about to turn twenty-one. As I threw a stick for August, I thought to myself: I'm in a gorgeous place; I'm so lucky to live here. So why on earth do I feel so shitty?

August dived into the breakers to fetch the stick, and I gazed across the ocean at the lights of Alcatraz Island, and the Golden Gate and Bay Bridges. I told myself that I was a young, talented guy living in the most beautiful place on earth. I had no reason to feel depressed.

I made a promise to myself there and then: I was going to quit everything that was negative in my life. From that night onward I was going to give up the drinking and the smoking, plus the negative mind-set. But I still didn't have the energy or focus to deal with the academic side of things. I decided to drop out of college so I'd have some time to sort out what I wanted to do with my life.

I moved home and got a job at the Richmond Wholesale Meat Company, a giant freezer-warehouse piled high with wrapped and boxed cuts of beef, pork, and lamb. My job was to take the orders, fetch them from the freezer, and pack them up so they could go out on the trucks. The warehouse was situated in North Richmond, the rougher side of town.

The guys I worked with were mostly ex-felons, and a number came from the Iron Triangle. But for some reason I got on well with those guys, and we had a blast. It was a raw and real experience for me, and perhaps that was what turned my mind again to thinking about joining the Marines.

During my first year at college, my high school buddy Daniel had visited me just about every other weekend. He'd been through Marine Corps boot camp and was now stationed at Camp Pendleton. He'd drive the two hours to Santa Barbara, and he'd bring a bunch of his Marine Corps buddies with him. Together, we'd hit the town. Over beers I'd hear all their stories about life in the Corps. I guess their tales of daredevil adventure seeped into me and had some kind of lasting effect.

One morning I was driving through Richmond to attend a community college. I had started doing some part-time study when not working at the meat factory. An urge took me inland, into the Berkeley hills, and I forgot about college for the day. I made for Grizzly Peak, a place that has a real resonance for me.

Grizzly Peak is a lookout point from which you can see the whole of the California coastline and the ocean rolling out beyond that. Throughout high school it had been a popular place to throw parties or take your dates to. At night the lights of San Francisco reflect across the water, and it is an awesome sight.

The road to Grizzly Peak winds through majestic forested highlands. As I made the drive in my beloved metallic green Ford Mustang, I had the sounds of my favorite band, U2, blaring over the speakers. I was just about to turn twenty-two years old, and I was thinking: I'm getting older, so maybe it's time to make some real, definitive decisions in my life.

As I drove, I couldn't get this thought out of my head: You know what you got to do. It's time to join the Marines. Ever since my stroll on the beach with August I'd kept returning to the same thought: If you can't find the physical challenge you seek at college, go for the toughest challenge of all—the Corps. There was a second thought too: I didn't want to spend the rest of my life asking myself "what if?" I didn't want to spend my life regretting not joining the Corps.

I turned the Mustang west and headed for the Marine Corps recruiting center in Hilltop Mall, in Richmond. It was a weekday, so no one was around. The recruiter sat at his desk looking bored. He saw me hovering in the doorway.

"Can I help you?" he called out.

I stepped inside. "I want to take the next bus to boot camp and join the Marines."

He started laughing. "First off, how do I know you qualify for my Marine Corps?"

I stood there staring at him in surprise. I'd expected him to say, "Well, come on in." Instead he was saying, "Son, you have to work hard to get into my Corps."

"So what does that mean?" I asked him.

"Take a seat and we'll talk about it."

The recruiter explained that all these kids fresh out of high school had just signed up for the Corps. They'd filled their quota for the summer, and the nearest he could get me in was October. If that was all he had, then that was all he had, and I signed the papers. I explained that I'd always wanted to be infantry, but as I was a little older than the average recruit, I figured I should learn a trade.

The recruiter was keen to get me in early, so he suggested I go on standby. Some young kid was bound to drop out at the last moment, so I could take his place. The only drawback with being on standby was that you went into the Corps on an "open contract." And it's the open contract guys who get the worst kind of jobs—always.

I drove home. My father was working in the front yard. He asked me why I wasn't at class.

"I didn't go to class," I told him. "I went to the Marine Corps recruitment office and enlisted."

He gazed at me for a long second before he spoke. "Is that what you want to do?"

I nodded. "Yeah. I've always wanted to be in the Corps."

He smiled. "Good. It's good to see you making a decision in your life."

I didn't care about anyone else's opinion, now that I'd got the blessing of my father. I spoke to my buddy Daniel to get some advice about going into the Corps.

"Whatever you do, do not go in on an open contract," Daniel told me. "Make sure whatever job you select is guaranteed."

I went to see my boss at the meat factory and told him what I was doing. He tried to convince me to stay. He offered me the job of warehouse foreman, which would have meant a huge pay rise, with benefits and the works. Normally, you needed a degree to get that position, but he said I'd proved myself and he'd give it to me anyway.

I thanked him but said this was something I had to do. I told him I was supposed to go to join the Corps in October, but I could be called at any time. My boss said that he'd like me to keep working at the factory until I got the call.

I had further meetings with my Marine Corps recruiter. I told him I wanted infantry experience and to learn a skill. He advised me to go into the communications field. I'd learn infantry skills, I'd learn a trade, and he could personally recommend it, for that was his job. I told him I was good with that, but I wanted it guaranteed.

I got the call in early August. Someone had dropped out, and I could take his place at boot camp. I headed for San Jose, and the Military Entrance Processing Station, the departure point for my journey into the Marine Corps. The marine there asked me to help him process the other recruits.

There were twenty of us, and the processing took longer than expected. Our flight to San Diego and boot camp was scheduled to leave soon.

Finally he came to me. "You're the last one, Dowling, so let's fly through this, as you guys are late for your flight."

We rushed through my form until we reached the point where I had to confirm my chosen job in the Corps. I told him that it was communications.

He paused, then fixed me with this look. "If it's comms, you can't get it."

"What do you mean?"

"Comms is full up. We've filled our quota."

I told him I'd got it guaranteed. He told me I did have it guaranteed, but only for an October entry date. It was August and it was closed out. I was completely blindsided by this. I'd come here burning with excitement, and now I was questioning everything that was happening.

"What exactly are my options right now?" I asked.

I could pick another specialty or walk away until October. The other specialties were closed out too.

"Fuck it, send me infantry," I told him.

"My friend, you are going in at the height of summer, and we've filled all our quotas. Infantry is closed out. We can stand

here all day and run down the list, or you can go on open contract. If you go open contract, trust me, the Corps won't waste
a good recruit on a shitty job."

I kept hearing Daniel's voice in the back of my mind warning
me against an open contract. But I had said my good-byes to
everyone at home, and I couldn't go back.

I shrugged. "Fuck it, send me open contract."

I signed the papers and off I went to boot camp.

As fate would have it, had I not gone in on an open ticket I
never would have gotten to be a military working dog handler,
and I'd never have teamed up with Rex. But as I headed off to
boot camp I had no idea that the Marine Corps uses dogs, or
that I would end up taking the best of them to war.

We're a few days into the Fallujah mission when Rex and I get
orders to mount up a convoy heading back to Camp Fallujah.
Gunney Trotter tells me there's a company from 2/2 getting left
at the Combat Operations Center, to dominate this new chunk
of territory that we've been fighting to gain control over. If they
need Rex and me, they'll send for us.

We get back to Camp Fallujah, and the first thing I do is
take a shower in the cubicle attached to my and Rex's room. It's
sheer luxury. I've been out there for days on that mission and
I've been using nothing but wet wipes to clean myself.

Kartune's preparing to make a resupply run to one of our
sister K9 units. There's a marine base a ways down the road at a
place called Baharia. Kartune figures Rex and I should come, just
so we can see how the other half gets to live. Baharia looks like
some tropical paradise. It even includes a man-made circular lake
of aquamarine water fringed with chaise longues and palm trees.

Baharia was built at the orders of Saddam Hussein to provide a holiday resort for him, his family, and their Ba'ath Party cronies. Originally, Saddam called the place "Dreamland." The Corps renamed it Camp Baharia. I tell the K9 handlers based there that they're living in sheer freakin' luxury. In paradise. They should go try a stint down at Mahmoudiyah.

Most nights a poker game kicks off in our K9 quarters. The night Rex and I return from our Fallujah mission is no exception. There're half a dozen handlers who are regular players. We gather in Kartune's room, because it's the biggest. Kartune's just been promoted to gunnery sergeant, so he's out working a lot of the time. He loves poker and is happy to let us use his billet as our gaming room.

The World Series of Poker tournament has just started being televised across the United States, and it's spawned a huge interest in the game. I've been carried along in the wave. There's a casino in Oceanside, just outside Camp Pendleton, called Oceans Eleven. I've been there a few times to play with Adam and Jason and my other Camp Pendleton buddies. I figure I'm a half-decent poker player by now.

Here at Camp Fallujah we each take a hundred dollars for an evening's poker. The betting's fierce, and mostly I'm up—I'm winning more than I'm losing. We're well into this game when Sergeant Nester Antoine, Kartune's second in command, walks into the room. He sits himself down, waits for a break in the game, then grabs a hand of cards.

"I'm getting bored shitless standing bone gate duty," Sergeant Antoine remarks. "If only we could go outside the wire all the time, like Dowling."

Fellow handler José "Chico" Chavez is playing. Chico's only

recently arrived in Iraq, and he's another of the guys stuck doing gate duty here on the base.

"Man, Dowling, what the hell were you and Rex doing out there in Fallujah?" Chico asks me.

"We got into a firefight, we occupied a compound, they RPG'd us all the time at night, and then we left," I reply in a flat monotone. I'm deliberately downplaying it, like it's a regular thing for Rex and me. "Now deal the cards."

Chico and the rest of the handlers tell me they want to get outside the wire on operations, just like Rex and I are doing. If there's an opportunity for me to take one of the teams with me, they're up for it. I say I'll do my best to get them along.

The following morning I'm woken at five-thirty by a marine from 2/2. He's been sent over to warn Rex and me to ready ourselves for a mission. We're leaving shortly for Zaidon, a shitty little place on the outskirts of Fallujah. The 2/2's Golf Company is already stationed there, and they've been getting smashed big-time by the bad guys. They're based in an old factory, and they've been hit so hard that all their Iraqi interpreters have quit.

They want Rex and me out there to help track down the enemy's arms and explosives. All Rex and I have time for is to eat, pack, and go. There's no time to tell the other handlers what we're doing, or to even think about getting one of them onto this mission. Rex and I join a convoy of Humvees heading out. When we reach our destination, it's like the Mahmoudiyah chicken factory revisited.

There are hundreds of marines crammed into a blasted shell of a warehouse, with a concrete floor and corrugated iron sides. Where enemy mortar rounds and RPGs have torn into the warehouse roof, the marines have made makeshift repairs using camo-netting. It provides zero cover from fire. All it does is cast a little shade, so that those trying to sleep during the day aren't doing so under the burning sun.

Rex and I have no option but to join the marines camped out on the bare concrete. There's nowhere else for us. Rex is in his travel kennel, I've got my sleeping bag beside him, and somehow we're going to have to try to stay sane here, in spite of the horrendous conditions. The Mahmoudiyah bunker strikes me as being close to civilized compared to where we are now.

That first night I bed down on the concrete next to Rex, and we get a taste of things to come. The insurgents have got our number now. They've realized they can't beat us in open warfare. Instead, they launch a fearsome mortar assault. They zero in on the factory, and rounds pulverize the thin metal roof above us, lethal splinters cutting through the air and tearing into the floor.

All I can do is crouch on all fours on the hard concrete, draping my body over Rex's travel kennel, to try to shield him. I've strapped his flak vest onto him, but I'm not kidding myself that it'll stop a mortar. In truth, I'm pretty much helpless to protect either myself or my dog. I try to keep him calm as death rains down all around us, but I feel horribly useless and exposed.

There's nothing worse than being under a mortar attack and feeling this vulnerable. It's like a lottery with death. A marine jumps into the turret of a Humvee to take cover, but the vehicle takes a direct hit and he's blown out of the turret and killed. It's the closest that Rex and I have come to having death unfold before us, and as the night bombardment grinds on we take scores more casualties.

By morning I can see how totally blasted apart the factory is. How Rex and I have survived is beyond me. I'd rather be in a full-on firefight than under a mortar assault like that. It's evil. We're losing guys and our morale's taking a hammering. We're desperate to go on the offensive and regain the initiative.

A patrol had gone out at night to search for the mortar team. Miraculously, they captured one of them alive. They managed to extract information pointing to where the insurgents are based and the location of their caches of weapons and explosives. Golf Company is going out to hunt them down, and Rex and I are going with them.

The marines know by now pretty much how Rex and I work, but this is a different kind of tasking. We're heading into an isolated, rural area, and we'll be searching farmland interspersed with the odd household. Golf Company's CO, Captain Conway, asks me how we're going to approach the mission.

"How d'you want to use Rex as we search? We'll be going house to house."

"Sir, secure each house and remove all the males," I tell him. "Keep all the woman and children in one room, or remove them completely. Get the guys out, but don't tear the place apart. Let Rex and me search first, so you tear it apart only if we find something."

The captain is good with that.

Captain Conway is a hugely respected commander, and he's loved by his men. He's the son of Lieutenant General James Conway, the commander who confronted me in my underwear when sleeping with Rex back in the Fallujah schoolhouse. I figure a strong Marine Corps pedigree runs through the Conway family.

We mount up the Humvees and head out into a patch of remote farmland. We form up on foot. I show Rex the Kong and give him the Seek command. Rex seems overjoyed to be out leading the marines again on a real search. There's a spring in his step and his tail's twitching from side to side as he lowers his head and starts to breathe in the scents all around us.

We start the walk, searching for weaponry and the raw materials for constructing bombs. It's early still, and the May heat has yet to start baking the flat, featureless landscape all around us. The morning cool lingers in the fields and the irrigation ditches, and along the dirt tracks where we're searching.

Captain Conway has asked for air cover as we do the search. I presume it's because we're entering a hard-core area, and the air cover is meant to intimidate the enemy. No sooner are Rex and I under way than a group of F-15s appears on the horizon. The pilots offer to fly low-level "shows of force," to deter any local bad guys planning to hit us. I've never experienced one before and neither has Rex. We've got no idea what's coming.

The lead F-15 arrows out of the sun like a burning spear, and it's streaking along at what looks like treetop level. It tears past overhead, and as it does so it pulls into a screaming climb, its afterburners kicking in red and fiery as they boost the F-15's thrust. The noise is like a jumbo jet landing right on top of us, and for a moment Rex and I are going for the cover of the nearest ditch.

I've been warned that the jets are coming in. But you can know the aircraft isn't going to hit you, yet it still doesn't sound like that when it's screaming right over your head. The marines of the 2/2 are crouched on their haunches, their hands over their ears. God only knows what the locals must think of all this thundering, deafening mayhem, plus the rumbling vibrations that seem to shake the earth at our feet.

I brush myself off and glance at Rex. He's looking at me as if to say: *Whatever the hell that was, partner, if they do it again I am not playing ball.* I give him a good stroke and I pet him. I explain that it's just some friendly pilots giving us top cover, and that they're there to keep the bad guys off our backs. Rex doesn't look too convinced.

The second time the F-15s come in, he gives a jolt and a jump, like he was half caught off guard, but then he looks to me to guide him. I crouch down and put my arm around his neck, pointing out the jets as they thunder toward us. I'm telling him, "Easy boy, easy boy," as they flash past overhead. He knows I'm trying to show him that they're friendly, but I figure to Rex they must look and sound like a flight of avenging dragons.

Once the F-15s are gone, I move around to face him. I crouch down and look him directly in the eyes, my face up close to his, my hands behind his ears. "There's nothing to worry about, buddy. It's just some friendly U.S. Air Force jets. We're okay."

The F-15s aren't the only distractions that Rex is facing. This being a farming area, there are goats, cows, rabbits, turkeys, and chickens around every corner. And with each comes a corresponding pile of poo. Rex is a very curious dog, and it's that curiosity that I harness in getting him to do the search. But he's a dog first and foremost, and he's intrigued by all these new smells.

We're walking along a track past a mud wall. Rex slows, then stops. I'm wondering if he's onto something when he leaps up and gets his front paws onto the wall. He peers over, and I join him. For Rex this is what it must be like being at the zoo.

There's an Iraqi woman sitting on a stool milking a cow, and she's surrounded by just about every farm animal you could imagine.

Rex's head is moving this way and that as he eyes the chickens. I know exactly what he's thinking. He's fighting against his instinct to go chase the lot of them. He'd like nothing more than to leap over the wall and be in among them, chicken feathers flying in all directions. His tail is wagging back and forth with furious excitement. He looks at me with a pleading expression on his features: *Please, can I, can I? Please?*

I tell him no, and we move on. Rex is cool with it. He doesn't go into a sulk or anything, or lessen his enthusiasm for the search. He loves the work we're doing here, it's just that the odd chicken chase thrown in wouldn't go amiss.

The security marines to either side of us have their hands full. As well as keeping their eyes peeled for the bad guys, they keep having to chase off stray dogs. They can smell Rex, and they keep fronting up to us as if they're going to fight him. With all the distractions it's a miracle that Rex finds anything.

But when he does, it's a bonanza of bomb-making materials. We're about to hit the jackpot big-time.

Chapter Twelve

OUR FIRST FIND IS A CACHE OF AK-47S AND RPK MACHINE GUNS HID-
den in a building. It's nice to find, but not unusual. Next, we're
walking along this raised bank that runs across an irrigated
field, and Rex shows a big change of behavior. We dig beneath
where he's sat his butt on the earth, and presto, the marines pull
out a sack stuffed full of RPG warheads.

Nice one, Rex. It's a real haul. Each warhead is a good four
feet long, and these are brand spanking new. I hold one up and
pose for a photo, Rex sitting at my feet on my left side. His
eyes are glued to the warhead, with a shining light blazing out
of them: *See, I got it! I got it!* He can't keep his gaze off those
warheads. It's like he owns them. They're his prize.

The RPGs were buried so deep that Rex couldn't have smelled
the warheads themselves. He must have picked up on traces of
explosives or related materials left on the surface by whoever
dug the hole. That's how sensitive his nose is. In the same field
he unearths old mortar rounds, detcord, and more RPGs. I'm
starting to get the impression that if I took a shovel and dug just
about anywhere in this area, we'd find something.

By midday we've discovered a ton or more of IED-making materials. There are several burlap sacks stuffed full of silvery-gray mortar percussion caps, plus khaki fins. They're from some seriously big mortars, and there are hundreds of them. The insurgents have buried this stuff with only one purpose in mind: unearthing it when they need it to build detonators and to make shrapnel for their IEDs.

By now it's boiling hot and there's not a scrap of shade anywhere in the surrounding terrain. Rex is still searching well, but I've learned how quickly the heat can sap him. There's a house on the far side of the field and we've got to get it cleared. Once that's done, I promise Rex he can have a good rest in one of the Humvees, with the aircon turned up full blast.

We head for the building, and the marines go in and clear it of any occupants. I sling my M16 onto my back; there won't be room inside the building for me to use it. I'll rely on my pistol in case we hit trouble. The woman of the house sees me and Rex heading inside, and she starts shrieking and wailing uncontrollably. I figure she's not exactly taken with my dog.

We've hit the jackpot in this area already: It's an IED maker's treasure trove. I figure we've had bad guys watching us as we unearthed all their bomb-making materials, and I'm hyperalert and threat-conscious as Rex and I move from the blinding white sunlight into the dark shadow of the building's interior.

Rex and I move through the kitchen area with two security marines a few paces behind us. I've got my dog going up and over the sink, the stove, and the obligatory broken, smelly fridge.

All of a sudden I feel a violent tug on the leash, and Rex has practically torn my arm out of its socket. He's lunged to attack something or someone just behind me. I figure the marines have failed to clear the house properly, and one of the bad guys has come out of hiding to attack us.

My hand goes to my thigh, I grab my pistol, flick on the flashlight that's attached to it, and spin around. I've got my weapon leveled at the shadows where Rex is straining to get his teeth into someone, my finger white on the trigger.

Then I see a furry brown blob caught in the beam of my flashlight. It scurries across the floor, and the marine to my right cracks up. He slumps against the flimsy kitchen table, holding on to it with both hands to stop himself collapsing with laughter.

"What you gonna fucking do, Dowling?" he gasps. "Shoot the goddamn rabbit?"

Rex is tearing this way and that, furiously pulling at the leash as he tries to catch a rabbit that's rushing around the kitchen. For some reason the lady of this household seems to keep a rabbit in the kitchen, and somehow it's got out of its cage. It's trying desperately to escape, and Rex is going crazy trying to catch it and bite it, and I can't say that I blame him.

I don't blame the marine for laughing at me, either. It is absolutely hilarious. Once we've recovered, we clear the rest of the house. That done, I throw Rex into one of the Humvees. The aircon's up high and it's like an icebox in there. Rex is used to the Iraqi heat, but not this degree of hot. It must be pushing 140 degrees out there.

I crouch in the shade by the rear of the vehicle and break out some water and an MRE. The Golf Company gunnery sergeant comes over to join me. He's Captain Conway's second in command and he's a great guy. He adores Rex.

"Rex, the superstar!" he announces. "How's Rexy doing?"

For a while we talk about all the material Rex found this morning. We've unearthed bomb-making kits buried in the fields and small arms in the houses. The marines have taken eleven guys prisoner so they can be properly questioned. It feels great to be part of a successful operation.

Captain Conway comes over to join us. He asks me how we train the dogs so they are able to do what Rex can do, and I talk them through some of the detection training levels.

"So how did you get into being a K9?" Captain Conway asks me.

"Sir, you're not gonna believe this: I went into the Corps on an open contract."

"*Open contract?* You're joking."

"No, no, sir, I'm serious. Open contract."

"Well, how the hell d'you get from there to K9?"

I tell them the story. At the end of boot camp and marine combat training, I got allocated my specialty. Every specialty has a code number, and I was given 58-11, which I knew meant the security field—military police. I was relieved—it could have been a whole lot worse. I'd never even thought of being an MP, but it was way better than being a cook or a sanitation engineer or a fridge mechanic, which were the kind of jobs I'd been expecting.

I moved on to MP School, at Fort Leonard Wood, Missouri, in the depths of a freezing, snowbound winter. On day one our instructor—a steel-hard Marine staff sergeant—gave us a pep talk. He spoke about why being an MP was a great job. You got to play so many varied roles: securing bases, checking vehicles, collecting prisoners of war.

You could even try for a specialized outfit, like the SWAT

or the SRT teams, or the HMX, the unit that secures the presidential helicopter. He rounded off his speech with these words: "You can even get to be a K9 handler, working with a military working dog."

I was mesmerized. I hadn't the slightest idea that the U.S. military used dogs. Our instructor asked if there were any questions.

I was the first: "How d'you get to be one of those K9 handlers?"

In response, he asked for all those who wanted K9 to raise their hands. More than half the class did.

The instructor laughed. "Here we go. We get this every time. Everyone wants to handle dogs because everyone loves dogs. That's great. But the problem is that in each class we only have two or three places. And there's such competition that you've got to come top of the class."

I was going to work my ass off. From that day onward, I wanted nothing else. It was K9 or bust. It was by total accident that I'd ended up here, but somehow I felt as if it was divine providence. Two weeks into MP School, the instructor took the names of all those who wanted K9. Again, half the class went for it.

He told us we were too many and he had to cut the fat out. He told those without a first-class Physical Fitness Test to lower their hands. He still needed more hands to go down. Those at less than an expert rifleman level, lower your hands. Those who'd scored less than 80 percent in their prelim MP exams, bug out. Twelve hands remained raised, mine included.

"Okay, it's between you guys. You guys have the dogfight."

I was three years older than most of the other MP recruits.

The majority were fresh out of high school. When they went drinking and partying, I was in the library or the gym. I was going to get K9 if it killed me. I scored 100 percent on all my written MP exams. But I knew that you could be the best on paper, yet if you didn't have the human-to-dog skills they'd never choose you for K9.

The final hurdle was going before the board. I faced my instructors, plus the Fort Leonard Wood commanders, and they asked me to justify why I should get K9. I had written a two-page essay on why I'd make a good handler. I'd written about growing up with a farm in our family's backyard. I'd written about how dogs had always been a part of my life, and about my work with August.

I ended the essay describing how August had come back to our family after he'd finished his stint as a guide dog. We still had him and loved him, old and slow though he now was. I stood before the board with a crisp and alert military bearing, and they questioned me on what I'd written. I told them that I felt getting K9 was my destiny, and that I was older and more mature than most of the other recruits, so better suited to the responsibility.

I walked away feeling like I'd done well. A week later I graduated from MP School the distinguished honor graduate. I'd been meritoriously promoted from private first class to lance corporal. The entire class stood in formation as each recruit was told where he was being stationed and what specialist role he was getting. I was assigned to the First Marine Division, based at Camp Pendleton.

Then our instructor got to it: He announced who had gotten K9. When I heard my name, I was over the moon. I'd gone from open contract to MP to K9. That was some evolution. And it was a journey that would end up with my getting allocated one of the best dogs there ever was, Rex.

I finish telling Gunney Massey and Captain Conway how I got K9 and they in turn tell me all about their dogs back home. So many marines reminisce with me about their dogs, it's starting to feel like some kind of field therapy. Some guys have German shepherds, others have hunting dogs that they stalk deer with in the woods, and others have dogs with whom they just love playing fetch-the-stick.

From the lowest to the highest ranks, I just let the guys talk about their dogs. At times like these Rex becomes a therapy and a morale dog. Seeing Rex and talking about their dogs remind the guys of life back home. It reminds them that there is a world outside the madness of Fallujah and Mahmoudiyah, and in part we're all here fighting for the right to survive this hell and get back to the world that we know so well and love.

Captain Conway has just finished telling me about his dogs when all hell breaks loose. I hear a massive *"AROOOF! ROOOF! ROOOF!"* from inside the Humvee. An instant later, Rex flies out the half-opened back of the truck. I feel like he's dislocated my shoulder, he's pulled so violently on the lead.

We've got the Humvees parked around the corner from a T-junction, and I've got my back to the intersection. An Iraqi kid of around ten years old has been leading a heard of sheep up to the T-junction, and he's just gone to turn the corner and pass us. Neither the sheep nor the boy has seen Rex, but he's seen them. He shot out of the Hummer and landed ten feet in front of them, barking his head off.

I've seen sheep like this before in Iraq. Normally, they have a slow, rolling gait. But right now, as Rex gets in their face, they turn into a flock of sheep attempting the world land speed record. They're off like a flash of brown furry lightning, and Rex is practically dragging me down the dirt track after them. The Iraqi shepherd boy takes one look at Rex, and he's off as fast as his legs will carry him.

I keep yelling, "No, Rex! Out! Out! Out!" but he's got sheep-chasing lust in his head.

Captain Conway and the gunney get a real kick out of Rex trying to chase that herd of sheep and dragging me along in his wake. As the animals disappear in a cloud of dust in the far distance, Rex is still barking fit to burst, and the marines all around me are laughing fit to burst too. It hasn't been too good for the poor Iraqi shepherd boy, but it's great for raising the spirits of the marines.

We search some more farmland and we're pretty much done. There's so much arms and explosives that we're overloaded with the stuff. The marine combat engineers gather it all together and pile it into a huge heap on an empty piece of scrubland. They prime the heap with some C4 plus detonators. There are cries of "Fire in the hole!" Then a massive explosion as they blow the lot sky-high.

It's like a mini–atom bomb going off, and it's great to see. That's a ton or more of deadly IED-making materials that the bad guys won't be using to build their killer devices. And that means a good number of American and Allied soldiers, plus Iraqi civilians, won't be getting their arms or legs blown off just because they stepped in the wrong place at the wrong time.

Rex and I are bang out of water by now. He is seriously hot and bothered. I pick him up and dunk him in one of the irrigation ditches. He comes out coat dripping wet and does one of his shakes—starting with his head and rippling down his body, and ending with his thick tail. He's showering water everywhere and half of it's going over me. It's kind of a Rex shower.

We return to our Zaidon base, and that night it's pretty much quiet. No one hits the chicken factory, and I hope the enemy's lack of appetite to hit us is linked somehow to the weapons and explosives that we found and destroyed today. The following morning, Rex and I head back to Camp Fallujah.

There's a military veterinarian visiting the camp, and he does the rounds of the dogs. It isn't until he gets to Rex that I realize just how stressed out my dog has become. With every dog before Rex there's no problem, including Rex's would-be girlfriend, Boda. But Rex hates veterinarians. Rex sees them as his evil archenemy, and he will fight them to the end.

I put Rex's mesh muzzle on him to stop him biting anyone, but still we have to sedate him before the vet can even touch him. Once Rex is out cold from the injection, the vet inspects him. His ears are full of dirt and crap, which the vet manages to expunge. But it's his anal glands that are the real worry. When a dog gets unduly stressed, those glands start to swell. Rex's are building up to be like a couple of hard-boiled eggs.

The anal glands are also called scent glands. Most carnivores have them, and they secrete small amounts of fluid. It's via that fluid's unique smell that one dog can recognize another, and they use it as a way to mark their territory. But the fluid smells unbelievably foul to us—like a lump of rotten fish left out in the Iraqi sun for a week.

The vet has a female assistant, and the three of us are debating who should pop Rex's glands. We know the stench is going to be horrendous. Dan Wheeler, a fellow dog handler, wanders over to watch the show. He volunteers to pop Rex's glands.

"Sure, feel free, go pop 'em," I tell Dan.

Dan knows exactly what he's let himself in for here. He's likely seen it before but never got to try it for himself. Dan and the vet gather at Rex's rear end while the assistant and I hold Rex's head and stroke him. They pull on some surgical gloves, and Dan takes the peanut-size gland between thumb and forefinger. The vet explains that the secret to popping the glands is to gently milk the fluid out, drop by drop, and not to force it.

Dan does the first gland, and his face turns a sickly shade of green. Before Dan collapses, the vet takes over and milks the other. Even from our end, the head end of Rex, the stench is unbearable, but the relief for Rex must be incredible. Having his glands done will help him face the stresses and strains of whatever the next few weeks and months will throw at us.

Kartune leaves Fallujah to head up to Al Asad, the air base we originally flew into. There's a new contingent of dog handlers being flown into Iraq, and he's gone there to receive them. It was obvious from our first week on operations that we need more K9 teams out here.

We've got U.S. Air Force K9 teams deploying alongside Marine Corps guys, and all told there are some twenty new K9 teams arriving in Iraq. The Air Force has far more handlers than the Marine Corps. These handlers are coming in to share the load so the Marine Corps doesn't get too thinly stretched in terms of its K9 teams.

The new contingent includes Adam and Jason, my buddies from Camp Pendleton. Kartune's promised that a fellow K9 team will be allocated to the 2/2, for when we return to

Mahmoudiyah. It looks likely that we'll be heading back there sometime soon now. The Second Battle of Fallujah hasn't really come to pass, and the word is that President Bush thinks the American public won't stomach a whole new load of casualties.

I was hoping to get either Jason or Adam to accompany me to Mahmoudiyah. Instead, they've been allocated duties around Al Asad. It looks likely that I'll get Chico Chavez coming south with me to the Triangle of Death. I met Chico at Camp Pendleton, although he's stationed out of Camp Lejeune. He's a good handler with a great dog, a Belgian Malinoise named Luki. It's going to be great having him with me down at Mahmoudiyah.

There are now seven K9 teams based at Camp Fallujah. Some of the newly arrived guys have been sent over to Camp Baharia and a couple of other bases. Kartune's plan is for the air force teams to stand gate duty, which will free up the marine teams to get out on the kind of ops that Rex and I have been doing.

The concern with the air force handlers is that they've had no combat training. Every marine is put through a monthlong training course, right after boot camp, which provides a basic grounding in combat skills. Plus there's a saying in the Marine Corps: "Every marine a rifleman first." It means no matter what job you're given in the Corps, you know how to pick up a rifle and fight.

Still, it's great having the air force guys with us. They take on a lot of the workload on the gates, which should free up the marine teams to work with the infantry and get outside the wire. Those air force handlers really know how to live. They bring DVD players and video games with them, plus all the newest film and gaming releases. They've also got choice military gear—including M4 carbines. The M4 is short, compact, and lightweight, and it's the rifle all us handlers really need out here on operations.

The air force teams are gung ho. They act as if they're just itching to get outside the wire. They keep asking the other handlers what it's like to be out on combat operations in and around Fallujah. By now Rex and I have been blown up, mortared, sniped at, and survived the fire of combat, and our reputation precedes us.

"Shit, go talk to Dowling," Sergeant Antoine tells the air force guys. "That motherfucker goes outside the wire all the time."

That night we're playing poker and the air force guys get dealt in. We joke around and have a blast, and it's great for team-building. Camp Fallujah gets mortared all the time, but by now it's become like background noise to us. Halfway through the game the base starts getting hit. The marines among us don't even respond. There isn't a break in the conversation, and no one so much as pauses or puts down his hand. But the air force guys are on their feet and peering out the windows, wondering what the hell's happening.

Boom goes a mortar. "Did you hear that? What the fuck was that?"

Boom goes another mortar. "Who's doing that shooting? Is that our artillery?"

"No, that's just like incoming," remarks Sergeant Antoine.

"Incoming? As in they're attacking the base?"

"Yeah. Incoming."

Sergeant Antoine and the rest of us keep playing the cards.

"Well, like, shall we suit up?" the air force guys ask. "Like, shall we put our gear on?"

We stop playing. "Yeah, like suit up and fucking grab your guns. We're being attacked here," Antoine remarks in his mock gung ho voice.

We're all laughing. Our quarters are situated bang in the midst of a huge base, with a ring of steel thrown around it. Our building is sandbagged and safe, and over time we figure the air force guys will realize this and get used to it.

Antoine says, "Look, it's no big deal. This happens every night."

"Shit, I don't care," says one of them. "I'm suiting up anyway."

They leave and go get their flak and Kevlar on. When they're back with us, they keep asking me about what it's like outside the wire. They keep talking about how much they want to get out there and get into action.

"Man, I so wanna go outside the wire," one of the handlers remarks.

It seems this is the sentiment of all the air force K9 guys. They figure they'll be bored out of their mind standing gate duty.

"Next time, I'll try and get you guys out with me," I tell them. "You guys sure you want to go?"

There's a chorus of replies. "Man, of course we'll go!"

"Shit yeah, we'll go."

"That's what we're saying, we gotta get outside the wire."

"Okay," I tell them. "I'll see what I can do."

A few days after our Zaidon mission, I get warned of another tasking with 2/2. I check in with them one afternoon, and Gunney Trotter tells me to ready Rex and myself for a mission to secure a route into Fallujah city itself. General James "Chaos"

Mattis—the same general Rex almost bit on our first day in Mahmoudiyah—is planning to have a one-on-one with Fallujah's tribal sheikhs.

He's going to warn them that the Marine Corps is going to take down the city unless they hand over the bad guys. Al-Zarqawi, the leader of Al Qaeda in Iraq, is in there somewhere, as are a whole card deck of Iraq's most wanted. The trouble is there's no safe route into Fallujah, so the Warlords' job is to clear a route into the heart of the city.

After the Blackwater deaths, and the First Battle of Fallujah, we know how dangerous it is in there. So far all the 2/2 missions we've been on have been around the outskirts of the city, and even then we've been met with a wall of fire. After the heavy and intense fighting of the First Battle of Fallujah, the city's pretty much off-limits to American troops. Now all of a sudden we're being sent in, and we know they'll have had plenty of time to ready themselves for us.

Rex and I are tasked to go in with Weapons Company. Weapons Company carries the heaviest firepower that 2/2 possesses: Their Humvees are mounted with .50-cal heavy machine guns, Mark 19 grenade launchers, plus TOW missiles. They drive everywhere, and they often carry mortar and sniper teams with them, to help provide security and firepower when needed.

We're to drop off sniper and mortar teams at the same compound where Rex and I experienced our first firefight. They'll cover us as we push ahead to the main bridge that spans the Euphrates, pretty much in the heart of the city. We're to secure the route in and the bridge itself, and only once the whole route is clear will the general head in to parley with the sheikhs.

I'm told to get Rex ready for a two-day mission. No one

doubts for one moment that this is the heaviest tasking that 2/2 has ever been given. I'm briefed on the mission on May 28. We're scheduled to go in two days later. When I listened to the mission brief, I thought, This mission is crazy. Everyone feels the same.

It's not a question of if we're gonna get hit, it's just where and when.

Chapter Thirteen

I FIGURE THIS IS THE IDEAL OPPORTUNITY TO GET ANOTHER DOG TEAM out on a combat mission. Rex and I could sure use the company on this one. I ask the Weapons Company commander if they could use another dog team.

"Absolutely."

I'm back in the billet that evening playing poker. There's myself, Sergeant Antoine, the air force handlers, and Chico. The air force guys ask me if there's much going on with the 2/2.

"Yeah, actually, I got this mission any day now to go into central Fallujah," I tell them. "All the marines think it's kind of bullshit, but we're doing it anyway, and there's a great chance that we'll get into some shit. But you wanna hear the good news?" I can't help laughing. "They say I can bring another dog team. Just what you guys wanted, right? So who wants to come?"

No one says a word. They're all glancing at each other, like who's going to volunteer, who's gonna break the silence.

I fix the air force guys with this look. "Hey, this is exactly what you guys were talking about over the last couple of days, right? Getting outside the wire."

"I want to go," one of them says, "but my dog's got to get acclimated to the heat out here first."

Another: "Well, me too, I'd go if the dog was acclimatized."

"And I'm scheduled to stand gate duty," the third guys says.

Chico has been watching the whole charade. He steps forward. "Fuck it, Dowling, I'll go with you."

I smile. "Chico! Great. Perfect." I glance at the air force guys. "You guys sure? This is your last chance."

They shrug and mutter their excuses, and that's that.

On one level I understand their reservations. They're fresh into theater and they don't have the infantry combat training or experience that we have. I guess it's a case of beware of what you wish for. In time I'm sure they'll find their feet and the courage to venture outside the wire.

Truth be told, out of all the guys at the Fallujah Hilton, I'm glad I've got Chico for this mission. He's a soft-spoken Hispanic marine, but he's hard as nails. I've seen him and Luki in training and they make a great team. Luki is a small Mal, the size of a pit bull, and he's strong and punchy, too. Chavez is short and stocky, and handler and dog kind of resemble each other. So it's Chico and Luki, plus me and Rex: That's the Fallujah mission team.

The Fallujah mission gets delayed for a couple of days. Chico and Luki plus Rex and I kill the time in training. I'm doing a center line drill with Rex. We're in a flat, open area of the base, and I've got two balls with me. I throw one ball in one direction, and as Rex comes running back with it gripped in his mouth I tell him, "Rex, out!" He spits out the ball and keeps running toward me, and I throw the other ball in the opposite direction.

We keep doing it back and forth, back and forth, and it's

great exercise for my dog. There's only sand and sunburned grass on the ground, so there's nothing to get in the way. Rex is turning faster and faster and his legs are a flashing blur as he sprints after one ball and then the other. I haven't the slightest idea that he's injured himself until we've finished the game. We're making our way back to our quarters, and I notice that he's limping.

I bend to check his left front paw, and he's torn one of his pads badly. It's half hanging off and bleeding heavily. It's not the first time that Rex has hurt himself in this way. A torn pad is a common injury for working dogs. Normally, if I keep him off it, it'll heal within a week. But right now we're unlikely to have a week, because we're on standby for the Fallujah mission. I'm worried that it won't heal in time, and we'll have to sign ourselves off the mission.

Before deploying to Iraq we were given a medical briefing by the Camp Pendleton veterinarian. She put together a medical kit for each handler so we can do some front-line medication of our dogs. She taught us how to insert an IV drip, to rehydrate the dogs. That's proved crucial out here in Iraq. Several times Rex has come in off operations so dehydrated that I've hooked him up to an IV.

She showed us how to check the dogs' gums: If they're whitish and lacking in color, it's a sure sign the dog's badly dehydrated. She taught us how to maintain the dogs' health, checking their ears and cleaning out any accumulated gunk. If you don't keep them clean, the dog can get bad ear infections, and it smells horrific. She taught us how to keep their nails clipped short.

She taught us how to check for signs of bloating, which can cause the dog's stomach to twist. A dog with bloating will have abnormal, heavy panting even at rest. Bloating and a twisted stomach is normally caused by a dog having eaten or drunk too much, and doing too much exercise on a full stomach. She taught us how to keep the dogs cool by using ice or water to douse them under the armpits and around the stomach area, the kind of thing that I've been doing with Rex when we're out doing a search.

She gave us doggy splints as part of the medical kit and taught us how to splint and bandage a break. You basically put one splint to either side of the wound and bandage it real tight. The medical kit is one of the pieces of equipment that I carry with me everywhere we go.

Rex had torn a pad once during training at Camp Pendleton. I'd watched the vet bandage it, and I decide to do exactly the same as she did now. We get to our quarters, and Rex is tired and lacking in energy to resist very much. I get water and disinfectant, and I sponge out all the dirt from the wound. I can tell how much it's hurting him. He keeps tugging his leg away, and I have to pull it back toward me so I can wash and clean it.

Rex knows that I'm trying to help him, but he keeps glancing at me from under his eyebrows with a pained expression: *I know what you're doing there, but hey, man, go gentle, it hurts.* Once it's clean, I put on some antiseptic cream, then some gauze, and wrap it tight with a bandage, starting with his foot and going partway up his leg.

I am the only person Rex would let do this kind of thing to him. If it was anyone else—the veterinarian included—Rex would need to be sedated first. But we've been together for so long now and grown so close that he knows I would never do anything to deliberately hurt him.

I'll clean and dress the wound daily, and I'll keep him in my room to make him rest and to let it heal. That way we may be fit for the coming mission. The Fallujah Hilton is so luxurious we've got proper beds with mattresses in each of the rooms. Whenever I'm out, Rex will be up there chilling on the bed. I let him lie there with his bandaged foot 24/7.

The toilet in our room has stopped working, so I head out one morning to use the outhouse. I'm wandering back when all of a sudden an Iraqi guy comes tearing out of our accommodation block and goes sprinting off into the distance. I know the guy, he's one of the Hajis working on upgrading our quarters. A Haji denotes someone who's been on the Haj—the Muslim pilgrimage to Mecca, their holiest of shrines. "Haji" is Marine Corps speak for local guys who are friendly.

There're a bunch of Hajis hanging new doors in our quarters, painting walls, and generally sprucing the place up. The Haji who's done the runner is a fairly decent guy. He even tried on Rex's bite sleeve for a laugh, and he seemed to find it funny when I threatened to make him do some decoying for me and my dog. But by the expression on his face he must have been caught trying to steal Sergeant Antoine's pants or something. He looked that terrified.

From our block up ahead I can hear commotion. Someone's shouting at my dog. I get into the hallway to see Sergeant Antoine yelling at Rex to get back into our room. Rex, of course, is refusing to do so. *That's my boy.* He takes orders only from me. Sergeant Antoine sees me and starts yelling at me instead.

"Dowling, get your fucking dog back into your room!"

I grab Rex, talk him down, and reverse him into my room. I shut the door and turn to speak to Sergeant Antoine. As handlers, we all know better than to walk into another guy's room, and we always knock.

"How the fuck did he get out?" I ask. "He didn't just open the door."

"The Haji came to work on your room, and he just barged right in," Sergeant Antoine explains. "So Rex tried to attack him."

"Well, that's good. I don't want any Hajis just wandering into my room when I'm not there. Is that the Haji I saw running off?"

"Probably."

"Well, the only reason Rex didn't get him is his bandaged paw."

All the handlers are out of their rooms, and by now we're all laughing. Sergeant Antoine and I go to look for the Haji who's done the runner. We find him hiding a few blocks away. We tell him that Rex is in his kennel now, so it's safe to return. But the guy refuses to go into my room if Rex is in there, even if he is locked in his kennel.

I take Rex with me to check in with 2/2 and get a heads-up on the Fallujah mission. We get introduced to the commander of CAAT (Combined Anti-Armor Team) White. Weapons Company consists of CAAT White, Red, and Blue. It's CAAT White that we'll be going in with to clear the bridge over the Euphrates. The commander tells me to keep checking in with him, because we're on standby and could be going out at any time.

I'm pleased the mission hasn't got the green light yet. The longer the delay, the better; Rex needs time to heal. I don't want the marines of Weapons Company to think I'm using a "sick dog" excuse to get out of going on this one. Last thing I want next time there's a dangerous mission scheduled is for someone to say, "Dowling, you wanna go? Or is your dog sick again?"

Rex and I return to the Fallujah Hilton. There's a brand-new lock and a door fitted to our room, and it's painted and good to go. The Haji's done it all in record time so he can keep his distance from my dog.

I'm rooming with one of the air force guys now. The increase in handlers means we have to double up, two guys and two dogs to a room. Still, he's got a portable DVD player, and he's brought the movie *Heat* with him, which is one of my all-time favorites. The guys in *Heat* are a small team working together as a band of brothers, just like we are in the K9 field. Plus Al Pacino and Robert De Niro are my two favorite actors.

The theme of an unbreakable brotherhood coupled with honor among thieves—the one last job—runs through the movie. They pull off the heist, only to get their vehicles ambushed by law enforcement guys as they try to make their getaway. Bursts of automatic fire cut lines of bullet holes through windshields, fountains of glass glinting through the air. Fire punches through the bodywork, chunks of metal spinning off in all directions. As I watch the movie's climax, I can't help thinking they're the kind of scenes I can imagine us driving into on the coming mission.

There's one other advantage to rooming with the air force guy. He's got an M4 carbine, and I'm determined to get my hands on it for the Fallujah job.

"Hey, you know I'm going into Fallujah, and we're gonna get into a fight," I tell him. "I don't want to be carrying my big-ass M16, so let me take your M4."

The guy gives this good-natured shrug. "Man, no worries. I'm only standing the fucking gate anyways."

I check in with CAAT White the following day. "We're heading out tomorrow morning," they tell me. "Mission kicks off at oh-six-thirty."

I've never mentioned that Rex has been injured, because I didn't want to risk being told to sit this one out. His torn pad is healing well, and I figure he's 100 percent fit for the mission.

At the crack of dawn the following morning we get driven over to the 2/2 by Lance Corporal Harrell, another marine handler, who's recently arrived in Fallujah.

Harrell, Chico, and I mill around the muster area, together with our dogs. There's a massive vehicle convoy formed up, and all we're waiting for is the CAAT White guys to show. The first to arrive is a marine called Showalter. He's munching on Lucky Charms cereal like they're potato chips. I ask him what's with the Lucky Charms. He tells me we're going to need all the luck we can get on a mission like this one.

There's the smell of hot metal, diesel fumes, and fear in the air. I've got a little Sony Cybershot camera tucked in my flak, and I pull it out and switch it to video mode. I film the Abrams tanks lined up next to us in a massive rank of armor. These are the tanks that are *not* coming with us today. Then I turn the camera on the column of Humvees, the very light cavalry that we're taking into the heart of the cauldron that is Fallujah.

I say to Chavez, "Chico, so I'm videotaping. We're going into Fallujah, how d'you feel?"

"Eerrr . . ." Chico shrugs. He's pretty much at a loss for words. He looks and sounds nervous as hell, which is fair enough, really.

I turn the camera on Harrell and ask him the same question,

but I turn away before he can answer: "Hey, it doesn't matter, you're not even goin'!"

I turn it on Showalter. "Showalter, you *are* going into Fallujah today. What you gotta say?"

He shrugs. "We're all gonna die."

I start laughing. "Oh, man, that's being optimistic."

He smiles. "You're definitely gonna die."

"So how d'you think Rex is gonna do?" I ask him.

He laughs maniacally. "He's gonna die. . . . Everyone's gonna die, and we're never going home."

"Oh, well, I guess we're all fucked, then. . . . All right, see you all later."

I stop filming. That interaction sums up what a great deal of the tour's been like so far. It's been disjointed, it's made little sense, and at every turn it's been pretty much bordering on the insane. But this is where Rex and I have found ourselves, and I wouldn't want to have missed it for the world.

Rex and I get introduced to Sergeant Brian Stokes, one of the two NCOs on CAAT White. He's not quite as tall as I am, but he's almost twice as wide. He looks like a charging rhino wouldn't stop him, and I can tell that he has ultimate respect from the marines on his team. Sergeant Stokes immediately falls in love with Rex.

"All right! We've got a dog! This is badass. We've got the dogs of war with us today!"

Sergeant Stokes rides in the lead vehicle in CAAT White's six-Humvee force. Rex and I ride with Lance Corporal Bob Tincher, the vehicle commander, in a Humvee more to the rear. Chico and Luki get allocated to a Humvee to the rear of us. We're both in open-backed—as opposed to up-armored—vehicles, and that's just the way it is.

At nine o'clock we set off. Rex does what he always does when he's in an open-backed Humvee full of marines: He barges his way through the crush until his nose is stuck out the side in the vehicle's slipstream. He's got his eyes everywhere and he's keen to check out what's going on.

Up front in the cab I notice there's a girlie picture tucked into the roof. It looks like a pinup from some magazine. I figure Rex should have a photo of Boda, his girlfriend here in Fallujah, pinned up somewhere, to help motivate him on the mission.

We've been on the road for fifteen minutes when our convoy pulls up at the compound where we got into our first massive firefight in Fallujah. We drop off a sniper and a mortar team so they can cover our backs. We push onward into central Fallujah, through streets that are sullen and darkly hostile. We've identified the choke point at which the insurgents are likely to try to hit the general—the priority route that's got to be cleared today. It's the approaches to the bridge that spans the Euphrates, and the bridge itself.

We reach the bridge without a sniff of resistance. But as Rex and I dismount, I can feel the air crackling with danger. The whole city is rippling with evil intent. The bridge lies before us and it's a monster. It's three-quarters of a mile long, and it's an open latticework of iron girders from end to end. There isn't a scrap of cover, and Chavez and I will be completely exposed out there.

The marines from CAAT White fan out to secure this end of the bridge. A force of Iraqi Civil Defense Corps (ICDC) and Iraqi police are there ahead of us, supposedly to secure both ends of the bridge. However, we trust these guys about as much as we trust the insurgents. We've all heard the stories about how they've been passing their weapons, and their intel, to the enemy here in Fallujah.

There have even been incidents where the ICDC have turned their weapons on U.S. soldiers and joined forces with the insurgents. They're supposed to be our allies here in Iraq, but I'd rather they weren't here with us at all today. It's impossible to know which of them you can actually trust and which are waiting to slit your throat at the first opportunity.

As we wait for the marines to get in position, Rex finds himself some shade under the Humvee. It's burning hot already, and it's not even ten o'clock. There's some kind of hydroelectric facility positioned at this end of the bridge, and it's covered in Arabic graffiti. I can't read a word of it, but I can recognize the distinctive image of a Humvee scrawled on one of the steel girders.

I ask Bob Tincher, our vehicle commander, what the graffiti says. He's a totally solid marine. He exudes a hard, professional confidence that is wholly reassuring.

"Well, that's a badly done picture of a Humvee," he remarks, "and the writing says 'attack these vehicles' or something similar. I got one of the terps to translate it for me."

Once the marines are in position, Chico and I get our orders.

"You guys are to secure the bridge," Sergeant Stokes announces. "Once you're done, maintain your positions, okay?"

I nod and turn to Chico. "Okay, let's start in the middle. We walk in opposite directions, me going the far side, you back to here."

Chico signals his agreement.

We cross the bridge in a couple of the Humvees. Rex and I dismount and start the walk. We have a security marine on either shoulder and a lone Humvee moving at a dead crawl behind us. That way, if we get hit when we're still on the bridge, we may just make the cover of the vehicle.

I try to concentrate totally on my dog, but I have never felt so horribly exposed. For a moment it crosses my mind to use the 360-foot leash so I can hang back and avoid the worst risk. And then I get a grip on myself. Every day Rex does the walk, risking his life for us, for the marines, for me. Who the hell am I to complain?

We're thirty minutes into the search and I'm drenched with sweat. I can feel it dripping into the small of my back and pooling in my pants. There's not a scrap of shade anywhere. The sun's beating down on us and reflecting back off the ironwork of the bridge and up off the smooth surface of the road.

But that's the least of our worries. All of a sudden my concentration is torn away from Rex by the howl of an incoming round. A mortar plows into the river just below us, throwing up a massive geyser high into the air. The water splashes down, soaking Rex and me. At the same time there's the fiery streak of a projectile hurtling across the open space above the river, and a rocket slams into the metal superstructure of the bridge above our heads.

I can hear a second mortar already in the air and screaming down upon us. I crouch down and grab Rex's flak jacket. It's blisteringly hot, and I've kept him out of it for as long as I can. But the mortars and rockets are too close, and I know that there are more coming, and his flak vest might just stop a flying lump of shrapnel. My hands fumble as I fasten the Velcro around his stomach and his chest, and the mortar tears into the riverbank just to the rear of us. *Kaboom!*

The enemy mortar team starts to fire for effect, shells screaming down all around us. Rex and I sprint for the nearest Humvee, hot shards of shrapnel hissing evilly around our ears. We dive into the rear of the vehicle and Bob Tincher gives the "Go! Go! Go!"

The driver guns the heavy vehicle, and we're doing the drive of our lives, careering back across the bridge through a tunnel of fire. At the same time there's a contact report coming in over the radio. Our backup sniper and mortar teams have been hit in a massive ambush back at the compound where we dropped them. We're getting smashed from all sides.

We rejoin the vehicles at the far side of the bridge. Stokes cans the mission completely. We make tracks for the backup position in full-on survival mode. It's a five-minute drive at full speed. We reach the compound in a snarl of dust, and immediately we're getting hosed down by burst after long burst of machine gun fire.

The last time Rex and I were here in the heart of a firefight, we had the entire 2/2 battalion with us, plus Abrams tanks. Now all we've got are two dozen grunts of CAAT White, plus a similar number in the sniper and mortar teams, and six Humvees. And by the looks of things we're up against the insurgent forces of the entire city of Fallujah.

The Humvees race to take up positions around the compound so each can put down fire with its .50-cal heavy machine guns and grenade launchers. Chavez is in a separate vehicle from Rex and me, and he's farther forward and more directly in the line of fire.

The enemy gunners are strafing our vehicles. We're in the

back of our Humvee, sheltering behind its steel flank. I can feel the rounds tearing into the far side of the vehicle, just inches from Rex and me, and snarling away into thin air as they ricochet off the armor.

All of a sudden there's a surreal scene. A lone Iraqi car comes trundling down the road that lies to one side of us and the enemy guns. Somehow, the driver hasn't woken up to the danger. The vehicle is hit in a barrage of blasts, and it rolls forward and into a ditch. I watch, dumbfounded, as the driver and passenger bail out and take cover, apparently unharmed.

The guy on the .50-cal heavy machine gun above us starts returning fire, the *thump-thump-thump* of the big weapon's percussions adding to the din. The noise is incredibly loud, and with each muzzle flash Rex goes jittery as hell. He keeps glancing up at me with a look of real pain on his features. Dogs have much more sensitive hearing than humans, so if it's this loud for me, it must be unbearable for Rex.

I lie across him holding his head down and covering his ears. I'm torn between trying to comfort and protect my dog as the bullets slam into us and returning fire. I go for a half-assed compromise. Keeping one hand on Rex's thick leather collar, and my body between him and the bullets, I draw my pistol and start taking potshots over the side of the vehicle in the direction of the enemy.

As I'm up firing, I keep glancing down at Rex. He's lying there staring up at me, mouth clamped shut and eyes saucer wide: *What the hell are you up to? And what the hell's going on?* It's the first time I've used my weapon in anger, and Rex is jumpy as hell. I crouch down with my smoking pistol and pet him some more. I tell him he's a good boy, a good dog.

But I'm having to scream to make myself heard over the deafening noise of the battle. There's a smell coming off Rex that is wholly new to me. I know instinctively what it is: the smell of fear. Rex is terrified. If he freaks out completely, he may bolt from the vehicle. If he does that, he's dead. But gradually my words and gestures seem to calm him, and I'm up on my knees firing again.

With my one free hand I use hand signals to keep Rex down and out of the line of fire. The roar of battle is too fierce for him to hear my verbal commands. The incredible thing is that Rex obeys those hand signals and keeps his nerve. I'm worried sick about him being in the heart of this firefight, and with our vehicle getting smashed like it is, but Rex is passing the test with flying colors. My confidence in him keeps on growing.

I see Sergeant Stokes bail out of his vehicle and sprint toward the enemy positions. He's yelling for us to move forward and to lay down fire. He scales a berm and stands on top of it, in plain view of everyone, and he's loosing off an entire magazine at the insurgents' positions.

Bob Tincher turns and yells at the rest of us to follow his lead. We bail out of the Humvee and start sprinting toward the nearest cover, a building some five hundred yards away. But we've barely gone five paces when a savage burst of rounds plows into the dirt right in front of Rex's paws. Further bursts kick up plumes of sand and dust all around us.

For an instant I'm glancing at the other marines, wondering what the hell we're to do. The cover's too far away for us to risk it. Instead, we make a mad dash back to our vehicle. We dive inside the Humvee and I'm crouched there trying to calm Rex, when suddenly I remember Chavez and Luki. I glance around the corner of our Humvee. I get just one glimpse before bullets snap past my face and I yank my head inside.

Chavez and Luki's Humvee is getting lit up, rounds sparking and hammering all along its exposed sides. There's a marine in the turret on the Mark 19 grenade launcher unleashing grenade after grenade at the enemy. Chavez is curled up below him in the rear, right on top of Luki, trying to calm and protect him.

He's got his body toward the bullets, desperately trying to shield his dog.

Chapter Fourteen

THERE'S A HALF HOUR OR MORE OF THIS INSANE FIREFIGHT BEFORE the mortar and sniper teams finally manage to move into our vehicles, and we fight and drive our way out of there. Apart from the very fact of us getting out of such an intense and massive battle, the unbelievable thing is that no one's been killed—Chico and Luki are okay—and the vehicles are just about usable. The Humvees are shot to pieces but somehow still drivable.

Five minutes out of the battleground, Sergeant Stokes calls a halt. He needs to do a damage inspection—the vehicles and his men. We've been ordered to set up a checkpoint on the road leading into Fallujah, and to hold it. We figure Command is still trying to call this one: whether to proceed with the mission or abandon it.

Rex and I dismount from the Humvee. That was as loud and as full-on as it's ever going to get. Rex stands there gazing up at me, and it's like he's bursting with relief that we're no longer in the midst of all that chaos and mayhem. He's standing tall and his eyes are shining bright, and he doesn't seem to be traumatized by what's just happened. I'm hugely relieved.

It's been proved that dogs can get post-traumatic stress disorder just like humans can. Troops exposed to brutal combat conditions can suffer lasting psychological damage, just as anyone who suffers intense trauma. It can hit immediately after the traumatic event, or many months afterward. Symptoms can include repeatedly reliving the event and the trauma that accompanied it.

Dogs feel many of the same emotions that we humans do, and I've been fearful about Rex getting PTSD. But right now he looks as if he's on the pure adrenaline high of cheating death, like he's loving the simple fact that he's still alive. Which means that he's feeling pretty much exactly like his handler is.

I take the opportunity to go check on Chavez and Luki. Chico greets Rex and me with a crazed grin and a burst of insane laughter.

"Man, what the fuck was that?"

I smile. "How you doin', bro? Congrats. You just survived your first firefight. What you gonna do now?"

Chico grins. "I'm gonna go to Disney World!"

I crack up laughing. Chico's comment is perfectly timed and perfectly suited to the crazed spirit of this moment.

"How's Luki?" I ask him.

"Luki's just great," Chico says.

"You see what those air force guys are missing out on now?"

Chico gives me a wide smile. "Man, yeah. I get it."

I figure Chico's in the same state as Rex and me. His adrenaline's pumping bucketloads, and he's on such a massive high that his senses are maxed out. There's no high that comes close to surviving a full-on firefight. I've heard people say that war is an addiction, and I understand that now. I have never felt so good as standing here with Chico marveling at how our dogs plus the two of us are still alive. And I've got a hunger—which I figure Chico shares—to go experience it all over again.

Rex and Luki are lying in the shade of the Humvee taking time out. They have their tongues lolling out lazily, and they've got a similar expression on their features. Rex is looking from me to Chico and back again, like: *You boys, you're becoming total adrenaline junkies. Take a leaf out of my and Luki's book, eh? Time to take a chill pill, the both of you.*

Rex is already older than I am in dog years. And he's beginning to act like a wise old dog. Rex has always been protective of me. That's the pack instinct thing. But now there's an element of me being the young pup, while he's the old gun.

Sergeant Stokes comes over to check on us and our dogs. I ask him what exactly a CAAT team does, apart from getting into insane firefights.

"We're the two-two's heavy guns," Stokes tells me. "But we also patrol, just like the infantry guys, only we've got the heavy guns with us on patrol, and when the shit goes down we're the QRF. We respond first to back up anyone who needs help. We're also the escort to EOD guys whenever they get called out to defuse something."

The QRF is Quick Reaction Force, a mobile unit that can go to the aid of units in trouble. Stokes explains that when they're out on patrol, the CAAT guys move around in the Humvees. It's the only way they can transport the Mark 19 grenade launchers and their other heavy weapons.

Five of the vehicles in CAAT White are open-backed. Stokes's vehicle is the lead, so it's up-armored and closed in, as it's most likely to get hit by an IED. It's also the only one with aircon.

I tell Stokes what I'm thinking. "So if Rex could patrol with you guys, he wouldn't get so exhausted like he does on the foot patrols. I figure he could last longer and cover more ground. So can Rex and I tag along with your patrols?"

Stokes loves the idea. "Hell, fucking yeah you can! I love dogs, and you guys have already shown you can handle a fire-fight!"

We're on the roadblock for a good two hours or more. Chico and I busy ourselves getting our dogs fed and watered. Neither Luki nor Rex can fight back in a full-on firefight, so Chico and I concentrated on safeguarding our dogs back there. That in turn meant our minds weren't busy worrying about getting killed. A dog can't shoot back, so it relies 100 percent on its handler to protect it.

Stokes, Bob Tincher, Showalter, and some of the other ma-rines gather around. The dogs draw them in. They get to talking about their pets back home. Their minds are off the firefight, and their nerves are calmed by the thought of the pets they and their folks have back in America.

I'm excited about this new patrol concept that we've thought up with CAAT White. If we can get out on their rolling patrols, there's no limit to what Rex and I can do out there.

Unsurprisingly, the mission to clear a route into Fallujah gets stood down. We return to base and Rex, Luki, Chico, and I make our way to the Fallujah Hilton. Luki and Chavez walk in ahead of us, their heads held high.

"Oh, man, we just got into this huge firefight," Chavez an-nounces.

I leave him to bask in the glory of his baptism by fire—one that a number of the other handlers had refused to come on—

and head for my room. Rex and I play one of our regular games to ease the tension of battle. I get on all fours and advance slowly toward Rex. He stands with his head down and turned slightly to one side. He's pretending not to see me, but out of the corner of his eye he's watching my every move. When I'm within range, I lunge for him. Rex knows what's coming, and he's ready.

He's nipping at my hands, trying to chew me off. I get a grip on his collar and start to drag him in. He's pulling back with all his might. I haul him closer and get him in a bear hug. Rex lets out a ferocious growl, but it's not a mean-spirited one. He's loving it. I pin him down and he's wriggling and thrashing like mad. When finally he's twisted free, he turns and starts swiping at me with his front paws.

After we're done playing, we lie down side by side on my bed to rest. I think back over what we've just been through. It's then that I realize something quite extraordinary, something I've never thought of before. Somehow, somewhere along the way, Rex and I seem to have gone from being combat newbies and guinea pigs to being a battle-hardened K9 team. And Rex has gone from being a dog who's terrified of gunfire to one who will walk into the fire with me time after time after time.

I ruffle his soft ears and wonder how on earth it's happened. Combat notoriety has crept up on us unnoticed, and part of me still doesn't believe it. I keep thinking that a time will come when Rex is gonna flee from the next explosion with his tail between his legs. Or I'm gonna come to my senses and realize that I just can't do another lonely, death-defying walk, like the one we did over the bridge.

But here's the thing: Having Rex beside me helps give me the strength so I *can* face it. Or maybe it's just that Rex helps me deal with the stress of it all. I've always known that dogs are great stress relievers. But a dog such as Rex also offers his human companion the ultimate in blind loyalty and courage. If I asked him to, Rex would advance blind to clear a cave stuffed full of Al Qaeda suicide bombers. And he'd do so without hesitation.

Likewise, never once has he faltered when I've asked him to do the walk with me, not even when we're under the enemy's guns. And because of this, he's put steel in my soul. I know I've got to step up to my dog. I've got to be the warrior that he needs me to be.

I don't hold it against those air force K9 guys for refusing to go on the Fallujah mission. I don't rub it in their faces or try to make them feel inferior. I saw a good deal of that kind of thing when I first got into the Marine Corps, during my three months of boot camp. I didn't like it much, although I realized that boot camp was a trial—to see which recruits were strong enough to make it and become one of the few and the proud.

Pretty quickly I figured out that boot camp was a kind of game. It was designed so the drill instructors could weed out the weak and the incapable. And more than physical strength, it was designed to weed out any mental and moral weakness in the recruits. You had to play the game and show initiative and be motivated the entire time. Those who didn't were singled out and given the hardest time possible.

I was older and more mature than most, and early on our senior drill instructor made me our platoon's "guide." The guide carries the guidon, the military standard that's specific to each platoon. I was part of Alpha Company, Platoon 1001, so our guidon was a rectangular flag with 1001 on it. The guidon embodies your respect for your platoon, and it's imperative that it is treated with precise care at all times.

I was fired from being a guide pretty damn quickly. We were in the chow hall one lunchtime, and I'd posted my guidon where it should be—upright against the wall. A rival platoon's guide came in and moved my guidon, replacing it with his own. Very slowly and gracefully my guidon toppled over until it all but whacked a drill instructor on the head.

The drill instructor picked it up and yelled out, "PLATOON 1001!"

Everyone on our table looked up. My drill instructor saw what had happened and exploded.

"Good to fucking go, Dowling! You're fucking fired! Get the fuck out of my chow hall!"

At first I was upset. I'd felt honored to be our platoon's guide. But as time went by, it soon became irrelevant. At the end of my first month, 9/11 happened, and overnight everything changed. In an instant the whole pace of boot camp geared up a level. The drill instructors started yelling at us: "Put your fucking war faces on, 'cause we're training for war." Things had gotten serious.

I learned ultimate respect for those drill instructors. They were physically hard and fit, and mentally they could run rings around any of the recruits. I never saw our instructors doing anything that wasn't aimed at turning raw recruits into super-motivated Marine Corps warriors, not even when they were chewing out the weak. And boy, did those guys know how to chew you out if you messed up.

There was one night I will never forget. We were getting ready for bed, and the drill instructor on duty had given us the regulation hour to prepare for the following day. That was also time to socialize with the other guys in the platoon. At the end of the hour you know the drill instructor will come out of his hut and yell for everyone to "get on line." You stand in two rows facing each other wearing nothing but your boxer shorts, ready for your final inspection of the day.

That night Sergeant Trenum, our senior drill instructor, was on duty. He was of average build, but he had a voice that could chew out recruits like no other. He called us to get on line fifteen minutes early. Everyone was rushing around trying to get ready, then shuffling into position. We lined up by height, with the shortest guys near the door and the tallest down at my end. There was a big, lanky, goofy bird of a recruit named Jones, who acted as if he had two left feet. As luck would have it, he was pretty much opposite me, so I was looking directly at him while standing on line.

As I stared front waiting for Sergeant Trenum to start making his rounds, I couldn't believe my eyes. Jones stood there at attention wearing only a jockstrap. He must have failed to find his boxers and didn't want to borrow a pair. The whole apparition was made even worse by the fact that Jones wore heavy black-rimmed glasses. At boot camp everyone had to wear the same regulation Marine Corps–issue glasses. They're nicknamed BCGs (birth control glasses) because no one can expect to get laid when sporting a pair. Jones managed to appear even more goofy and ridiculous by wearing his BCGs all crooked.

Sergeant Trenum had started his inspection, so it was far too late to try to fix Jones. I tensed myself for the whirlwind that I knew was coming. We were all issued a jockstrap, but we never

ever wore them. Sergeant Trenum had barely even started his inspection when he glanced over and noticed Jones.

"What the fuck?" he exploded.

He stalked over and stopped bang in front of him. Jones was staring straight ahead as if there was nothing wrong. Sergeant Trenum looked Jones up and down. He was shaking his head in despair, as if he were thinking, Fucking Jones, why's it always Jones?

"Jones, there's something about you tonight that separates you from everyone else. I can't put my finger on it, literally and figuratively. I can't figure it out. So, help me out here, Jones. What makes you different from all the other recruits in this room?"

"Sir, there is nothing different about this recruit, sir," Jones yelled.

Sergeant Trenum put his head down and shook it some more. "Jones, let's try that one more time. Why the fuck are you so different from the rest of 1001?"

"Sir, because this recruit is wearing a jockstrap, sir."

"What the fuck? Are you so fucking retarded you can't tell the difference between boxers and a jockstrap? I'm surprised you don't have it around your neck, you fucking retarded Big Bird–looking lanky fucker."

It was funny, but of course you couldn't laugh. If you laughed, Sergeant Trenum would turn his ire on you. He sent Jones into the middle of the squad bay and made him do push-ups and jumping jacks, with his balls hanging out from one end of the jockstrap and his ass from the other.

Eventually, he called a halt. "Jones, that's enough. I can't stand looking at your ass anymore."

Sergeant Trenum sent Jones back into line. But it wasn't over yet. The recruit to my right was a big, hefty guy called Myers. The trouble with Myers was he looked like the Sasquatch. He had a carpet of hair all down his front and all down his back. Sergeant Trenum was about to move on past Myers, but then he stopped. He was staring at Myers's stomach. He bent down and squinted, then stood up.

"Myers, give me your tweezers."

"Sir, yes sir!"

Myers opened his medical box and handed the sergeant his tweezers. He went back to attention, and Sergeant Trenum reached forward with the tweezers and pulled something out of Myers's belly button. It was an enormous ball of belly-button fluff. I could see out of the corner of my eye that the drill sergeant had the most disgusted look on his face.

He held the fluff up right in front of Myers's face. "Myers, you are so fucking disgusting," he rasped, speaking real slowly. He held the fluff under one of Myers's nostrils. "Myers, cover the other nostril. Now breathe your disgusting funk in and keep your mouth shut."

Myers breathed in and the drill instructor squeezed it up his nostril. "You leave that fucking disgusting ball of shit in your nose." He threw the tweezers down. "Myers, did you shower tonight?"

"Yes, sir, this recruit showered tonight, sir."

"Well, you magic-carpet-riding Sasquatch son of a yeti . . ."

Sergeant Trenum started laying into Myers verbally, doing one of his classics. I was still trying not to laugh over Jones and the jockstrap incident. Now this. I heard a snicker from a guy opposite me, which triggered another recruit to laugh, and I couldn't hold it in anymore. That was the trigger for the entire 1001 to start.

I felt Sergeant Trenum shift his gaze from Myers to me. "Jones, Myers, Dowling—this shit is everyone's fault," he declared, gesturing at all of us pissing ourselves laughing. "The lot of you are all fucking disgusting. Get to fucking bed and wait until tomorrow: I'm gonna kill you guys and enjoy every minute of it."

To get thrown out of boot camp you had to mess up real bad. Even Jones made it through, as did Myers. But via the process the drill instructors put them through, those guys went into boot camp boys and came out pretty much men. I made it through boot camp just fine, and I was strengthened hugely by something that my mother revealed to me during my first weeks there.

She'd found out from her own mother that the man she'd always believed was her father was actually her stepfather. Her real dad had been killed when she was a baby. He'd been in the Korean War, serving with the Marines. That meant that my maternal grandpa was actually a marine before me, and that the Corps ran in my blood.

I'd always felt a need to test myself and to join the ultimate warrior brotherhood. Maybe this went some way toward explaining this urge and why I'd been so drawn to the one iconic fighting force—the Marine Corps.

Shortly after the Fallujah mission has proved nearly the death of us, 2/2 is ordered to return to Mahmoudiyah. The Fallujah Hilton has been like paradise for Rex and me, but Mahmoudiyah is where the 2/2 is going, and that means my dog and I are going with them.

Chico Chavez and Luki are supposed to go with us, but for some reason our kennel master decides that instead we're to get Lance Corporal Harrell and Falco, his Dutch shepherd. Harrell is a big, wide-eyed, slow-moving, soft-spoken guy from the prairies, but I sense his eagerness to get out there with his dog. He's not afraid to go outside the wire, and it's going to be a huge relief having another K9 team with us at Mahmoudiyah.

But before we leave Fallujah, some shocking news does the rounds. According to one of the air force handlers, a marine from the 2/2 has been kidnapped by the insurgents. A marine kidnapped? I figure the air force guy has to be kidding. I go check with the Warlords and it seems it is for real. Well, kind of.

The marine who's been kidnapped is Corporal Wassef Ali Hassoun, the Arab guy whom I'd never got more than a word out of when trying to talk to him down in Mahmoudiyah. Apparently he kept telling his fellow marines that he was freaking out because he was "shooting at his own people." Word is that he befriended some of the Hajis on the Fallujah base, and they arranged to do a fake kidnapping.

The marines of 2/2 figure the Hajis have spirited him away to a safe place, in return for him deserting the Corps. He's got family in Jordan, so it'll be easy enough to get him home. They've made it look like a real kidnapping by showing the corporal's ID on videos that have been released to the media. Either way, "kidnapping" a U.S. Marine is a real propaganda coup for the insurgents. But everyone is convinced that the whole thing's been staged.

A day or two later, news breaks that confirms our worst fears. Marine Corps corporal Wassef Ali Hassoun hasn't been kidnapped at all. He's jumped ship. Deserted. We're none of us too pleased. The corporal represents a very valuable asset to the enemy. He knows all about our bases and their security. He knows all about how we operate when on patrol. He knows our greatest strengths and our weaknesses. It's a real blow that a once fellow marine with that level of insight and knowledge has gone over to the dark side.

Still, the show has to go on. Rex and I are offered a lift back to Mahmoudiyah with CAAT White. The Humvees are loaded with marines and festooned with their rucksacks hanging off the sides. Rex mounts up in the lead Humvee—Stokes's vehicle—and he's raring to go. He's looking at me with a gleam in his eye and his tongue lolling out big and pink and hanging halfway down his chin: *Come on, partner, I can sense it. We're going home!*

It says it all when Rex considers Mahmoudiyah and the Bunker his home. But oddly, heading south feels a lot like going home for me too. This place—this war—is getting under our skin and into our blood. It's June 24 as we set off to return to Mahmoudiyah. We're approaching four months in and well over halfway through our Iraq tour.

Stokes likes playing the joker big-time, especially when it come to Rex. As soon as we're under way he's radioing in sitreps to base, and each time he grabs for his roof-mounted radio he shoves Rex's head to one side. Rex snaps it back again and takes a playful nip at Stokes's hand. And so they start roughhousing in the front of a speeding Humvee.

"Rex, what the hell, man?" Stokes laughs. "You don't want me speaking on the radio? You want to radio the orders?"

Stokes's driver is named Winkler, another Eminem look-alike. Like Stokes, he loves having Rex sandwiched between the two of them. Up in the .50-cal turret sits Robinson, a good old country boy who's never without a half-smoked cigarette perched on his lip. Even in a firefight he's got one jammed in his mouth.

We know we're almost home when we see the shot-up Mahmoudiyah road sign hanging above the Mixing Bowl. We count the number of bullet holes, and we're glad to see there are a few more. We'd expect nothing less from the Triangle of Death. We pull up on the roadside on the approach to the base because there's a holdup.

The guys dismount, and Bob Tincher and Stokes start handing out crayons and coloring books to the crowd of kids who gather. I like the way these guys do things. They're good to the right people, the Iraqi women and kids. They're doing their hearts-and-minds stuff. But they're not going to take one iota of shit off of anyone, either.

We drive into the base, and we do a rapid handover with the army unit that's been stationed here. Those guys can't wait to leave, because they've taken a real pounding. In our absence, they have been shot to hell. They've taken twelve KIAs in the short time that they've been here, plus dozens more wounded. They can't wait to get the hell out.

Rex and I move back into the Bunker. It's changed beyond recognition. The army engineers have been all over it. One wall has been racked out with shelving, and they've put locks on the doors. They've also punched a hole in one wall and inserted an aircon unit, which is hooked up to the electricity.

It's a damn sight more civilized in the Bunker now. We can close the door and keep the aircon running, and the army boys have even left us a TV and DVD deck as a bonus. It's not quite the Fallujah Hilton, but it's getting there. Harrell and Falco move into the Bunker alongside Rex and me.

Rex and I at Camp Fallujah, Iraq, June 2004. As usual, Rex is on my left, but it's odd for him to be lying down. He's usually on his feet, curious about his surroundings and eager for some bomb-detection work, which to him is just an enjoyable game. I guess he knows he's only posing for a photo here, so he's not particularly interested!

Corporal José "Chico" Chavez and his military working dog Luki, the morning of the Fallujah mission we did together. Chavez and Luki were a great team and good friends.

Rex and I searching a vehicle at a Camp Fallujah gate, May 2004. I'd get the occupants to dismount and remove any electrical devices—cell phones, in particular! With the doors and trunk open, I'd put Rex all through the vehicle, using his nose to search for arms, explosives, or VBIEDs (vehicle-born IEDs, aka car bombs).

Rex in his regular place in Sergeant Stokes's Humvee, surrounded by all our gear. We're about to leave Camp Fallujah after our stint there and return to our regular stalking ground, Mahmoudiyah. Oddly enough, by now this almost felt like going home for Rex and me.

Rex standing duty at a Camp Fallujah gatehouse. The barriers behind him are HESCO—wire mesh walls filled with dirt and rock, for blast protection; the marine on duty mans a Browning .50-caliber heavy machine gun.

Rex and I sit atop an Abrams M1A1 main battle tank in the staging area of FOB Mahmoudiyah. We had experienced the combat effectiveness and firepower of the Abrams back in Fallujah when we were in our first major firefight alongside the Marines of 2/2, the Warlords.

Rex in his shrapnel vest moments after we started getting mortared on the south side of Fallujah, when we went in to clear and secure the bridges across the Euphrates River. It was often pushing 100 degrees in Iraq, and I'd try to keep Rex out of that flak until the last possible moment for fear of him overheating.

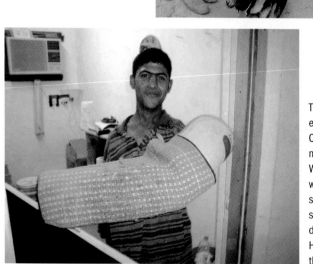

Me, Rex, and Bob Tincher, a vehicle commander for CAAT White, in Fallujah. Rex isn't wearing his flak vest, but moments after this photo was taken we started getting mortared, which is when I strapped it on to try to protect him from flying shrapnel.

The Haji—the local Iraqi—who unexpectedly walked into my room at Camp Fallujah to put a new lock on my door and ran when he saw Rex. We had a good laugh about it afterward. Here he is wearing Rex's bite sleeve—worn by decoy "suspects" so Rex could practice grabbing and detaining them, without harm. The Haji wasn't about to volunteer for this job!

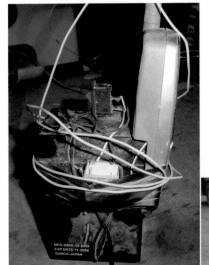

A defused IED detonator. It's a cell phone strapped to a battery with wires connected to explosives. A watcher would call the cell phone when he spotted a Marine Corps patrol passing the hidden device; this would send a charge through the battery and on through the wires to the explosives—crude but very effective. Some 80 percent of these bombs ended up killing Iraqi civilians instead of the US forces, so by sniffing out such devices Rex and I were safeguarding the locals as much as we were our own guys.

Explosives ordnance disposal (EOD) marines doing maintenance on their bomb-disposal robot that assisted with defusing IEDs. Whenever Rex and I found a suspicious device, we'd call in the EOD teams.

A cache of RPGs Rex and I found with the help of the Marine combat engineers. The metal detectors they carried around with them located dozens of weapons and caches of explosives that were deeply buried.

One of Rex's best finds. It doesn't look like too much but he located these weapons in several different areas in and around the house these insurgents were using. This happened during our joint mission with the Army.

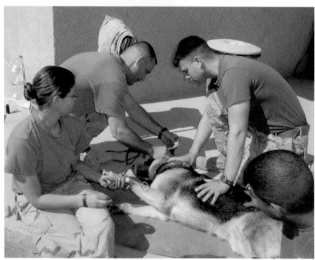

The Army veterinarian and vet technician, stopping by Camp Fallujah to check on our dogs. Rex is muzzled and sedated while being inspected, since he didn't enjoy being looked at by the vet at all. Our dogs got their ears flushed out and anal glands popped, which kept fluid from building up within the glands and causing added stress and soreness. What a relief for Rex!

Compared to the bunker at Mahmoudiyah, the K9 quarters at Camp Fallujah were like the Hilton. Here's Rex stretched out and enjoying a well-earned rest on my luxurious bed.

Rex and I standing duty at the FOB Mahmoudiyah gatehouse. Rex has got his paws up and his head out, watching for any new arrivals. We did our fair share of gate duty, and it was here that I'd first run into Suraya, an Iraqi interpreter I befriended, much to the displeasure of the insurgents.

A Humvee mounted patrol of the Warlords, moving out on a mission around Fallujah. We used the skeletal-like building at the rear to muster in prior to staging an operation in the area. This shows the typical terrain we'd patrol through: flat, dusty, sunbaked, and littered with rubble—in short, ideal IED-planting territory.

Corporal John "Red" Walls after receiving a Purple Heart for being wounded in action when he took shrapnel in his leg. Red was a great guy and one of the first marines Rex and I had met upon arrival at Mahmoudiyah. It was with Red that Rex and I found the hut we were to make our home—the Bunker. Red felt his wound was minor and that he didn't deserve a Purple Heart.

Me, Rex, and Gunnery Sergeant Trotter from the 2/2. Gunney Trotter was my first in line chain of command while we were with the 2/2. He made sure that Rex and I were taken care of, and over time he really warmed to my dog.

With my parents after deployment. My father was not supposed to have been alive when I got home but I got to see him one last time before he finally passed.

Rex in his "house" at the Camp Pendleton kennels. Not a fan of small dog treats, Rex enjoyed these big mammoth bones more than anything!

Gunney Trotter decides to take the tiny hut next to ours. It's small and cramped as hell, but he seems happy enough in there. "To hell with bunking in one room with another five marines" is the way he explains it to Harrell and me.

It's good having Gunney Trotter next to us. I can walk next door to clear ops, rather than having to struggle trying to raise him on the radio. As we're neighbors now, I seize the moment and suggest to Gunney Trotter that instead of having us stand gate duty until someone asks for us, why not let us go out on the mobile CAAT patrols? Gunney Trotter's good with that.

I take Harrell around the base and introduce him to the 2/2 guys. I'm senior in rank, so I'm nominally in charge. But in reality Harrell and I, plus our dogs, will form a team of equals. We decide to rotate duties. When one team's standing gate duty, the other will be out on patrol. Plus we'll train together and keep our dogs sharp.

The main problem now is that it's late June, midsummer, and burning hot. When first we opened the door to the Bunker it was like a furnace in there. Even at night it's pushing 100 degrees. I feel kind of crazed, like my brain's being fried the whole time. I feel like a semizombie.

Our medical kit for the dogs contains doggy thermometers. After putting on the dog's muzzle, you're supposed to stick them up the dog's rectum to check its temperature. Mine is so hot the mercury has gone off the scale and won't work anymore. Harrell's thermometer has done the same. God only knows what it must be like for Rex and Luki in their thick fur coats.

The first morning that we're back in Mahmoudiyah, I'm using the Porta Potty. I've taught myself to go quickly—no one wants to die on the crapper. I've just settled down to my business when there's the scream of an incoming mortar round. It slams into the muster area in front of me, and I'm telling myself I really do not want to get hit here on the throne.

That first mortar is quickly followed by a sustained barrage as the enemy rains rounds upon us. This is a serious, concerted assault on the base, and here I am caught with my pants down. I finish up quick as I can and dash out pulling up my trousers as I go.

I dive under the nearest concrete shelter as more rounds slam down around us. *Welcome back to Mahmoudiyah.*

Chapter Fifteen

WHILE STANDING ONE OF THEIR VERY FIRST GATE DUTIES HERE AT Death Central, Harrell and Falco prove their mettle. Harrell calls me on my radio. We've given ourselves call signs to use over the air to avoid any confusion between dog teams. I'm K9 One and he's K9 Two. There's a squelch of static on my radio, and I hear Harrell's voice sounding clear but tense and strained.

"K9 One, this is K9 Two. I got a local vehicle and Falco's showing a change of behavior. I figure there's maybe a bomb in there, but I can't find nothing. Can you bring Rex to verify it's not a false respond?"

I tell him we're on our way.

I grab Rex and hurry over to the front gate. All the time I'm thinking it's got to be a vehicle-borne IED (VBIED), or in layman's terms, a car bomb. It could be poised to blow just as soon as there are enough marines—or dog teams—within range. If so, it won't be the first time that we've been menaced by a suspected VBIED. And as is always the case, it makes my blood run cold.

* * *

Before we managed to get out of Fallujah, the place had a nasty surprise in store for us. An Iraqi had driven up to the Camp Fallujah base and bailed out of his car, leaving it bang in front of the main gates. There was only one possible explanation: It had to be a VBIED.

The first Rex and I knew about it was when Kartune came and had words with the handlers gathered in our quarters.

"We just got word they need a dog team on one of the southern gates, to search a vehicle."

"What, like a checkpoint?" I asked.

"No. Some Iraqi drove up in a car and ran. It's been left in an area where vehicle convoys pass and patrols walk by to get to the gate."

"So why don't they send EOD to check it out?"

"EOD won't respond until we make a positive ID first."

"What the fuck?" I said. "If it walks like a duck and talks like a duck, it's probably a duck. They should send EOD."

Eventually, Sergeant Dan Wheeler, a handler based out of Camp Lejeune, volunteered to go check it. It was a ballsy move, because Wheeler was pretty much fresh into Iraq and everyone hated VBIEDs. I volunteered to go with him as his spotter. A spotter checks the area and vehicle for signs that there's been a bomb planted, while the handler concentrates on getting his dog to do the search. The spotter can keep a watch out for suspect wires, which the handler may not notice as he's focused on his dog.

We geared up in flak and Kevlar, strapped Wheeler's dog into his doggy flak, and drove over there. The battered white Toyota Corolla was isolated and exposed in the fierce midday sun. It was visible for miles around, and it was clear that we wouldn't have a scrap of cover as we approached it. If there was a watcher out there waiting to trigger a VBIED, he'd be able to see us coming a mile off.

We parked a little ways off and sat there examining the area. Back at the gate the marines were at their posts, watching over us. Finally, we could put it off no longer. We walked up real slow to the vehicle. Twenty feet away, we stopped and gave the Toyota a visual inspection. I lay on the ground and tried to see if there were wires poking out underneath it, or anything else that pointed to a VBIED.

I couldn't see anything obvious. We had no choice but to move in and search the vehicle proper. We stepped farther into the blinding glare and the heat, and closer to the vehicle. We circled it once, twice, and still nothing obvious. Wheeler started to search with his dog. As he did so I was trying to keep my eyes everywhere, plus I was trying to get my thumping pulse under some kind of control. I was certain that this one was going to get us.

I was hoping to God that his dog didn't find anything, because we were horribly exposed out here. For a split second his dog looked like he was showing a change of behavior. This was pure terror. I kept glancing in the car windows for anything deadly, but I could see nothing obvious. Finally, Wheeler said he was done and it was all clear, and we got the hell out of there.

Walking up to a suspect VBIED is intensely nerve-racking; the fear of getting blown up is almost as debilitating as actually getting blown up.

On this call, Harrell's done a fine job. He's got the car to stop a good distance from any marines, and he's kept them well away from it. He's got the driver to turn the engine off and open all doors, the hood, and the trunk. Crucially, he's also got the driver to remove any electrical devices, including cell phones.

I get Rex to search all over the vehicle, and sure enough he shows a strong change of behavior at the rear end. He's standing beside the trunk and sucking in the scent, and he won't move. Harrell tells me that Falco did the exact same thing.

My heart's thumping fit to burst as we search the entire vehicle, but there's nothing to be found. We figure the dogs must have picked up the residual odor of an IED, which means the vehicle's most likely been used for transporting one or more explosive devices.

The driver seems dodgy as hell. He's a bag of nerves as he watches Rex and Falco work. The dog find is the perfect excuse to take him in for some proper questioning. It also makes the marines on the gate doubly glad to have us working alongside them.

I'm wondering where Suraya has gotten to, because I've yet to see her on any of the gates. I was looking forward to spending some time with her again. I'm facing another month or more on MREs now, and some of her home-baked bread and chicken kebab sure wouldn't go amiss. I've also been looking forward to being in her company and picking up on our conversations.

I figure the marine standing gate duty is sure to know. "Where's Suraya got to?" I ask.

He gives me this weird look. "Man, are you serious?"

I shrug. Of course I'm serious. "Yeah, where is she?"

He shakes his head. "Man, didn't you hear? Suraya was killed."

I feel as if I've just been struck in the stomach by a speeding truck. *Suraya dead*. She can't be. "What the fuck . . . what the hell happened?"

He tells me the story. A couple of weeks back, Suraya was followed home from the base. The insurgents have made it a priority to track any Iraqi civilians working for the American forces so they can kill them. They stormed into Suraya's house and interrogated her for hours. Then they executed her "for working with the Americans." For good measure they shot dead her entire family as well.

The news comes completely out of the blue. All I can think is, What a complete and total waste of life. This is a turning point for me. It makes me wonder what on earth is the point in all of this. What is the point of us being here if it just gets a woman like Suraya killed? Suraya had her whole life ahead of her, and now she and her entire family are dead, and for what?

Suraya wanted to build bridges and understanding between us and the locals. Her killing is senseless and evil. The insurgents are murdering their own people, and they're not even combatants. They've realized how hard it is to kill American soldiers, and that we will hurt them back, so they've decided to kill those Iraqis who work with us. Killing fellow Iraqis and fellow Muslims is incomprehensible.

I feel horribly dark and torn up with anger inside. I go find a quiet place with my dog, and I try to mourn Suraya's senseless murder and that of all her family. She was such an innocent, lovely person. Her killing makes me think of my father: *Suraya's gone and my dad's supposed to be dead right now*. It's midsummer and way past the deadline by which he was supposed to have passed away. It makes me think that I just want out of here.

I just want to get myself and Rex home safely and to go see my father before he passes away.

It's been days since I last was last able to check how he's doing. I go try to call my folks, but as usual I can't get a connection. I check the e-mail instead. The news is that he's still tenaciously clinging onto life.

I return to the Bunker. Rex hops on my cot, and we bed down together. He knows I'm suffering, and he's doing his best to comfort me. I lie there stroking his ears, and I offer up a prayer for Suraya's soul and that of all her family. I am sure she has made it to heaven, and her folks too. And I pray that I get to see my father one more time while the three of us—him, Rex, and I—are alive and still breathing.

One life is brutally taken away, and another is given. I get a mail delivery. There are letters and big boxes of snacks for me, and bones for Rex, plus photos of my folks back home. Mail means so much to me that I keep every last letter and card that anyone's sent to me.

In among the messages there's wonderful news. My brother Kevin's wife, Maria, has just given birth to their son. They've named him Joseph Patricio Dowling, after my father—Patricio being the Latinized version of Patrick, as Kevin's wife is Hispanic.

I manage to get a phone link through to my brother. He tells me about the birth, then asks if I'd be willing to be the godfather to his son. I'm deeply touched and honored. My dad is over the moon to have survived long enough to see his second grandchild born. It's fantastic to speak to them all at such a warm, happy time, and in a way it's the antidote that I needed to the killing of Suraya.

I tell my folks few details of what's been happening out here. How can I communicate that a lovely Iraqi woman in her early twenties has been murdered along with her entire family, and simply because she was working as our translator? How could I ever get anyone back home in America to understand all that? I tell them that I'm fine and that Rex is fine, and that we're doing good out here. I don't want to worry them.

In among the mail there's a cigar from Kevin. It's as big and thick as a prize carrot, and it's got my godson's name printed on it, plus the date of his birth. It's never going to get smoked. I'm going to keep that cigar forever.

There's also a letter from my mom's sister, Auntie Debbie. She's just been on a trip to the Canadian Rockies, and she's sent me a postcard of snowcapped peaks and mountain meadows full of pink and yellow wildflowers. It's looks so calm and cool and peaceful compared to where I am now. She talks about her holiday and signs off with a funny little doodle of a dog, followed by a PS: "Do you like my drawing of Rex? Yes it is a dog. Now you know why I majored in Business and not Art!"

Auntie Debbie's doodle makes me laugh. I contrast her letter and her life to where I am now. I've got a dog tag around my neck with my personal details on it, plus one sewn into my boot. The one in my boot is in case I get blown up and they need to ID whose foot it is that they've found. That's one side of the brutal logic of the war that we're fighting out here; the other is the pointless, senseless murder of Suraya and her entire household.

Suraya's death epitomizes all that is crazed and evil about this war. The enemy is targeting anyone they can connect to the Coalition. They're sowing the city with IEDs, disregarding that most of them kill their own people. And any of our patrols hit by an IED now face a murderous follow-up ambush. Death Central is a very, very dangerous place to be—especially for the man and the dog doing the walk.

A couple of days later, Rex and I are tasked with a new mission. The CO of the Warlords, Lieutenant Colonel Keyser, plans to have a meeting with the city's clerics and tribal sheikhs. He wants a route cleared into downtown Mahmoudiyah so he can meet them at city hall. There's one upside to the mission: We're going in with CAAT White.

Rex and I mount up in Stokes's Humvee, and Rex takes his regular place, nose pressed to the windshield. Stokes has got a video camera taped to the dash, and he's filming anything crazy that happens on their patrols. He's burning through a lot of videotape.

Stokes has a ghetto blaster jammed between him and Winkler. He starts every mission with a hot blast of Metallica or Godsmack, just to get everyone in the mood. We were out on a mission and Stokes grabbed a bar of C4 plastic explosives. He stuffed it in his mouth, teeth bared like he was going to bite a chunk off it. That pretty much sums up Stokes's character. He's a crazy, fearless, badass marine, and a great leader of men. You just got to love him for it.

During our downtime, Stokes and I have become addicted to a PlayStation football game called Madden NFL 2004. I keep winning, and it bugs the hell out of Stokes. He hasn't yet won a single game. I've been yanking his chain about it when we've been out on patrol. "Can't wait to get back to base and kick your ass at Madden!" I tell him. But Stokes is a big old boy and he can handle it.

After a few games of Madden we generally sit around shooting the shit. Stokes talks about how much he misses playing football. Like me, he did two years of college, then dropped out to join the Marines. He's thinking about trying to complete his studies, and doing so on a football scholarship. His mom's doing the rounds of colleges back home, trying to secure him a place.

I try to encourage him. I had the same passion for playing football when I was in high school, before injury made it an impossibility for me. I tell Stokes to keep persevering, that if he believes in it strongly enough, it'll happen.

We head out of base on the mission to clear a route into Mahmoudiyah. Stokes and Rex start their messing. Stokes makes a grab for the radio, Rex tries to stop him, and in no time they're wrestling and thumping around. Winkler seems to love it, though I can't understand how he can drive with Rex thrashing around like that. As for Rex, I've rarely seen him warm to someone as quickly as he has to Stokes.

We've got a new passenger who's tagging along for today's ride. Shawn Rhodes is a marine combat correspondent. He's riding with us to report on today's mission, for the Marine Corps' own publications and for the media in general. Part of his job is to file reports on what we're up to here so our families can read about it back home. He's fascinated to come across a K9 team in combat, and he's asked to shadow us for the day. I've told him he's more than welcome to tag along, because you never know what will happen in downtown Mahmoudiyah.

We drive into the center of the city, Rex and I clearing a couple of nasty bottlenecks en route. We haven't even pulled to a halt at city hall before we're getting plastered with gunfire. Across the street a bunch of gunmen are assaulting the local police station. There are tracer rounds and RPGs scorching through the air, and we're caught bang in the middle.

The marines of CAAT White lay down a wall of counterfire, and the insurgents quickly realize they're outgunned. They drop their weapons, mingling in with the crowd. We can see them running and hiding, but they're doing so in a street crowded with civilians. They blend in, and just as soon as they do so we're forced to stop shooting. We can't keep firing if it risks civilian lives.

These are the kinds of tricks the insurgents are using all the time now. When they're not planting IEDs or executing entire families in cold blood, they're hiding among women and children, using innocents as human shields. It's cowardly, and for us it's hugely frustrating. It makes the marines' blood boil when they won't stand and fight with us man-to-man.

We pull over on a dirt parking area between the police station and city hall. This is the place where Lieutenant Colonel Keyser plans to hold his meeting with the sheikhs. Rex and I pile out as the marines surround and secure city hall. The police station next to it is an ugly concrete structure painted sky blue, with a couple of palm trees towering over it. It's pockmarked with bullet holes and the blackened scars of grenade impacts.

The insurgents have been trying to overrun the police station, in all likelihood so they can execute the policemen stationed there. As with Suraya, the Iraqi police are seen as being "collaborators" and fair game for murdering. The arrival of CAAT White has promptly put an end to their assault, but even so, one Iraqi policeman has been killed and there are several wounded.

An ambulance turns up. It's total chaos as a crowd of civilians mixed with Iraqi police try to help evacuate the wounded.

All of a sudden, there's a blast of gunfire right in front of Rex and me. Men, women, and children dive for cover as the CAAT Whites aim at the gunmen, poised to open fire. It turns out it's some idiot Iraqi policemen firing their weapons into the air, in an effort to clear the crowd.

They finally get the injured policemen into the ambulance, and it's on its way. Rex and I check and secure city hall and the surrounding area. When we're sure that it's clear of IEDs, we hunker down in the shade of a palm tree. The fierce sun's beating down from a cloudless sky, and I douse Rex with bottles of water. It's like we're in a furnace.

I notice a group of Iraqi police and civil officials standing nearby, pointing at Rex and me. They're having words with our interpreter, but I haven't a clue what they're saying. When they're done, I go ask the terp what's up. He explains that the police and officials were saying that they know Rex is here to sniff out the bombs, and they need their own dogs to do the same so they can clear their own buildings of any threat.

They were discussing how much a dog like Rex must be worth, and what kind of breed he was, and whether they could breed their own dogs with him. They figure Rex's bomb-sniffing abilities are largely a result of the breed of the dog, not the training. It's all fairly innocuous, apart from one thing. If these guys know so well what Rex is here for, you can bet the insurgents do too.

It's a long day's search by the time we're done, and Rex is pooped. Rex and I are chilling in the air-conditioned cool of the Bunker, and Shawn Rhodes joins us. He's blown away by the day we've spent together in the Triangle of Death and he wants to ask me some questions about our work. He's wondering about search dogs versus metal detectors, and which is more efficient at finding the bombs.

I tell him there are no specific numbers, no in-depth studies have been done. But I know for sure that a dog is far superior. The problem with a machine is that you can't give it directions and allow it to track a scent to its source, as you can with a dog. A machine goes wherever you take it, so it offers a blunt, unintelligent form of bomb detection.

The man-dog relationship means the search is a two-way process, and it's infinitely quicker to clear an area with a dog. With a metal detector you have to cover an entire patch of terrain section by section, foot by foot. A good working dog can give you can accurate clearance in a fraction of the time. In many scenarios a metal detector is next to no use anyway, because the kinds of places you have to search are full of scrap metal, shrapnel, and garbage.

I explain how we train the dogs to search in an inverted-V pattern whenever they're clearing a building or a vehicle. Your dog starts low and moves his head up as high as he can and back low again, and repeats that pattern over and over. A good dog learns to search in that wave pattern and not to come off pattern unless he's onto a target scent. The pattern ensures that the dog detects scents at ground level and higher up, and at all levels in between. A good dog learns to follow that search pattern independently and with little direction from his handler.

As we talk, there's a knock on the door. It's a messenger announcing, "We need a dog team to go on a mission at sixteen hundred."

I ask him the nature of the mission. He explains that the 2/2 have received intel that there's a massive VBIED factory in a

rambling compound on the outskirts of town, just south of the Mixing Bowl road junction. A patrol's going in to raid it, and they need a dog team. For a moment I consider sending Harrell and Falco, but I know they're out on patrol on the far side of the city.

I have a cold, pathological hatred of VBIEDs. I'm convinced one of them is going to be the death of Rex and me. But I take the mission anyway. It's what I came here to do. Shawn Rhodes can't believe that Rex and I are going out again. He asks if he can come with us. I tell him he's more than welcome.

We mount up the Humvees, and we head out into the 130-degree furnace of late afternoon.

Chapter Sixteen

THE SUSPECT VBIED FACTORY IS A MASSIVE, UGLY COMPOUND SUR-rounded by a high concrete-block wall. The entire place is well hidden, and it feels brooding and like it's got something to hide. There are buildings two and three stories high, plus large low-rise sheds interspersed with patches of waste ground. The marines throw a ring of steel around the place. They've got Humvees parked out on the street covering the road, and guys are standing guard on the flat roofs of the buildings.

One building is a pile of flattened rubble, as if it's been hit by a bomb. For a moment I wonder if there was a guy con-structing a VBIED in there, and he touched the wrong wires together and blew himself to shreds. If so, he got exactly what he deserved.

The entire compound is crammed full of old metal pipes, wires, cables, broken-up vehicles, and war debris. There are pools of old oil and God only knows what else on the ground, and the place stinks to high heaven. I slip Rex's doggy booties onto him.

Then we start the search. We're a good hour in and Rex

has found stacks of weaponry—AK-47s and ammunition by the bucketload—but no explosives. It's baking hot inside the buildings, and I've got sweat pouring off me. My light desert-camo uniform has gone dark where it's soaked with my own body fluids.

I take a pause so Rex can drink and rest. He's so exhausted he can't even sit up to drink. He lies on his front, immobile, and I have to pick up his blue plastic water bowl and slowly pour the water onto his tongue, hoping some gets into his mouth and down his throat. It does seem to revive him.

We go to clear a warehouse. The stench is at its worst in here, as if someone's died. We're halfway across a metal platform that's lying on the floor when Rex spies a rat. He lunges for it and goes shooting around a corner—he is a dog, after all. Moments later there's an almighty metal-on-metal explosion.

For an instant I'm convinced that my dog has just set off some kind of killer device. The marines behind me have hit the deck. They're on their belt buckles about to open up. I race around the corner after Rex, and there he is, a sheepish grin on his face. He's knocked over a huge oxygen cylinder that's about five feet tall. It's slammed into the metal platform, making a noise like an explosion.

I breathe out a long sigh of relief. I realize that I've been holding my breath ever since I thought they'd got my dog. I try to get my heart rate under control again, and I give Rex a look that says: *You and your drive to chase freakin' animals. You almost gave me a heart attack!*

I turn to the security marines behind me. "Sorry about that, guys. Rex just knocked over a gas canister is all."

After two hours of searching we're finally done and can declare the place clear. We've got a good haul of weaponry but no VBIEDs or the materials used to manufacture them. I guess the intel was off the mark. But all I really care about is that Rex and I haven't been blown to smithereens, and neither have any of the marines. Rex is totally exhausted, and I'm not far behind him.

Back at base, the marines manage to rustle up a big, juicy beefsteak for Rex. There's a cook trying to run a tiny chow hall of sorts at our Mahmoudiyah base. It's not up to much, and most of the marines are still living on MREs. But they figure Rex has done a world-class epic search today and he deserves the biggest treat ever.

It's eleven o'clock at night by the time we've got ourselves cleaned up and eaten. We're totally pooped, but still I've got an urge to go check my e-mail for news of my father. We head for the Internet café. The base is eerily still and quiet at this time of night. It's lit up by the occasional light, but it's dark and sinister outside the perimeter.

From a good distance away I hear a roar like an express train bearing down on us; incoming. I hear it from far away only because everything else is so quiet. I glance up in that direction as the roar becomes a deafening snarl, and an RPG tears over the base perimeter. It misses the watchtower by a few feet, skips over the razor wire in a shower of sparks, and explodes in midair.

Rex and I have thrown ourselves onto the deck. We get up and brush ourselves off. I check him over and he's perfectly all right, as am I. But Rex gives me an unmistakable look: *Partner, I've had more than enough of this shit for one day. Let's hit the hay.* He's right. Maybe we can call my folks tomorrow.

We head back to the Bunker and Rex is pretty much instantly asleep. He's snoring away and making little yelps as he dreams. I figure the heat must have completely finished him. But for some reason I can't sleep.

Just for a moment back in that suspect VBIED factory, I thought the bad guys had finally succeeded in killing my dog. I practically had a heart attack on the spot, and I guess the shock of it has messed me up. Or maybe it's just the cumulative stress of all that we've been doing here and of the series of near misses we've had.

Either way, the last time I felt anywhere near this shitty was when I faced the prospect of my K9 career being finished for good, and pretty much before it had even started. After graduating Dog Training School, I'd been overjoyed to get sent to Camp Pendleton K9 unit. It had a soaring reputation, and its handlers were seen as being second to none.

I was in awe of their skills. A couple of the handlers could walk their dogs through hours of detection work without even needing a leash. Balto was one of those dogs, and he seemed alert to his handler's slightest command. It was as if that handler could communicate with his dog in a special, secret language. And so I started living the dream and learning all I could from these superexperienced handlers and their dogs.

But overnight, the dream became a nightmare. A few weeks into my time at Camp Pendleton's K9 unit, every handler there—the new guys like me included—was arrested. For six months the Naval Criminal Investigative Service (NCIS) had been investigating the unit, and now we were facing some serious charges. In an instant, my dream of being a K9 handler pretty much crashed and burned.

The handlers were so hot at their jobs that I guess they had got a bit cocky. You're not supposed to keep nonmilitary dogs at your kennels. But a local police department had a dog that was totally unmanageable, and they had asked our guys if they could fix him. If the animal's aggression could be managed, they felt that he'd make a great police dog. But the dog turned out to be so aggressive he was fighting everyone—handlers and the other dogs included.

This was before my time, but someone had reported it to NCIS, which had started an investigation. Rumor fueled rumor, and soon NCIS agents had our unit slated for the worst imaginable crimes: hazing (aggressive bullying of new recruits), falsifying documents, and drug trafficking. There were even rumors that our unit was going to be charged with prostitution.

We did have drugs at the unit, because we needed samples to train the narcotics sniffer dogs. And we did have some pretty female handlers in our unit. But that didn't make us drug pushers or pimps. The NCIS charge sheet was outrageous; even the accusations of hazing were totally over-the-top. Sure, the way the handlers trained new guys like me was hard and relentless, but I wouldn't have had it any other way. That didn't make it "hazing" and it didn't make it wrong.

The first I knew of the NCIS investigation was when our kennel master asked us to gather in an open area adjacent to the kennels. It struck me as an odd place to hold a briefing, but I was the new guy and orders were orders. We stood in a circle, and he told us that at 0700 the following morning we all had to be at the Security Battalion headquarters—our parent unit—for questioning.

He told us that our K9 unit was under investigation by NCIS, and that he suspected our phones were being tapped. He told us to answer all questions to the best of our ability. He rounded off with this: "I have an idea what's going on, but to protect you guys I'm not telling you. You're safer that way." What the hell did that mean?

The following morning the NCIS agents arrested all the handlers. Colonel Leo Mercado, CO of the Security Battalion, started bawling us out, accusing us of disrespecting his command and being a disgrace to the Marine Corps. When he was done, the NCIS agents handcuffed us and drove us to their facility.

I was marched into a cramped interrogation room. One agent stood, the other sat, and they read me my Miranda rights: "You have the right to remain silent. . . ." Then they threw a bunch of photos across the desk—close-up shots of me and the other handlers with our dogs. I realized then how intensively they'd been spying on us. I was confused and angry, but I had no idea whom I should be angry at.

"Are you willing to waive your rights and answer our questions?" one of the NCIS agents asked.

"Why would I not want to answer your questions?" I countered. "I got questions I want answers to—like what the hell is going on here?"

The standing guy launched into a twenty-minute diatribe. I was part of a unit accused of all these heinous crimes. He finished by accusing me of falsifying government documents, by forging the dogs' training charts.

"Are you fucking kidding me?" I retorted. "I'm the new guy. I'm the boot marine. I'm in no position to falsify *anything*. Why would I want to do anything wrong, like freakin' manipulating charts?"

They moved on to hazing. I accepted that the training was hard, but so was boot camp, and in neither was my life in any danger. No one ever made me do anything embarrassing or degrading. They said I'd seen the other new handlers getting hazed, and I was culpable for not reporting it. I couldn't believe these guys.

"Like I said, I'm the new guy, the boot marine," I told them again. "In boot camp you're taught never to break the chain of command. I see something bad, I report it to my seniors. Fact is, I never saw anything bad. If I had, I'd have reported it to the noncommissioned officers in my unit."

They accused me of being in on a conspiracy, the evidence being the photos of us gathered in the field for our kennel master's briefing. "You're all in it together." I said that if my kennel master told me to meet him in the ladies' room at 0600 hours, I'd be there. I obey orders. That's my job. It's what marines are trained to do.

The grilling ended with them asking me if I was willing to make a statement. I told them that of course I was. I had nothing to hide. I asked them if I was going to jail. They told me that for now at least I wasn't. I'd be released back to my unit. I asked them if I could still be a dog handler.

They glanced at each other. "Only the Security Battalion commanding officer, Colonel Mercado, can make that call. As it stands right now, you are all relieved of your duties as military working dog handlers," I was told.

I left the room distraught. I'd done nothing wrong, yet my

world and my life were collapsing. All I'd ever done was obey orders. That's what I'm trained to do. That's my job.

I obey orders—whether I'm in Camp Pendleton or out on the burning hot streets of Mahmoudiyah.

It's early July and Rex and I are tasked to do the walk of all walks: We're to clear IED Alley.

The first we know of it is when Stokes strolls over to the Bunker. "Hey, Dowling! We're heading out. Let's roll!"

We're so used to working with these guys that's all Rex and I need to hear. We head out in the Humvees and Rex is up front play-wrestling with Stokes. *WOOF!* Rex barks in Stokes's left ear.

"Damn, Rexy, you just deafened my—"

Before Stokes can finish, Rex has barked in his right ear. Stokes realizes he's outbarked and covers his ears with both hands. Winkler's pissing himself laughing in the driver's seat, and from the rear I'm also enjoying the Stokes and Rexy show.

We're approaching IED Alley when Stokes turns to me. "Hey, bud, can you clear the route before we head down it, like real quick?"

He's acting as if he's asking me to go fetch him a carton of milk from the corner shop, or something. I really do not want to do this. But how will I feel if I don't do the search, and we ride down it and one of the Humvees gets blown to pieces? It'll haunt me for the rest of my days.

"Yeah, sure," I tell him. "Sure I can."

I'm trying to act all casual and unconcerned. Truth is I am absolutely crapping myself. Of any mission, I fear that clearing IED Alley's going to be the one that gets Rex and me killed. But just as soon as that thought comes into my head, I try to block it out. Instead, I tell myself that this is what Rex and I came here to do.

IED Alley is a key transit route for the 2/2. It leads between two intensely hostile areas. It's a dirt road running along a raised bank with a palm grove on one side and buildings on the other. It gets patrols directly into the back side of a neighborhood that's a known hotbed of insurgents and where we've been hunting for their bomb factories. That's why we're always using it, and that's why they keep hitting us here. And because it's a dirt road, it's easier for the enemy to dig in and hide the IEDs.

The convoy pulls to a halt. Stokes gives me a curious look, half admiration, half pity. "Dowling, you sure you wanna do this?"

"Sure I am," I mumble. "Sure."

Rex and I dismount. I can't afford to hesitate or show indecision here. If I do, three things will happen. One, the marines all around me will pick up on it, and they'll start to lose their confidence in me and my dog. Two, it'll give the insurgents longer to prepare for an attack, that's if they are out there readying themselves to hit us. And three, that indecision will run down leash to my dog.

I've got a sick, cramped feeling in the pit of my stomach. Rex and I turn to face the way ahead. Pits and craters dot the road's surface, signatures of scores of IEDs. I worry I've lost my mettle, that I'm going to flunk it.

I'm quietly falling apart here, and I'm doing all I can to hide it from my dog. There's not a patrol drives down IED Alley that doesn't get targeted by an IED, the enemy following up with murderous machine-gun fire and RPGs. We're heading into the fires of hell.

I show Rex the Kong. Instantly, he's bright-eyed and eager. To him this is a game; to me it's a death walk. We take a first step, then another. We're a third of the way down IED Alley, with the vehicles parked up back where we started. Two security marines have volunteered to go with us and they're on our shoulder.

My dog starts to show a change of behavior. His tail, which has been wagging happily to and fro, suddenly goes rigid and upright. His whole body freezes, apart from his nose.

He lowers his muzzle to the ground. Up ahead is a small patch of dirt that looks as if it's been recently disturbed, or like it's been tampered with. It's a classic indicator of where an IED may be buried. Rex has got a manic look in his eyes, and he's fixed that patch of dirt with his laserlike gaze.

Rex inches forward, his nose going like a suction pump. He flicks his head around and he gives me a quick, intense look, his amber eyes burning with the excitement of the chase: *Freakin' hell, check this out! I'm onto something big this time!*

I feel my blood run cold. I am absolutely convinced that patch of rough ground is the source of the killer scent. I'm certain there's some kind of explosive device buried just in front of Rex's nose.

Rex is so good at this. I know he's trying to trace the heart of the scent cone—where the deadly package of explosives, circuit boards, cell phones, and shrapnel that make up the IED sits waiting for the call to detonate it.

A few feet short of that disturbed patch of dirt I can sense that Rex is about to go down on his haunches. The instant he does I'll know he's found the source, and I'll make a quick mark there on the ground. Then we'll get the hell out of there as quickly as we're able, while yelling out a warning to the security marines to do likewise.

I try to concentrate on what my dog is doing as he creeps forward, paw by paw, his nose sucking up the scent in great throaty gasps. But my mind is screaming at me wildly: They're gonna blow it right in our faces, then pound us with gunfire and rockets just to make sure they've really smashed us.

Suddenly, there's an almighty *BOOM!* The earsplitting crack of the explosion reverberates around us, and all four of us— three marines and one dog—dive for cover. I elbow forward and dive on top of Rex, to shield him from the blast. But an instant later I realize that it's not the bomb in front of us that's gone off.

Above the palm trees to our left there's a massive, pluming ball of orange flame punching skyward, spurts of blasted debris fingering out in all directions from the epicenter of the blast. An IED has been triggered over there, and from the looks of it, it's a freakin' monster. I wonder who the hell's been hit this time.

Powerful waves of gunfire thunder out of the smoke and dust as the insurgents unleash a barrage of machine-gun fire in a follow-up attack. I roll closer to Rex, getting my body between him and the enemy guns. I'm wearing my flak; Rex isn't wearing his. I wrap myself around him and pull his powerful body tight in against me. Months spent working in the heat and dust have turned Rex into one taut and muscular dog.

As I whisper calming words in his ear, I can hear the marines behind me yelling at each other above the deafening noise of the battle.

"Load up! Load up! We're moving out!"

I turn to the security marine nearest me. "I'm certain Rex was onto something."

"No time!" he yells. "There's no time! We got to go give the other guys backup."

We sprint for the Humvees. Stokes is in his vehicle yelling into his radio. I can't manage to break in and warn him about the IED that Rex sniffed. He's too busy trying to work out who's been attacked, and how and where, and how we should respond.

Then we're in the Humvees and we're moving out. The IED hit a fellow patrol from 2/2, and they're being smashed in a follow-up ambush. We've got to get our asses over there to help our fellow marines. There's only one way to get to them: to drive down IED Alley, which I now know for sure has been laced with at least one IED.

I finally manage to get a warning through to Stokes: "Halfway down, Rex was onto an IED!"

Stokes doesn't falter. "Fuck it, we got to chance it. We got to go help our guys."

Winkler guns the Humvee's powerful motor and puts pedal to the metal. We race ahead and I'm tensing myself for the hit that I'm sure is coming. But we roar safely past the patch of earth where Rex indicated an IED was buried. The Humvees behind us follow, and there's still no explosion. For an instant I wonder if Rex was mistaken—that there was no bomb hidden there—but I can't believe it of my dog.

We reach our fellow patrol and go in guns blazing, helping beat off their attackers. It's CAAT Blue, and they've got to get their vehicles and their wounded out of there pronto. In the confusion and red mist of the battle, they set off back to base without telling us which route they're taking.

Rex and I are out searching the road where CAAT Blue has

been hit. I'm focused on my dog, and I miss the fact that they're returning to base via IED Alley itself. A few moments later, a second enormous explosion punches into the air. I wheel around to see a dark, pluming smoke cloud fisting into the sky, right above the stretch of road where Rex had indicated that he'd found the hidden device.

I know instantly what's happened. Rex was right; he had found an IED.

I can hear Stokes's voice screaming over his radio: "Is anyone hurt? Is anyone hurt?"

There's a moment's echoing silence before a voice comes back, tense, tight, fearful: "No, we're all okay. Repeat, all okay. Moving back to base."

CAAT Blue has been hit by two IEDs in quick succession. Miraculously, every marine on their patrol has survived both of them. From my heart I thank God.

The CAAT White marines fan out in all-around defense. They're flat on their belt buckles on the fringes of the route. The gunners on the Humvees have got their .50-cals and Mark 19 grenade launchers scanning the palm groves to either side of us. Stokes says we're going to pull security for some time here and hold this road.

Rex and I finish clearing the route, and there are no more IEDs as far as we can tell. But everyone is tense as hell due to the repeated explosions and the firefight. It's now that Rex chooses to pull a stunt that has us all in stitches. In the midst of the insanity that is the Triangle of Death, Rex is the greatest stress reliever of all.

I'm chewing the fat with Stokes and the other guys as we scan the terrain. We notice a young Iraqi couple walking down the road toward us. Rex has wriggled on his belly under the Humvee, and I figure he's trying to get into some shade. In truth, he's getting ready to ambush the strolling lovers.

They're a couple of feet away when Rex lets rip: *"AROOOOF! AROOF! ROOF! ROOF!"*

I spin around and see the Iraqi woman collapsing and the gallant Haji at her side sprinting away for all he's worth. He vaults a fence and he is haring off into the palm trees, abandoning his lady. It's unbelievable. She's lying there like someone has shot her, and her man has done a runner.

The woman must have fainted with fright at Rex's performance, and I do feel bad. But at the same time I can't help laughing. As for the other marines they are pissing themselves.

Stokes goes to splash some water on the woman's forehead, to revive her. Rex meanwhile has a huge, goofy grin on his face. He's acting like he's done a great job of protecting us, but he's been so good at it that he's made that poor Iraqi woman pass out. It's that woman-in-the-drive-thru-McDonald's situation all over again.

Stokes's water splashing brings the Iraqi woman around, and she appears to be perfectly all right. But I figure she must be pretty pissed off at her man for running off. It's hardly gentlemanly or gallant.

We finish standing security on the road, and we load up to head back to base. The only way to do so is back up IED Alley. Halfway down there's a massive crater surrounded by burned and blackened vegetation. It is exactly where Rex had indicated that the IED was buried. *Trust your dog.* It's more than likely been detonated by a cell phone. I can't for the life of me understand why the watchers hadn't called it in on Rex and me.

The CAAT patrols don't have any electronic countermeasures—jamming equipment—to block cell-phone signals. That means there's nothing to stop the bad guys unleashing a command-detonated IED on anyone in a CAAT patrol, including the dog team. As it happens, the IED has blown up between two of CAAT Blue's speeding Humvees. The watchers just got their timing wrong is all.

I figure Rex and I were five feet away from the device when we were called off by Stokes, so pretty much right on top of the thing. We had no vehicles with us, and only our two security marines. So maybe the watchers were waiting for a bunch of marines to gather around the device before they set it off.

Either way, that's how close the enemy has just come to killing me and my dog.

Chapter Seventeen

WE DRIVE BACK TO BASE IN A TENSE SILENCE. I FORCE MYSELF TO face the hard, unpalatable truth: Rex and I were a hairsbreadth away from getting blown to pieces out there. But I've learned the hard way that sometimes when you're knocked back, you've got to come right out again fighting.

After the NCIS agents had busted our K9 unit, it took two months for my case to come to trial, during which we seemed to be the gossip of the K9 world. In spite of my innocence, I felt tainted, like I had to hang my head in shame. I was told I had a choice in terms of trial: I could opt for a court-martial, in which I'd get a military judge, or I could go before Colonel Mercado for a Non-Judicial Punishment (NJP). I was advised that at an NJP I could be punished only to a certain level, whereas a court-martial could max it out.

I opted for an NJP, as did all the lance corporals and some of the NCOs at our now-defunct K9 unit. The ten of us gathered for the hearing. Two handlers, both lance corporals, went before me, and each was found guilty as charged. I was led into an outer office, then marched before the colonel. I stood at attention, eyes staring at the wall above his head. To my right were seated the NCIS agents who had questioned me.

The colonel read the charges—falsifying government documents and conduct unbecoming a marine—and asked how I pleaded.

"Not guilty, sir," I replied.

He gave me a hard look and told me that I'd better have some damn good reasons for pleading not guilty. I told him everything I had told the NCIS agents, plus a whole lot more. I finished by stating that if I had my time again, I wouldn't change the way I had behaved in any way at all.

Then the colonel hit me with this: "I know you're guilty, Dowling, because you refused to cooperate with the NCIS agents. You refused to write a witness statement. That amounts to conduct unbecoming a marine."

"That's not true, sir," I replied.

The colonel was incredulous. "What did you say?"

"That's not true, sir. I answered all their questions. I said I was happy to make a statement, but it was so overwhelming because I'd already been interrogated for an hour, I asked if I could take a break. They said I could go home and they'd call me back to do my statement. They never called me back in. There was a video camera in the room that I guess recorded it all. Ask the agents who questioned me. They're sitting right there. They can verify what I've said."

The colonel glanced across at the NCIS agents. They shrugged, in a guess-the-kid's-telling-the-truth kind of way.

The colonel scanned the paperwork, then fixed me with a look. "I can't believe that I'm doing this, but Lance Corporal

Dowling, I hereby exonerate you of all charges. You are to be reinstated as an MWD handler here at Camp Pendleton."

The joy and elation I felt upon leaving that room was incredible, but it wasn't over yet. The colonel had made it clear that he'd be watching me like a hawk. I was the only one from the entire unit cleared of all charges, though most of the other handlers would be exonerated in due course on appeal. The only charge that was made to stick with any handler in our unit was hazing, and that with an NCO who was something of a hard-ass.

Shortly after I was cleared, Jason and Adam joined me, and we started working flat out to rebuild the Camp Pendleton K9 unit. We were green, but we had enthusiasm and love for our dogs. Jason and Adam were soul mates, and in no time we became close. We were having the time of our lives training with the dogs right across the base and working to rebuild our unit into an unbreakable team.

Then a head dog trainer got parachuted in from another unit. He was tasked with recertifying all the dogs after the NCIS shakedown. I presumed it was simply a formality, but unbelievably the guy failed *every single dog*. He couldn't face telling the colonel that Balto, Brian, and the rest were some of the best dogs in the entire U.S. military, so he retired them from service.

None of those fantastic dogs ever got to serve again. But I guess what doesn't break you makes you stronger, for it was losing our dogs that led me to finding Rex. He was the first new trainee dog sent to Camp Pendleton. The day came when I had to certify Rex as a fully trained MWD. I had to take him through an explosives-detection course in front of the only person qualified to certify him—Colonel Mercado.

The day arrived. I had to certify Rex, Jason was doing Robby, and Adam had a dog called Bruno. Rex and I were first up, but my dog didn't put a paw wrong, and we passed with flying colors.

"You and Rex look great as a dog team," the colonel told us as he handed us our certificate. "And Lance Corporal Dowling, you're doing a fine job. I'm proud of how you're helping rebuild Camp Pendleton's K9 unit."

And so Rex and I became Camp Pendleton's first newly certified MWD team, and the colonel became one of our greatest supporters. Colonel Mercado even handed me his the provost marshal coin, with the Iwo Jima flag on one side and the U.S. eagle on the other. This was his personal coin, which he would hand out to marines as a reward for outstanding achievement.

In a matter of months I'd gone from facing a court-martial to winning the colonel's full support. It was some turnaround. And two years later, Rex and I would find ourselves in Mahmoudiyah, involved in the fight of our lives.

Just as Colonel Mercado had warmed to Rex, so the commanders of 2/2 are falling for my dog. One evening shortly after our IED Alley walk, I'm over by the H&S building chatting with Captain Conway, the commander of Echo Company. He asks if he can see Rex do some patrol training, as opposed to search work. I tell him I'll fetch Harrell, and we'll give him a demonstration.

We gather in an open area to the rear of the base. A good twenty marines have seen us heading out with our dogs and they've come to watch the show. Harrell and I decide to run through the five basic stages of patrol work. Harrell's just about to prepare to decoy for me and Rex, which means putting on the bite sleeve, when Captain Conway intervenes.

"Say, Dowling, you think I can get bit by Rex?" he asks.

I smile. "Sure, of course, sir."

I help Captain Conway on with the bite sleeve, a thick, impenetrable tube of tough jute. The jute sleeve is designed to take a dog's bite while preventing the wearer from coming to any harm. I send Captain Conway off a good few paces away. I'm thinking that he is the highest-ranking person Rex will ever get to bite, so this had better go according to plan.

In real life we call the guy we send the dog after the "suspect." Ideally, you want the dog to bite the suspect on the back, to really stop him and bring him down. The dog has to bite and hold and bring the suspect to a halt—to "apprehend" him, as we call it. Once he's done that, you'd normally get the dog to transfer his bite to an arm, to better control the suspect.

I coach Captain Conway on how to present the bite sleeve to Rex, to make sure he bites the sleeve. I hold Rex by the collar and show him the suspect, Captain Conway. Rex knows what's coming and he's looking at me with an expression of pure excitement: *Oooh! Can I? Can I go get him? Can I grab the suspect?*

I give him the command: "Rex, get him!"

And he's gone, like a bullet from a gun.

Rex streaks across the ground between us, launches himself into the air, and clamps his jaws on Captain Conway's arm. Thank God he's bitten the bite sleeve, although I never really doubted that he would. He knocks the captain a good few feet backward, and I can tell that both man and dog are loving it. We do a repeat with Falco, so Harrell's dog also gets to bite the captain, and all the while the marines are cheering and applauding.

Rarely have I had to use Rex's patrol skills out here in Iraq, but still the marines love to see the dogs in action. A couple of the guys step forward and ask if they can take a bite too. We do some more of this, and it's real therapy for guys who've been at war for months now. I spot Gunney Trotter in the midst of the growing crowd, and even he looks like he's enjoying the show.

I walk over to him. "Hey, Gunney, d'you want to get bit?"

He gives me a look that could kill. "Fuck that, do I!"

Gunney Trotter's well at home in the midst of a Fallujah firefight, but he's still a little apprehensive of my dog.

As far as Rex is concerned, the guys who now make up his dog pack are the marines of 2/2. He's grown to be protective of each and every one of them. After the patrol demos are done, Rex and I go for an evening stroll around the base. We're heading for the telephones so I can call my folks. We pass by the shed where CAAT White is billeted. As soon as the guys spot Rex, they're calling for him.

"Rexy!"

"Hey, T-Rex!"

"Come here, buddy!"

By now they're competing to see who can be best buddies with my dog. The CAAT White guys love horsing around with him. They've learned his character well. If you try to pet him he won't necessarily bite you at first. He'll take a moment's petting, and then he'll start play-biting to get you off. If you don't stop, he'll growl very, very, very loudly, and that's the signal that trouble's coming.

It's like a threat game with the CAAT White guys. They love it when they can get Rex to do his low, rumbling, throaty growl. They think it's fantastic, like playing with fire. It's reached the stage now that whenever they have a patrol going out, these CAAT White guys send for Rex and me, which makes it doubly great that Rex gets on so well with them all.

It's August now and the heat is killing. We're five months into our tour, Rex and I are still alive, and back home my father is hanging on. I'm starting to believe that he, my dog, and I might make it through this okay. I get another mail delivery and there's another letter from Grandma Trujillo. She never seems to tire of writing. "How's my handsome Marine? Hope you're still getting mail and lots of packages. Let's see—what has this old lady been doing . . ." Grandma gives me the news from home— my dad's just about the same as when last she wrote—then finishes with this: "It's been pretty hot here lately, but I know it's a lot hotter where you are. Wish I could send you a bucket load of ice. Lots of ice! As usual, I'm sending you stuff to read. I couldn't find any reading for Rex, though! Time to sign off and now it's time for you to read the paper! Grandma."

She's enclosed a copy of our local newspaper, the *San Gabriel Valley Tribune*. I pay special attention to the sports pages, but I can't help taking a look at the articles about the war in Iraq. It's weird. From reading those reports, you'd have thought there was some clear intent and purpose to what we're doing, some grand master plan. Here on the ground it often feels like a war of bitter attrition and random chaos and bloodshed.

But at other times it's feels as if we are doing good. What gives it a unified sense of purpose for Rex and me—what makes it worthwhile and keeps us going—is that we are saving lives.

Iraqis as much as Americans. And the marines are helping rebuild schools and parks and bridges and other vital infrastruc-
ture, plus providing the locals with medical supplies. And I
remember Suraya telling me how liberated the Iraqi women
felt . . . before the insurgents decided to murder her.

Rex and I get a surprise tasking. We're getting a day's break
from the Triangle of Death. A patrol from the 2/2 is heading up
to Baghdad, to link up with an army unit stationed there. The
northern border of our area of operations meets the southern
border of theirs on the outskirts of Baghdad. A bunch of houses
up there are suspected of being a hotbed of insurgent activity.
The marines and the army are planning a joint operation to hit
them from both sides, with the army being in overall command
of the mission.

We drive up to Baghdad in a convoy of Humvees. Baghdad
feels like a real, working city after Mahmoudiyah and Fallujah.
The streets are thronged with people and the highways choked
with vehicles, some of them gleaming new. I sit in on the mission planning, and the army commander asks how I want to use
Rex.

I tell him just as I've been doing with the Corps: His men
should remove and secure all people from a building, leaving
it untouched. I'll go in with my dog to clear it, and we'll move
on to the next target. We'll turn a place over only if Rex finds
anything. I'll need two security guys on my shoulder as I search.
That's it.

By now it's predictable: Nothing remotely like I've asked
happens. We go in at crack of dawn the following day. We reach
the first target building, and the soldiers go right in and ransack

the place. By the time Rex and I are allowed inside, it's chaos. We try our best to ignore the balls-up and complete the search.

In one of the bedrooms Rex drags me over the upturned furniture and the debris straight to a metal locker. He's showing a massive change of behavior, sniffing all up and down the door, and he won't be pulled away. The locker is chained with a giant padlock. I check with the soldiers outside: Has anyone searched the locker? No.

I ask why they ransacked the whole building but left the locker unopened and untouched. They tell me that there are a lot of buildings needing searching, and they figure they've got to get a move on. I turn to one of the handful of marines who've accompanied me on this mission. I ask him if he has bolt cutters on him. He informs me that he does.

"Let's crack it open," I tell him.

We do just that, snipping through the padlock and chain that secures the locker, and presto—it's Aladdin's cave in there. The locker's stuffed full of assault rifles, ammo, and explosives. There's even a kukri in there, a heavy, curved fighting knife that the British army Gurkhas use. I wonder where the hell they got that from. We get the army guys to remove the lot and pile it by the roadside. I guess that's another few dozen lives that Rex has saved today.

The house is set back deep in the bush. I figure it's worth doing a thorough search now; there have to be more munitions or weaponry hidden in the grounds. Rex and I start to clear the surrounding bush. It's full of trash and debris, but Rex is fixated on one board lying on the ground. He keeps sniffing at it and he won't be moved.

I lift it. Underneath what looks like trash casually thrown into the undergrowth, there's a cache of old mortar rounds. It's prime IED-making material. I move an adjacent slab, and there's a cache of artillery shells. Under another pile of trash they've stashed lengths of detonation cord. It's an IED maker's paradise out here.

I call in some of the soldiers to gather up all that we've found. They're catching on now, and they start poking their way gingerly through the bush themselves. The grass is high, a couple of feet or more, and Rex keeps sniffing in a dense patch of vegetation. I part it and see a hulking great machine gun.

It looks like a Soviet-era "Dushka," a 12.7mm antiaircraft gun that's equally devastating when used against ground forces. Rounds from that could shred a Humvee's metal skin, rip through a soldier's body armor, or tear a man limb from limb. One bullet would certainly make mincemeat out of my dog. It's big, bulky, and heavy, so I ask the soldiers to lift it out.

They do just that, but as they're piling up all that we've found I hear them mouthing off to the officer commanding the mission.

"Hey! Sir! Look what we just found!"

Rex and I complete the search, then rejoin the soldiers. They have everything—the mortars, the shells, the detcord, the small arms and ammo, plus the monster machine gun—lined up on the roadside. The army officer asks me if Rex and I have found anything. I guess his guys have claimed credit for the entire haul.

I tell him that yes, we have found some bits and pieces. I point to the individual items and I list what Rex's nose has sniffed out. It's the entire lot. I tell him that the soldiers who helped move it can confirm that Rex deserves the credit. He challenges them and they nod, sheepishly, confirming that it's my dog who's the real hero.

"Great job, dog team," the army officer remarks. "That's why we asked you out here."

It's not that Rex and I need the credit. By now we've found enough arms and explosives to start a small war. I just don't appreciate anyone taking credit for Rex's hard work.

Rex and I move on to the next house. Again it's been ransacked, but not so badly this time. The house sits on the banks of the Euphrates River, and it's a pretty plush kind of residence for an Iraqi home. Rex and I search every room, until finally we open a door to discover the snazziest bathroom that I have seen in Iraq.

I stand there, mouth agape. There's a sink, a proper sit-down toilet, a shower, and even a bidet, all in matching light blue marble with gold trim. It wouldn't look too out of place in a plusher Richmond suburb. It's the first house I have come across in Iraq with a toilet that actually flushes. Normally they have an outside loo, which is a hole in the ground with a bucket of water to sluice it down.

I'm tempted to drop my pants and enjoy a relaxing, sit-down crap, but time's pressing and we've got to finish the search. When Rex and I are done clearing the house, we push into the backyard to start scouring the bush. We've been out there a good twenty minutes when I glance up from where Rex is searching. I can't see our security guys anywhere. I stand and listen. I can't hear them, either.

I risk a shout. "Hey, where you guys at? You guys there?"

There's no response. It's a big area and it's starting to feel very lonely out here. There's a flash of movement to my left, and suddenly a crowd of Iraqi women comes running through the bush toward Rex and me, their faces radiating hatred. I guess the men aren't far behind.

I recognize them from the houses that we've just searched. The soldiers are supposed to have rounded everyone up, and kept them corralled until Rex and I are done. Instead, they've let them go, and there's not another friendly soldier in sight or hearing distance of my dog and me.

As the crowd advances toward us, several thoughts crash through my mind. First: The soldiers have let the women and children go because they think the operation's over. Second: Rex and I have been forgotten and the soldiers are leaving. Third: There's every chance there could be a suicide bomber among them.

The crowd's trying to force us back away from the house and the road, but I know that's a trap. All that's back there is open palm groves and bush. It's farther away from any friendlies, and it's a perfect hunting ground. Our only chance lies in doing exactly what the crowd least expects—running at them.

I grab Rex and yell, "Go! Go! Go!" We sprint forward. I spot a gap in the mass of bodies, and we make a break for it. Figures dive left and right to escape Rex's snarling jaws. They're terrified of him, and I'm so glad I've got him by my side. Having Rex there gives me an incredible sense of power, in spite of the fact we're outnumbered and alone.

Hands reach out to grab us, but Rex is growling and snapping like a thing possessed. An instant later we're powering past, and my boot crashes open the back door to the house. We sprint through, hurtling over upturned chairs and tables and smashing through debris. Above the din I can hear the screaming mob coming after us. We power through the front door and onto the street.

I glance around, breathless in the heat and dust, and there's one of my army security guys standing idly by, acting like there's nothing amiss, like he's waiting to catch a bus on the corner of his neighborhood back home. I stride across to him, Rex at my side. I figure there are enough tough-looking men-at-arms out here to deter the would-be mob that was on our backs.

I front up to the army guy. "What the hell!" I yell in his face.

"Oh, yeah, you guys," he remarks. "So, did you find anything?"

"Fuck did we find anything! You guys just took off! You're security for the dog team! What the hell?"

He starts mumbling excuses. "Oh, yeah, well, we couldn't see you. So we thought, like, you'd taken off on your own. The brush was getting too thick for us. We figured you'd just left."

I'm so goddamn angry. I'm tempted to tell Rex to bite him. I've got nothing more to say to the guy, or his army buddies. I rejoin the handful of marines tasked to the mission, and I make a promise to Rex and myself there and then: From now on, Rex and I work only with marines who know how we operate. We have a little over a month more on our tour, and those guys supposedly standing security for us almost got us captured or killed.

As we drive off from the location, the women and kids are screaming at us and hurling rocks at the Humvees. I have no doubt whatsoever that they were aiming to corral Rex and me into some remote area, where they could isolate us from any help and do us serious harm.

What I can't face right now is losing Rex, or failing to see my father.

Chapter Eighteen

Back at our Mahmoudiyah base, there's some half-bad and half-good news. The bad news is that John "Red" Walls, the guy who'd first welcomed Rex and me to Mahmoudiyah, has been injured while out on a patrol. The good news is that it's only a light flesh wound.

Red is going to be awarded the Purple Heart for getting wounded in action, but he's pissed as hell. He figures that he doesn't deserve a medal any more than the rest of the guys of 2/2. Marines from 2/2 are racking up Purple Hearts because the battalion has taken some of the largest amounts of casualties of any unit. We figure not many of us will escape as a minimum the odd flesh wound by the time we leave Death Central.

Two days after the army op near Baghdad, Rex and I are given our next tasking. We're out with CAAT White at first light, heading for an area of run-down low-rise housing and scrubland adjacent to IED Alley. We're continuously getting hit from this area, so the searches for the bomb makers and their IED-making factories are relentless.

We're clearing the bush to the rear of some houses, and there are packs of stray dogs howling and slavering at Rex. They're dying to have a go at the unknown dog on their patch. Marines to either side of us are throwing rocks at the savage mongrels whenever one or another tries to go for my dog.

Incredibly, in spite of all the aggression and the distractions, Rex is keeping completely focused on his task. It's like he knows what we're up against it here—that this is where the bomb makers are cooking up their deadly cocktails—and that he's got to sniff them out of hiding. I can sense that once again Rex has upped his game. We're both totally focused on the search, and we're determined to find the bomb makers' hidden stash.

We round a bend, and all of a sudden Rex comes face-to-face with a stray. It's a giant, wild-looking dog, and Rex and he are eye-to-eye with each other. I can tell how utterly startled Rex is. One moment he had his head in search mode, sampling various scent cones and trying to sift out the one we're all after; the next, he's faced with a snarling stray the size of a wolf that seems determined to fight him.

Rex knows the dog is about to bite him. It's barking wildly and showing the whites of its fangs through its wide-open jaws. The thick, foamy saliva all over its teeth and gums is a sure sign that the dog has rabies. Sadly, the stray dogs in Iraq are riddled with disease, and rabies is one of the most prevalent.

"Back the fuck off!" I yell at the dog. "BACK THE FUCK OFF!"

But the stray isn't moving. I yell and scream but I can't get it to back away. Instead, it's creeping forward to launch itself at Rex. Rex is going crazy—he knows he's about to get attacked.

He's straining to leap forward, snarling and dragging to get free of the leash. When a dog on lead faces one off leash, it feels insecure and vulnerable, just as Rex is now.

One bite from that stray and Rex will get rabies, sure as eggs are eggs. Rabies is a killer. I might get Rex treated in time to save him, but it would be the end of Rex sniffing out bombs in Iraq. There's even a chance that he wouldn't survive.

I know what I've got to do. I slip my hand down, flick open the catch of my pistol holster, and draw my M9. I do not want to do this. I'm a dog lover, not a dog killer. I especially don't want to do it in front of Rex. But I've got no choice.

I tell myself that wild dog is going to die of rabies anyway, and it will be a slow, lingering, horrible death. It's much better this way. I don't even have time to yell a warning at the marines behind me. I level the pistol, aim, and fire, putting a bullet into the dog's heart. He drops to the earth, dead.

I yell out: "Friendly fire! Friendly fire!"

I feel terrible, but there was no other way to save Rex. It strikes me as ironic that here I am, dog handler and dog lover, and the only thing that I'm certain I've killed in Iraq is a dog. In another world and another life that stray could have been one of our pets back home. He must have been a powerful, magnificent animal before the rabies got him and sent him loco.

I move Rex away from the area so he can't smell or see the dead dog. Then I get my face down close to Rex's so we're eye-to-eye. I give him a little talking-to, explaining what I've done and why. He looks at me with his bright, shiny eyes and head cocked slightly to one side, as if he's listening real hard. When

I'm done explaining, I give him the Seek command, and Rex is immediately back on the search. If he's traumatized at all by my shooting that stray, he's not showing any signs of it.

Twenty minutes later Rex reaches one particular bunch of bush and shows a slight change of behavior. He keeps leaving the area, having a good sniff around, and then returning to it. It's like he's checking all around the scent cone and repeatedly tracking it to its source.

He's not certain what he's got here. I've seen him like this before. It's a pattern of behavior that means: *I can't be sure, but I think there's something buried real deep somewhere under that bush.* I let him work his nose for a while, and he's not leaving this one patch of scrubby grassland.

I call up the boys with the metal detectors. They run their machine over the area where Rex's snout is pointing. *Bleep, bleep, bleep, bleep.* The marines start digging, and the first thing they pull out of the ground is a white sack of the kind used to make sandbags. It's packed full of detonation cord. It's followed by two big rolls of electrical wire. Then they pull out three more sacks, stuffed full of PE4 explosives, old mortar and artillery shells, plus several plastic bags full of cell phones.

There's enough kit here to make dozens of command-detonated IEDs, and Rex's find is nothing short of a lifesaver. The marines rounded up the males of the house prior to our starting the search, so we've got the detainees in the bag already. We've unearthed their bomb-making kit, and somewhere among those prisoners are the bomb makers themselves. Rex has hit the jackpot.

We leave the area and take with us the detainees and all their

IED-making materials. We pull out with Rex on the rear of an open-backed Humvee, flanked by a couple of marines. He's sitting on his haunches and peering over the side, just like the marines are. His head's level with theirs—two guys with helmets on, and Rex with his ears pricked forward, real interested in what's going on.

The way he's sitting there racked up with the marines, Rex looks totally human.

I guess it's inevitable that something has to happen to shatter the myth of Rex. We return to the same area a couple of days later, hoping to sniff out more of the bomb makers' deadly materials. I'm clearing the road with Rex up ahead of me on his leash, and all of a sudden he goes absolutely rigid. I've never seen anything like it. His muzzle is pointed directly at a bush, and he's totally certain.

The bush is thick and green. It's impossible to see through it. If there is an IED hidden in there it has to be some monster device, the way that Rex is reacting. My stomach's gripped tight with fear. I have never seen my dog like this before: His tail's bolt upright like a lightning rod; his head's on the deck snorting in the scent real hard.

His paws are going one in front of the other, *pad, pad, pad,* right up to the base of the bush, and then he's sticking his head inside. I figure he's got to be tracking the scent cone to its very source, but I'm on the verge of yanking at the lead and pulling him back from whatever killer device he's found there.

I turn to the marines on my shoulder. "Rex is onto something! Get ready to run!"

I can read the fear in their eyes. I guess they can see it in mine too. They see how Rex is behaving, and they know enough about him by now to realize when he's onto something. I turn back to Rex, and he's still got his head stuffed in that bush. All of a sudden his tail starts wagging fiercely back and forth. I was expecting him to sit down at the source and turn and give me the look. Instead he's doing this tail-wagging shit. Why on earth is he wagging his tail if he's just found a monster bomb?

"What the hell?" I exclaim.

I step forward and stick my head into the bush beside him. At the base of the foliage there's a litter of newborn puppies. One is black and white, and there are a couple of sandy-colored ones, and they're wobbling and stumbling about with their fat tummies and their bandy legs.

"What have you found? What have you found?" I ask Rex gently. "So, who wants to be the daddy, eh, Rex?"

He turns and gives me a look: *Cute! Can we take one home?*

The very sight of it melts my heart. The marines on my shoulder move forward to join us. They crack up laughing.

"Hey, you know, I don't think those puppies are gonna blow!" one of them remarks.

The relief on their faces—and on mine, I guess, too—is crystal clear. Their expressions have gone from tense fear to sheer relief and joy. That's puppies for you. We'd rather come across a newborn litter any day—innocent, fresh life—than an evil killer device.

Rex keeps snuffling at the puppies, but I can't let him go forward and actually touch them. Who knows what diseases they might be carrying?

We return to base that afternoon and Captain Dahle gives me the word: Rex and I are scheduled to leave soon. We're getting rotated out the way we came in, via Al Asad air base back to the United States. In the meantime, we're to keep doing the missions.

The Warlords are scheduled to leave Mahmoudiyah in early October, so Rex and I will be getting out just a few days before they do. I box up all our gear so we're ready. Every day is suffocatingly hot and I'm done with it. I'm so ready to get back home. Iraq for me is like a beach without water, and I've lived all my life beside the sea. At heart, I'm a California beach-dreamin' kind of guy.

I start making the rounds, letting the guys know that we're soon out of there. Over the last couple of months I've made a big point of hanging out with the marines all through the chicken factory, because Rex is a therapy dog for them. Everyone's petting and fussing over Rex, and taking souvenir photos. If there's a celebrity at Death Central, it's Sexy Rexy.

I've really appreciated having Harrell and his dog, Falco, here alongside us. They lightened the load for Rex and me. Harrell and Falco have had IEDs go off on them as they're out doing vehicle patrols. I've even heard and felt one of those explosions. From the base I saw a massive plume of dark smoke barreling into the sky, and that was where an IED had targeted my fellow dog team on patrol.

I'm not getting any mail anymore, because I've told everyone to stop writing, in case the letters and parcels don't reach Mahmoudiyah before we leave. But I check every day that I can on my dad via e-mail, and the news is that he's hanging on. I can't wait to see him for what I figure will be the last time. But before that can happen we've got missions still to do here in the Triangle of Death.

Our next tasking is a night patrol with CAAT White. We've done a lot of night patrolling since returning to Mahmoudiyah, and Rex and I dig being out during the hours of darkness. It's cooler at night, so Rex can last longer on the search. Plus, a dog can see far better at night than a human, so the darkness doesn't hinder him that much.

The canine eye is built to see at night, with a larger pupil to suck in ambient light—that thrown off by the moon and stars—plus a concentration of rods and cones arranged to boost available illumination. I know how amusing Rex finds it that I can't see in the dark: *Why do you need that flashlight to see where you're going?* He finds my night blindness almost as funny as my need to lace on my boots anytime we go walkabout. *Bet you wish you had paws, pads, and claws.*

Stokes has adopted a new modus operandi for CAAT White patrols. He's so frustrated at getting hit by an invisible enemy using IEDs and follow-up ambushes that he's decided to drastically alter the way they do things. Instead of working to standard operating procedures—evacuate the kill zone as quickly as possible—they're going to do the opposite and pursue the enemy at every turn. Rex and I are going to get a taste of Stokes's "hot pursuit" tactics on this coming night mission.

We gather in the muster area, and Stokes is ribbing me about Madden NFL 2004. We've just played the first game where he finally managed to beat me.

"I got your ass, Dowling," he gibes me. "You have been de-throned!"

"Stokes, man, come on. I just felt bad seeing you lose all the time. I told myself I had to let you win the one game!"

Everyone in the Humvee's loving it as Stokes and I give each other shit. Even Rex seems to be enjoying the joking around. Stokes gets Metallica thrashing out of the ghetto blaster, and we head out of base with the heavy rock blaring. It's Stokes's way of saying, We're on a hot pursuit patrol. Come get some.

We burn down Route Jackson, the main highway leading toward the concrete overpass the Mixing Bowl. The aim of this patrol is to stand security on Routes Jackson and Michigan, and to see if we can't catch some of the insurgents out planting bombs under cover of darkness.

Stokes flips off the music. It's a sign that we're getting into Mahmoudiyah proper now, seriously hostile territory. Stokes turns to Winkler and asks him something about a recent football game. They're chatting away about the game as we disappear beneath the tangle of concrete highways.

We shoot out the far side, and the instant we do there's a violent flare of flame to our left and the roar of a rocket launching. Rex and I have both heard it, because I've got the side window down a little to give him some air. I flick my head around just as Rex does the same, and I'm staring at a flaming RPG warhead coming right at us.

Time seems to freeze. From the trajectory of the flaring rocket trail it looks as if it's aimed right at our heads. Instinctively I duck as the warhead thunders over the hood of the Humvee, missing it by a bare few inches. It goes right across the hood, like metal scraping metal, a great big fuck-off rocket before our very noses. It practically takes Robinson's head off where he's perched in the .50-cal turret.

The RPG explodes on the far side of the road, the white-hot heat of the detonation lighting up a wide stretch of the highway in an eerie, smoke-enshrouded halo of light.

Robinson yells, "Holy fuck, that was close!" I glance up at him, and he's got a cigarette butt glued to his lip.

We've just escaped death yet again, and I can sense that Rex feels it too. I figure we're done: We've just used up number eight of our nine lives.

Stokes is yelling into his radio, "RPG! Contact left! Contact left! RPG!"

Without a word, Winkler ramps the Humvee around in a screeching turn, and he's gunning it down the barrel of the rocket launcher. I haven't the slightest doubt that Winkler will ram it right into them, smashing through the makeshift barricade they're hiding behind. Or more likely, Robinson on the .50-cal will shoot them dead before the Humvee manages to reach them.

The RPG team sees our vehicle thundering toward them and they throw down the rocket launcher, turn on their heels, and run. The Humvee skids to a halt in front of the abandoned barricade. Winkler can't drive any farther, because there's rubble and crap all over the place.

"Okay, this is close enough!" Stokes yells. Being the maniac he is, he piles out of the vehicle. "I'm goin' after them!"

With that he's gone, sprinting forward, vaulting the barricade, and charging off into the badlands. I glance out the side window and see the lone figure of Stokes tearing down the darkened slipway, running off into the blankness of the night.

One part of me needs to be there alongside Stokes, watching his back. The other part of me needs to be here with my dog. I know if I leave without him, Rex will go crazy left alone in the vehicle, pawing and tearing at the doors and the windows. But if I take him, I'm needlessly exposing my dog to enemy bullets, rockets, and bombs. Plus it's no place for Rex out there: We'll be vaulting barriers and debris all the way.

For an instant I'm torn. Then I turn to Rex: "STAY!"

And I'm gone.

I'm pounding after Stokes, and everywhere there're marines bailing out of the vehicles to join the pursuit. I hurdle the barrier from where the rocket was fired, and there's the launcher lying on the ground. For several minutes I push deeper into no-man's-land, thundering down this debris-strewn concrete slipway, my rifle aimed ahead of me, but there's no sign anywhere of the enemy—or of Stokes.

Then a figure comes looming out of the darkness. It's Stokes, and he's breathless and deflated.

He looks at me, eyes burning angrily in the night. "I guess the motherfuckers got away. *Again.*"

We have to accept that they're gone. We figure they had a getaway vehicle with a driver at the wheel. They piled into that and they're out of here. I'm standing there with Stokes surveying the scene. We know the rocket attack was that close to frying our vehicle. We're talking about what is our next best move when something brushes against my leg, and I feel a wet nuzzle to my hand.

It's Rex. Out of nowhere he's sat there on my left at the Heel position. Somehow he's got out of the vehicle and come and found me. He gives me a look: *Buddy, you're crazy if you think you're going out on this one without me.* It turns out that he's managed to paw down the Humvee's window and leap through it. He must have tracked his way to me by my scent.

I can't help laughing. This frigging dog—there's no stopping him.

We return to the Humvees and load up. We head down Route Michigan, then pull over. We're close to an off-ramp, and it occurs to me it's a good place for the enemy to have set an IED. They tend to plant them on stretches of road where vehicles are forced to slow, to increase their chances of hitting their target.

Stokes must be thinking the same thing. "Hey, Dowling, you figure can you search that exit ramp to make sure no one's planted any bombs?"

I ask for two guys to stand security. It's dark as pitch out there, and one of the security marines suggests he bring a Chem-Light, a plastic tube full of a chemical liquid that glows when opened. We use them to provide low illumination, or as markers.

He cracks the light stick, but he snaps it so hard all the fluid flies out, and most of it lands on Rex. In an instant Rex is transformed from a black shadow to a great big fur ball that glows in the dark!

Rex glances down at his fluorescent green coat, then gives me a baffled look. It's hilarious, but there is a worrying side to it. Once we start the search, Rex will be a big glowing ball of fur racing about, and he'll be highly visible. If I can see him, so can an Iraqi sniper, or an RPG team, or a watcher waiting to trigger an IED. But we're here now, and we're committed and have to do the search. I wipe as much of the glowing gunk off him as I can, then we head out to clear the road.

No one shoots my glowing dog, or blows him up or hammers him with an RPG, and there's nothing much to find. We stand security for a couple of hours, but Route Michigan is quiet as the grave. We're back at base before sunup, and no one's dead and no one's been injured.

That's about as good as it gets on a lot of our missions.

Chapter Nineteen

REX AND I GRAB A FEW HOURS' SLEEP. WE'RE WOKEN BY A KNOCK ON the door of the Bunker. It's one of the marines from H&S, and he tells me that Captain Dahle wants to see me. I wander over to the H&S building, and the captain tells me to report to the Combat Operations Center in twenty minutes. I'm to bring Rex with me.

The COC is situated inside the chicken factory, in an upstairs, officelike area. It's the nerve center of two-two. It's where the CO of 2/2, Lieutenant Colonel Keyser, plans operations with his senior commanders. I wonder what they want me for, and I wonder why they're asking me to bring my dog.

It's an odd one. For obvious reasons, Rex isn't normally needed to attend briefings or to receive orders. I mean, he's certainly sharp, but he doesn't speak human. Sure, he can talk to me—but that's in a language that no one else can understand.

Rex and I ready ourselves, then head over to the building. At the top of the stairs, Captain Dahle is waiting for us. I enter with Rex at my side. I'm expecting maybe to see the CO of 2/2 there, with his XO and sergeant major. Instead, every officer from 2/2 we've ever worked with is gathered in that room.

At the head of the gathering sits Lieutenant Colonel Keyser. It feels kind of formal, and I'm about to take a place at the back, but he signals me over. He fixes me with a look, then gives the same kind of look to Rex.

"Corporal Dowling, I know that you and Rex are due to leave any day now, but before you leave I want to show our appreciation for the work you and Rex have done for the War-lords. I hear that when the company commanders have brief-ings, they argue to get the dog team, because you guys really look after them and their marines."

He pauses and gives me a firm smile. "They're pretty much fighting each other over who gets Rex! And that tells me you guys have done a great job out here. So, on behalf of 2/2, the Warlords, we want to adopt you and Rex as two of our own. You've always been Warlords when you're been here with us, so as a way of us demonstrating that, here is our coin."

He hands me the 2/2 Battalion coin. This is the Warlords' formal send-off for "their" K9 team, and I'm moved almost to tears.

I take the coin in my hand. "Thank you, sir."

There's a small round of applause.

"Take care of Rex," says Lieutenant Colonel Keyser, "just like he took care of us."

I nod. "Always, sir. And thank you."

I turn and Rex and I are gone. I can hear the officers calling out, "See ya, Rex!" and "Thank you, Rex!"

Back in the Bunker, I take a good look at the coin. It's got "United States Marine Corps—Semper Fides" emblazoned on

the one side. On the other there is "2/2 Warlords" superimposed over a dagger, around which are listed the theaters in which the Warlords have served: Iraq, Lebanon, Haiti, Kuwait, Cuba, Tarawa.

As I turn it over and over, admiring its look and feel, I'm overcome by this sense of achievement and well-being. Rex and I have done exactly what we came out here to do. We haven't once faltered.

The following day is September 15 and we're waiting to get the word that we're leaving. It's five-fifty in the morning and still dark when Stokes knocks on our door and warns me and Rex to ready ourselves for another mission. CAAT White is heading out on a standard patrol through Mahmoudiyah, and they want us with them.

We head over to the muster area and mount up. Rex is in the rear of the Hummer, paws up on the side.

Stokes comes striding over to me. "Man, Dowling, you're an asshole."

I laugh. "Why? Just 'cause I keep beating you at Madden . . ."

Stokes shakes his head. Smiles. "No. You're an asshole because you get to go home before I do. Get down from the Humvee. You're not going on this patrol. They just called me. You get to go home, you lucky bastard."

I get Rex out of the vehicle, and we say our farewells to the CAAT White guys. We exchange numbers and e-mail details, and promise to get in touch for a reunion back in the States.

The six Humvees of CAAT White leave the base, then Rex and I head to the Bunker. Harrell is going to be left here, and a replacement dog team will be brought in to cover for Rex and me. I know the guy who's coming to take our place. It's Adam

Lawson, with his dog, Tino. They're a great team that I know well from Camp Pendleton. I couldn't have asked for a better handler or dog to replace us. Mahmoudiyah is going to be left in good hands.

I say my final farewells and snatch a few last photos. I'm grabbing my gear to load onto one of the trucks when I hear a sharp explosion echo across the city. I pause for an instant, my brain processing the sound and shape and feel of the blast. IED. A big one. And most likely on Route Tampa or thereabouts.

I think little more of it. There are bombs going off all the time in Mahmoudiyah. That's life in Death Central. But unbeknownst to me, that IED has detonated at the very instant that Stokes's convoy was speeding past. If you're close enough to an exploding IED, it kills you via traumatic brain injury. In an instant the power of the blast alone shakes your brain to death.

The IED has detonated right on top of Stokes's vehicle. The savage blast has ripped into the side of his Humvee, throwing a tornado of deadly shrapnel through it, tearing off its doors, and hurling them into the dust at the roadside. The puncture point of the explosion is directly behind the two front seats, or exactly where Rex and I would have been sitting had we gone out on that patrol, had Stokes not told us at the eleventh hour to get off. But I know none of this right now. I have no idea of the horror that has engulfed CAAT White. I'm heading for a convoy of trucks with Rex at my side, and we're loading up our gear to get the hell out of Death Central.

Rex and I leave Mahmoudiyah as we arrived, hitching a lift on a resupply convoy. We head back to Fallujah. I arrive looking like a hobo—again—my cammies all ripped to shreds by razor

wire and stained and dirty from the weeks and weeks of search work.

Rex, however, is a picture of good health, his coat shimmering, his nose wet, his caramel eyes bright. My daily grooming and care routine has kept him in tip-top condition, in spite of the pace of ops and the heat.

We catch a ride in a CH-46 helicopter back to Al Asad, where Rex and I are reunited with the K9 teams with whom we arrived seven months ago. We shoot the shit and swap stories from our deployments. The other guys can't help ripping the piss out of my appearance. I'm rake thin and I've got a big hole in the crotch of my one serviceable pair of cammies, the other pair being covered in shit and torn to shreds by the wire.

During the last few weeks of relentless operations in Mahmoudiyah, my buzz cut's grown long and floppy on top. The handlers keep teasing me that I've reverted to the laid-back California beach dude I always was. They break out the electronic hair clippers, sit me down behind one of the tents, and shave my head practically bare.

Every single K9 handler has done our tribe proud, as have their dogs. We've found tons upon tons of weaponry, ammo, and bomb-making kit, and discovered countless IEDs. To a man and dog we've all done good here in Iraq.

I came to Iraq doubting myself and deeply unsure of taking my dog into the fire of combat. I'm leaving knowing that Rex and I put total trust in each other, and together we achieved the seemingly impossible.

Adam and Jason, my Camp Pendleton handler buddies, recently deployed to Iraq, just as they always wanted. Jason's stationed at Al Asad, and Adam's at an air base north of there. We manage to get together at Al Asad and play poker and exchange war stories. It's great to see the guys again, and we make plans for the good times we're going to have when we're all back in the States.

There's one last surprise in store for me. I manage to phone home, and my dad is still with us, thank God. But my mom's got some bad news for me. She's been holding back telling me until the day I was scheduled to leave Iraq. A few weeks back, my beloved green Ford Mustang got totaled. I'd left it in the care of my brother, and he smashed it up big-time. They didn't want to worry me with it while Rex and I were still doing the walk in Death Central.

Oddly enough, I'm not particularly bothered. After surviving the hell of the Triangle of Death, it doesn't seem so important anymore. All that matters is that my dog and I are still alive, and that we have saved lives down there in Fallujah and Mahmoudiyah. The rest is all meaningless fuzz and noise. A distraction. The life-and-death existence that we've been living here has put it all into perspective and shown me what truly matters in this world.

We board the C-17 for the long flight back to the United States. All I'm hoping and praying for now is that my dad holds on long enough for me to see him. I park Rex in his crate and tell him to get some shut-eye. He's earned it. And even though I hate flying with a passion, I ride in the cockpit with the pilots, I'm so desperate to get a first glimpse of the lights of home.

We touch down at March Air Reserve Base, and there's a group of volunteers who have formed a reception party. They're a bunch of senior citizens, and they have home-baked cookies, tea and coffee, and cell phones for us. I give the cookies a miss but grab a phone. I speak to my dad. He tells me the doctors have let him home for his last few days. I tell him to hold on. I'm coming home.

But there's one thing I've got to do first. I head to Camp Pendleton and take Rex to his kennel. He runs inside right to his water bowl and takes a long, satisfying drink. I sit in the kennel, feed him, and watch him eat. As I do so I'm reminded of a mirror image, from the time before we deployed to Iraq. I sat with Rex, just like this, and told him we were going to war and pondered what Iraq might hold in store for us.

Well, now we know. Together, we've slain our demons, done good out there, and survived. Rex wolfs his chow like he always does, like he's never gonna eat again. He lies down next to me, with his head cradled in my lap, and soon he's falling asleep. Iraq has exhausted him.

Gently, I remove his thick leather collar. I hang it where it lives, on top of his kennel. As I do so, I caress the scratched and battered leather. It is so broken in. I reflect on what it's been through, and what that signifies about Rex and me and Iraq. Our bond is stronger than ever now, man and dog. We know each other in a way that I might never know a fellow human being. Our understanding is instinctive and primeval and it runs so deep.

In Iraq we put our lives in each other's hands (and paws) day after day. We took care of each other no matter what. Rex and I have a bond that will last for the rest of our born days. If ever there was a marine who lived up to *Semper Fidelis*, the motto of the Marine Corps, it's Rex.

I'd joined the Marines to test myself, to be the toughest of the few. Yet barring that one exception in Fallujah with my pistol,

I've come away from the war in Iraq barely having fired my weapon in anger. And so it is that my time with Rex has taught me a different kind of warrior creed—a toughness that over-arches all of that.

It is to walk into the fire day after day after day, all but defenseless, knowing the enemy is hell-bent on killing us, and doing so in an effort to save lives. It is to do so knowing that I am being watched and targeted, but never once feeling alone, for I have my dog at my side. And knowing that Rex will be there for me, whatever I ask of him, always.

With those thoughts foremost in my mind, I close the gate to Rex's kennel and leave him to sleep, and I head out to see my father.

Epilogue

I HAD A MONTH'S LEAVE AFTER IRAQ AND I SPENT AS MUCH OF IT AS I could with my father. He told me that every day I was away he prayed for me and for Rex and that we'd make it back safely. While I was at home I sent an e-mail to Stokes. He called me up, and it was via that call that I learned about the IED that had blown up their patrol on the day that Rex and I left Mahmoudiyah. Somehow, Rex and I had cheated death yet again. How and why we'd done so, God only knows. Perhaps it was the protection provided by my mother's bear statue and my father's by now very battered rosary beads. I like to think that it was.

I'd met several private security contractors during my time in Iraq. They were fascinated to see a K9 team at work, and they told me that if ever I wanted to work as a private operator they could sure use me and my dog. I'd thought long and hard about it and had decided to do my four years in the Corps and then go private.

It was Stokes's phone call, and his news about the IED strike, that made me change my mind. Rex and I had survived snipers,

IEDs, mortars, rockets, rabid dogs, and gunfire in Iraq. How many times did I want to roll the dice?

My father died on January 5, 2005, which meant I got to spend one last Christmas with him, and was there at his funeral. I returned to Camp Pendleton, and Rex and I picked up our training routine. We were out on the beach, and Rex swallowed a bellyful of ocean water. I put him in his kennel to rest, and one of the handlers went to feed him. She told me that Rex wasn't eating his food.

I went to check. Sure enough, he was lying on his side unresponsive, and his food wasn't half gone. He didn't even get up to greet me. I knew something was badly wrong. I called the base veterinarian, who told me that maybe Rex was tired. I told him that my dog wasn't tired: He was sick, and I needed him looked at.

I drove Rex over to the vet's surgery. He did an X-ray, and it was immediately clear that Rex was bloating. The vet called in a colleague, and they prepared to do emergency surgery that would last long into the night. They sedated Rex and sliced him open right down the middle, releasing the gas as they went. Then they sewed his stomach to the lining of his insides so it couldn't twist with the accumulating gas.

The surgery saved Rex's life, and he was soon back to his old self.

Tragically, Adam Cann, my K9 buddy who helped rebuild the Camp Pendleton K9 unit, was killed by a suicide bomber and died from the sheer concussion of the blast. His dog, Bruno, was hurt but still conscious. Bruno lay down on Adam's body and would not allow another person to go near him. Bruno survived and is still working today. Adam Cann was the first

American dog handler killed in combat since Vietnam, roughly thirty years ago.

Rex is still serving as a military working dog at Camp Pendleton, and he is one of the oldest and most combat-experienced K9 veterans there and in the entire Marine Corps. He's too long in the tooth to go on combat missions now, so he's relegated to working in the United States for the reminder of his career.

After our deployment to Iraq, he went on to complete two more combat deployments, and he and his new handler were blown up by an IED. Thankfully, they both survived, as the IED was buried too deep and the ground took the brunt of the force. His handler was awarded a Purple Heart. Rex did not receive one because sadly military working dogs are not officially allowed to receive medals in the U.S. military.

Due largely to his mother's relentless determination, Stokes went on to Appalachian State, playing football for them. In spite of the injuries he'd suffered in Iraq, he was a key player on their team, helping them to win the NCAA Division One championship in 2005 and 2006, the first championships the school had won in its hundred-year history. It was a story of such heroism that it made the local papers and soon went nationwide.

When I joined the Marine Corps, there were only a couple hundred K9 teams in the entire U.S. military. There's been a massive increase in numbers since. A few months after my return from Iraq, two Israeli dog handlers spent a few weeks with us at Camp Pendleton. The Israeli military boasts some of the most experienced soldiers in the world when dealing with IEDs.

Those Israeli handlers were experts in Specialized Search Detection, where the dogs search remotely off leash, using hand commands and/or voice commands via radio links. With their help, the American military K9 community learned how detection dogs could be remotely operated. During the search, the handler speaks to and instructs his dog via a radio collar and can do so from one thousand yards away. The U.S. military now has its own Specialized Search Dog Teams trained to operate in this remote way.

We had learned a lot of lessons in Iraq, and as a result we set up K9 units specifically trained for deployment to war zones. Those teams form a part of the Marine Expeditionary Force, and they are dedicated to active operations. There's now a training school to prepare K9 teams for offensive operations, and predeployment exercises take place to simulate combat situations. There are also specialist K9 Mine Detector Teams and Cadaver Detector Teams.

Military working dog gear has evolved to include vastly improved shrapnelproof vests and Doggles—goggles that protect their eyes from dust and sand. Such developments in K9 training, operational capability, and kit evolved directly out of that summer 2004 deployment of the first K9 units to Iraq.

There was none of that when Rex and I went to war. Back then we were the guinea pigs, and we made it up as we went along—up close and personal.

Afterword: Update on Rex

AFTER TEN YEARS OF EXEMPLARY SERVICE, MILITARY WORKING DOG Rex E168 is now retired from the United States Marine Corps. In those ten years Rex was assigned to ten different handlers— nine others after me. Following my service in Iraq, I was honorably discharged from the Marines and I had to pass Rex onto a new, younger handler. Giving him up after all we had been through was one of the most difficult things I have ever had to do, and I advocated very strongly that he be assigned a handler who would show him the love and dedication that I had.

I kept close track of his progress throughout his career, visiting him many times at Camp Pendleton, keeping alive my hope of adopting him upon his retirement. Every time I saw Rex he knew right away who I was, and despite the years that had gone by, the bond was so tight and right between us. Sometimes I even got to take him out for a run and to do a few exercises, and Rex seemed just as happy as ever to be at my side again. Whenever we were together it always brought back for me the buzz and the sheer joy of working with Rex.

Late in his career the handler Rex had directly after me,

Megan Leavey, told me of her plans to adopt him when he retired. Megan had deployed to Iraq on two separate tours, and during one she and Rex were blown up while searching for explosives and IEDs. Both survived their injuries and went on to continue to serve, and Megan was awarded a Purple Heart as a result of that incident. Although I wanted Rex myself, I supported Megan in her efforts to adopt him, largely because I knew all too well of the long-term needs of wounded warriors.

Since my deployment to Iraq I have worked extensively with the Wounded Warrior Battalion and similar nonprofits that help wounded servicemen and women recuperate and return to normal civilian life. During my time working with wounded warriors, I have worked to have therapy and service dogs placed with wounded warriors and have seen the dramatic and positive effect this has on them. The faithful companionship and support of a dog provides huge therapy for injured servicemen and -women.

All I ever wanted was to adopt Rex, so I could be the first and last handler he ever had, and so we could be reunited after all those years. But since Megan was wounded with Rex in combat, I knew that the right thing to do was to support her in her effort to adopt him. Despite how much I wanted to have Rex, it would have been wrong for me to get between a wounded warrior and the dog that could be her therapy for years to come.

When the process for Rex's adoption began, the Marine Corps called and gave me an opportunity to adopt him. I told the Marines that since Megan was a wounded warrior, it was right for her to get Rex. It was one of the toughest things I've ever done, but it was the right thing to do—helping clear the way for Megan to adopt. I don't regret it for an instant, though

I shall miss having Rex at my side for the rest of his life, now that he's become a civilian dog.

Because military dogs are trained to attack, as well as to sniff out explosives, they cannot simply be retired and allowed to live in a civilian population right away. They must go through a series of evaluations and de-training, so that they can make a successful transition to civilian life and not become a liability. This process can take several months, especially if there are other military dogs in the system about to retire—which there were when Rex was going out for adoption.

Understandably, Megan wanted to speed the adoption process. In an effort to do so she contacted Senator Chuck Schumer, her state senator, to enlist his help in pushing it forward. The Senator put out a press release and campaigned for Megan to be allowed to adopt Rex in a speedy manner, and tens of thousands of American citizens signed a petition in support of her doing so. An owner of the New York Yankees got involved, and the media was suddenly full of stories of the military working dog hero and what his life might be like after the Marine Corps.

At the time I told Megan to let me know if there was anything she needed me to do—and I wrote to Senator Schumer's office endorsing Megan's adoption of Rex. I appeared in the media helping endorse the adoption, and the press coverage certainly helped speed up the process. The end result was that Megan was able to adopt Rex more quickly than most dog handlers who are waiting for a military working dog that is being retired—this was great news!

On April 6, 2012, I attended Rex's retirement ceremony at Camp Pendleton. It was one of the most fulfilling days I've ever had. When I first began handling Rex he and I were as green as any new military dog team. I was there to pick him up and bring him to Camp Pendleton for the first time, and of course it was a bittersweet moment for me to see him leave Camp Pendleton for the last time, and not by my side. But I knew it was the right decision all the same.

During our early days together I often wondered what Rex would go on to accomplish through his career. He was recognized for his achievements and performance as a military working dog during his retirement ceremony. His citation read:

FOR SUPERIOR PERFORMANCE OF DUTY WHILE SERVING AS A PATROL/EXPLOSIVE MILITARY WORKING DOG, MILITARY POLICE COMPANY, SECURITY BATTALION, MARINE CORPS BASE CAMP PENDLETON, CALIFORNIA, FROM 14 MAY 2002 TO 06 APRIL 2012. MWD REX PERFORMED HIS DUTIES IN AN EXEMPLARY AND HIGHLY PROFESSIONAL MANNER. MWD REX PROVIDED OVER 11,575 HOURS OF MILITARY WORKING DOG SUPPORT CONSISTING OF SEARCHING OVER 6,220 VEHICLES DURING RANDOM ANTI-TERRORISM SEARCHES, 7,800 BARRACKS ROOMS SEARCHED DURING 260 OFFICIAL COMMAND AUTHORIZED HEALTH AND COMFORT INSPECTIONS ABOARD MCB CAMP PENDLETON. IN ADDITION TO BASE OPERATIONS, MWD REX SUCCESSFULLY COMPLETED 3 COMBAT TOURS IN SUPPORT OF OPERATION IRAQI FREEDOM IN WHICH HE CONDUCTED NUMEROUS COMBAT OPERATIONS AND WAS CONSTANTLY PUT IN HARM'S WAY DURING MULTIPLE FIREFIGHTS, MORTAR ATTACKS, AND IMPROVISED EXPLOSIVE DEVICES. FURTHERMORE, MWD REX WAS ASSIGNED TO SUPPORT THE UNITED STATES SE-

CRET SERVICE ON MULTIPLE OCCASIONS FOR THE PRESI-
DENT OF THE UNITED STATES, VICE PRESIDENT OF THE
UNITED STATES, AND THE UNITED NATIONS GENERAL
ASSEMBLY. MWD REX'S ENTHUSIASM, INITIATIVE, AND
LOYAL DEVOTION TO DUTY REFLECTED GREAT CREDIT
UPON HIMSELF, AND WERE IN KEEPING WITH THE FINEST
TRADITIONS OF THE MARINE CORPS AND THE UNITED
STATES NAVAL SERVICE.

—B. K. WOOD
COMMANDING OFFICER
SECURITY BATTALION, MCB CAMP PENDLETON

Thank you for your service, your dedication to duty, and
your sacrifice, Rex. *Semper Fidelis.*

Mike Dowling

Acknowledgments

A VERY SPECIAL THANKS IS DUE TO THE FOLLOWING PEOPLE, WITHOUT whom this book would never have been written. A special thanks to Damien Lewis, who sought to recognize military working dogs and convinced me that Rex and I had a story worth telling. Without his passion and enthusiasm, this project would not have happened. Thanks also to my literary agent in the United Kingdom, Annabel Merullo, and in the United States, George Lucas, who helped make this book a reality.

Very special thanks also to Peter Borland, my editor at Atria, and everyone else on the Atria team, including Nick Simonds, Judith Curr, Dana Sloan, Mara Lurie, Larry Pekarek, David Brown, Aviele Fredman, and Jeanne Lee.

Being a military working dog handler in the Marine Corps was one of the greatest experiences of my life. A good military working dog team doesn't depend only on the handler spending a lot of time with the dog—it is a team effort. I am grateful to so many people who helped Rex and me become a good dog team. First and foremost I thank my kennel master at Camp Pendleton, Staff Sergeant Greg Massey. At the time Staff Sergeant Massey came to Camp Pendleton, the unit was essentially starting from scratch all over again. Under his leadership and guidance, the MWD section is now one of the Marine Corps' elite K9 units.

I thank my fellow handlers and chief trainers at Camp Pendleton, especially Sergeant Jason Cannon, Sergeant Adam Cann (RIP), Sergeant Jesse Maldonaldo, Sergeant Lester Huckey, Sergeant Lori Luna, Sergeant Vincent Amato, Sergeant Alex Reeb, Sergeant Jason Wood, Sergeant José Prado, and Corporal Brendan Poelaert. I looked forward to coming to work every day not just to work with Rex, but just as important to train with my good friends. Through our training and the social times we spent away from the kennels, we built everlasting relationships I will cherish forever.

I also thank my kennel master in Iraq, Staff Sergeant William Kartune, for looking out for all the dog teams and providing us with valuable knowledge, supplies, and training throughout our deployment.

I thank the veterinarians at Camp Pendleton while on my deployment: without their constant and immediate care for our dogs and training us how to take care of them in the field, we might have lost some.

While deployed with Rex, I received many letters and messages from friends and family that showed an incredible amount of support. I have kept almost every letter, postcard, and photo that was sent to me. These people were generous to take time to send me a package, letter, picture, postcard, or some other support. Many of those letters and parcels also included words and gifts—a bone!—for Rex.

The people I must especially thank are the entire Trujillo

family, especially Grandma, Chris and Margie, Rosella, Chris Jr., Debbie, Brian, and Matthew; the Haig family; Aunt Patsy and Patrick Malloy; the Paasch family; the Bruce family; the Iliff family; the Roberts family; the Metzger-Jones family; the Canotal family; the Flannerys; the Davalos family; the Luries; Ben Maple and his family, and Kathy; my friends Brian, Pooya, Karlo, Daniel, Brittany, and Annie; and all my other friends and family who graciously offered their support.

I also thank the entire Dowling family for sending support throughout my deployment, especially my parents, Joseph and Lorraine; Shane, Patrick, Darcy, Shannon and Mychael, Kevin and Maria, and my godson Joseph.

I thank the dog teams of previous wars, especially those that never came home. You pioneered the military working dog profession under extraordinary circumstances and set a standard of excellence we can only hope to match.

I thank the marines of Second Battalion, Second Marines, the Warlords. Rex and I couldn't have asked for a better-trained and more professional fighting unit.

To all my brothers and sisters in the armed services, you have become family to me and I love you. To all the wounded warriors, and those who sacrificed it all, you will never be forgotten. Thank you.

Finally, thanks to Rex E168, the most crazy, aggressive but calm, stubborn, loyal, dedicated, obedient, courageous, devilishly handsome son of a bitch I have ever had the honor of working with. We did it, bud. Seek, Seek, Seek.

Roll of Honor: Marine Corps K9 Units Deployed to Iraq, March–September 2004

Staff Sergeant William Kartune, kennel master, from Marine Corps Base Hawaii

Sergeant Charles Allen and Rocky, from Camp Pendleton

Sergeant Nester Antoine and Boda, from Marine Corps Logistics Base Albany, Georgia

Lance Corporal Denise Causey and Ricky, from Marine Corps Base Okinawa, Japan

Corporal Darin Cleveringa and Rek, from Marine Corps Logistics Base Barstow, California

Lance Corporal Kevin Collier and Art, from Marine Corps Base Hawaii

Corporal Mike Dowling and Rex, from Camp Pendleton

Lance Corporal Goers and Ringo, from Marine Corps Base Twentynine Palms, California

Lance Corporal Joe Kang and Marcie, from Marine Corps Air Station Iwakuni, Japan

Corporal Eric Mathers and Bepo, from Marine Corps Air Station Yuma, Arizona

Corporal Donald Paldino and Santo, from Marine Corps Base Quantico, Virginia

Corporal Eric Vasquez and Boris, from Marine Corps Recruit Depot San Diego, California

Corporal Mark Vierig and Duc, from Marine Corps Base Hawaii